WILHELM REICH

WILHELM REICH

Psychoanalyst and

Radical Naturalist

ROBERT S. CORRINGTON

Farrar, Straus and Giroux

New York

Farrar, Straus and Giroux
19 Union Square West, New York 10003

Copyright © 2003 by Robert S. Corrington
All rights reserved
Distributed in Canada by Douglas & McIntyre Ltd.
Printed in the United States of America
First edition, 2003

All illustrations are courtesy of Mary Boyd Higgins
and the Wilhelm Reich Infant Trust Fund.

Library of Congress Cataloging-in-Publication Data
Corrington, Robert S.
    Wilhelm Reich : psychoanalyst and radical naturalist / Robert S.
Corrington
        p.   cm.
    Includes bibliographical references.
    ISBN 0-374-25002-2 (alk. paper)
    1. Reich, Wilhelm, 1897–1957. 2. Psychoanalysts—United
States—Biography.   I. Title.

BF109.R38C67 2003
150.19′5′092—dc21   2002044767

Designed by Jonathan D. Lippincott

www.fsgbooks.com

1   2   3   4   5   6   7   8   9   10

To my friends and colleagues at Orgonon

Contents

Preface

Wilhelm Reich (1897–1957), the brilliant psychoanalytic theorist and protégé of Sigmund Freud, is one of the most restless figures in modern thought. His outer journeys led him from his native Austria to Germany, to Denmark, to Sweden, to Norway, and finally to the United States (partly because he had to flee the Nazi government after Germany's annexation of Austria in 1938, which automatically made him an inhabitant of the Third Reich). He was persecuted by the psychoanalytic establishment, by the Communist Party, and by the Danish, Swedish, Norwegian, and U.S. governments, and died in a U.S. federal prison, where he was being held on trumped-up charges made against him by the Food and Drug Administration. His life had genuine tragic components, many clearly self-caused, but not all. He had a turbulent personal life with three marriages and many love affairs. Unlike his one-time mentor and father figure, Freud, he remained fully sexually active until his imprisonment and felt he could not endure to live without fairly regular sexual connection.

Reich is rarely written about these days, let alone read by serious students of psychology or historians of ideas. The standard view is that he had some promising ideas about character formation, emotional armoring, the latent negative transference, stasis anxiety, orgastic potency, the formation of the fascist personality, and defense mechanisms, but that by the mid- or late 1930s he had succumbed to a latent psychosis (probably paranoid schizophrenia) and strayed from psychoanalysis into pseudoscientific terrain with his explorations into so-called bions, the cancer biopathy, and cosmic orgone energy.

This standard view is based on a profound misreading both of Reich's texts and of his own life story. Moreover, work coming out of his research has not been properly attended to by outsiders (one glaring example being the neglect of his 1933 book *Character Analysis*, revised and expanded in 1945 and then again in 1948, but not published until 1949), who would have had to pay serious attention to the *detailed* experimental procedures undertaken by Reich, especially in his last years, in order to understand it fully. Typically, Reich is demonized (often by people who have never read him) or his work is split apart and the so-called "good" Reich is contrasted to the "insane" Reich. Consequently, the situation is not one that has lent itself to a focused examination of his categorial scheme or of his own complex psyche.

My own view is that there is much wisdom to be found in almost all of Reich's writings, including his sometimes ridiculed philosophical texts of the early 1950s. I also take very strong issue with the common claim that Reich suffered from paranoid schizophrenia. No paranoid schizophrenic could have written the brilliant and conceptually consistent books that Reich did year after year after year, whatever their ultimate empirical merits or failings. In fact, very few writers in any field, whether healthy or diseased, show such amazing lucidity in their texts over a lifetime of writing.

I do think that Reich manifested forms of hypomania with an attendant psychic inflation, but it is not at all clear that he suffered from, say, manic-depressive disorder. If one listens to his recently reproduced clinical lectures from 1949, entitled *Orgone Therapy* (available in a six-disc CD format from the Wilhelm Reich Museum in Maine), one hears no indication of the pressure of speech or of any kind of manic ideation. In fact, his interaction with his peers and interlocutors in these lectures shows him to be fully in command of his ideas while being engagingly open to critique. Was he paranoid during his final years in America? Probably, but new evidence has begun to reveal just how extensive was the harassment of him and his work, and it suggests that external events exacerbated his paranoid traits.

It is my conviction that Reich provided an extremely important component for what a sexually liberated life-philosophy would look like. I will also argue that in such works as his *Ether, God and Devil*, and *Cosmic Superimposition*, written mostly in English in the early 1950s, Reich was

creating his own version of an ecstatic naturalist and universalistic religion.[1] Although he would have been profoundly uncomfortable with such
language, as he often was intensely critical of what he called "religious
mysticism," for example, as it manifested itself in the Nazi movement, my
sense is that he sought a deeper religiosity that came from the core of the
self (the primary drives) rather than from neurotic or even psychotic forms
of religion that ultimately came from the violent and sexually suppressed
secondary drives.

Reich had a kind of hypomanic intensity in his dealings with the
world, leading his student and biographer Myron Sharaf to give his conceptually weak and negative biography on Reich the title *Fury on Earth*.[2]
His astonishing energy was manifest in both positive and negative ways.
On the positive side, it was manifest in his unrelenting quest to get at the
heart of things, to probe into the ultimate structures of psyche, soma, and
cosmos. On the negative side, it was manifest in his direct and nonevasive
tactics with patients and with analysts in training (as he tried to pry loose
the latent negative transference) and with his unrelenting focus on the
validity of his own ideas. (Of course, the astonishing hostility facing
his work only deepened this focus, catching him in a vicious cycle.)

Given the astonishing distortions that have been imposed upon his
work, it is once again time to do a very careful textual reading of his
pertinent major and minor writings so as to rescue them both from the
encrustations of history and from the willful distortions of the psychoanalytic establishment. It will be impossible in this limited study to examine
all of his writings, but we can get a very clear picture of his conceptual
system from the texts that we do examine, and I will be mindful of his
whole corpus as I unfold his categorial framework. I will also slightly
stress the earlier psychoanalytic material, as I feel that some of it has
been neglected, especially the works of the 1920s, the brilliant political
and psychoanalytic material of the 1930s, and the fascinating philosophical works from the late 1940s and early 1950s, in which I think Reich is
giving us a genuine foundation for a new global "religion."

I am not in the position to give a final scientific assessment (whatever
that would be) of the bion theory, although I have, of course, seen professional slides of what are believed to be bions and have talked to researchers who now are working with what they hold to be bions. There
may be some further experimental glimmerings in that direction, but we

must await the unfolding of detailed inquiry. The orgone theory strikes me as having some strong metaphoric value, but it may also have some direct phenomenological warrant. My sense is that the current direction of physics, with the correlations among string theory, relativity, quantum theory, and classical thermodynamics, is moving in a different direction from Reich's, which in any event had to do with a different set of issues (primarily, for Reich, those issues that point to a biological energy that is even more basic in structure than electromagnetic energy). But the foundations of physics have shifted more than once since Reich's death and will shift again. I also suspect that biologists may find their own way of doing viable research into orgone energy.

Reich held that orgone—the basic primal energy of the universe and, by implication, all living systems—had thermodynamic and organic properties, while not being strictly electromagnetic, and that any conceptual elaboration of its ways of behavior must be functional/organic rather than mechanistic. My growing sense is that something like orgone exists and that Reich appeared on the scene too early (and thus lacked the proper paradigm) but had it basically right, and the public paradigm has yet to catch up to him. The other possibility, namely, that no such energy exists, flies in the face of worldwide experience as embodied in the history of religions, esoteric practices, and cumulative practical and self-critical awareness of life processes. I do not think that this energy can be explained away by classical psychoanalytic theories of projection, the childhood omnipotence of thought, or misplaced object cathexis.

A scholar who is also a participant in Reich's amazing odyssey has to avoid the temptation to be overly defensive of Reich, but it should be clear to any intellectual historian that his colleagues often treated him unfairly, both out of very complex personal motives (certainly envy, in the early Freudian circle of the 1920s) and for deeply held conceptual reasons (pertaining, for example, to his orgasm theory). Most of his interlocutors simply lacked the intellectual equipment to follow his many-faceted journey into depth psychology, biophysics, literary analysis, political theory, sexology, energetics, and philosophy. I am persuaded that Reich was a genius of the highest order, with all that this disruptive force entails for healing and destruction, and that almost no one he knew was in a position to comprehend the full depth or scope of what he was struggling to manifest. Is this a nineteenth-century romantic, even patriarchal, view, one that is ripe for deconstruction? Perhaps. But I ask the reader to suspend judgment as the story is told. The genius myth has not fared well in these self-styled postmodern times, but it may thrive again in the decades to come.

I approach conceptual issues as a philosophical theologian (an enterprise that functions at the place where radical philosophical inquiry intersects with the insights of world religions) with an almost lifelong interest in depth psychology. When I was eighteen, I discovered Carl Jung and was immediately transfixed. This interest has continued now into my fifty-second year, leading me to lecture on his work both at my own university and at the Jung Institute in Zürich, as well as into six years of ongoing Jungian analysis with first a male and then a female analyst. Jung's ideas will be seen in much of what follows, in what I hope is an illuminating and nonintrusive way. I have also published a number of books and articles probing into the basic structures of the self, with my own form of reconstructed psychoanalysis.

At the age of twenty-five I discovered a strange book with the evocative title *The Function of the Orgasm* (*Die Funktion des Orgasmus*), part 1 of *The Discovery of the Orgone* (*Die Entdeckung des Orgons*)[3] and had another epiphany. Here was an author who took me out of my internal introverted intuitive world into the body, into the physical world of sensation and physiological response, and into absolute immediacy and relationship with another human being. This author was to be the second great depth psychologist in my life, although one who would continue to puzzle me and for whom I would develop, as he would have predicted, a kind of latent negative transference, namely, a largely unconscious resistance to the growing identification with a parental figure. Reich frightened me in a way that Jung did not. Both thinkers were boundary-transgressors, but while Jung's transgressions could be internalized, Reich's were external and had interpersonal and social implications. Neither man kept within the bounds of monogamy, although Jung attempted to keep this side of his life hidden. Reich was more honest in his sexual dealings and argued against what he called "enforced monogamy."

Reich also had a very curious relationship to his own Judaism. In a fascinating short book written in German in 1946 (*Rede an den kleinen Mann*) and translated into English in 1948 with the more aggressive title

Listen, Little Man![4] (*Rede* simply means "speech"), he argues that Jews should assimilate totally into a new world civilization and cease to exist as a separate people with their own unique religion and special history. Does this mark him as a self-loathing Jew, or are there more complex motives at work? I am not persuaded that the former idea is a possibility. The latter prospect suggests itself because in the same book Reich also takes a vigorous stand against the then–especially virulent forms of American racism (lynchings were still being widely practiced against sexual "transgression") and argues for the full sexual rights of interracial couples. (Again he seems to have been pushing toward the idea of a posttribal internationalism.)[5]

I write as someone sympathetic to Reich's views, but with some reservations. My intended relationship for this book is threefold: (1) Reich enthusiasts who are interested in a fresh interpretation of his life and work, but also (2) people with some basic knowledge of the psychoanalytic tradition who would like a "brush up," with a focus on Reich, and (3) people with almost no knowledge of Reich who want a (hopefully) thorough and accurate introduction.

The issue of validity will be uppermost in this analysis. By "validity" I mean to ask whether Reich's categories, such as "latent negative transference," actually have some phenomenological (experiential) warrant and, if they do, whether they are logically consistent with his other key categories. I approach this task more as a philosopher than as a clinician, as my strategy is to move into what might be called a philosophical anthropology in the existentialist tradition of Martin Heidegger (1889–1976)[6] or the neo-Kantian tradition of Ernst Cassirer (1874–1945).[7] The goal of philosophical anthropology is to develop an encompassing perspective on the whole self-in-process as it manifests its cumulative directionality in both its conscious and its unconscious dimensions. For philosophical anthropology, psychoanalysis represents a subaltern discipline, albeit one that must be highly privileged if it is to complete its own work as philosophical anthropology.

In addition, I am concerned with the semiotic issues of depth psychology, namely, with how the self processes signs and renders its world intelligible. Semiotic anthropology is a new field that has a lot to offer to psychoanalysis precisely because it provides a language and a structure for embedding the self in an evolutionary nature in a way that Reich,

in particular, likely would have found deeply congenial.[8] Each self-
in-process moves through what the Euro-American philosopher C. S.
Peirce (1839–1914) called signs, objects, and interpretants (new signs
that emerge out of the original sign/object relationship) so that meaning
can be had in a chaotic world. In this study Peirce's model, which has become the standard worldwide model for semiotic theory, will prove invaluable for framing key aspects of Reich's theory of character formation
and even for understanding some aspects of his more elusive orgone theory. In terms of more recent work in semiotic anthropology and psychoanalysis, I think of the post-Freudian and neo-Hegelian Julia Kristeva,
whose work in semiotics has broken new ground in the self/world correlation.[9]

While examining Reich's views from the perspective of philosophical
anthropology, I have also undertaken a psychobiography in which I probe
Reich's expressed and latent myths about himself. Like Freud, who identified with the historical figure Hannibal, and like Jung, who identified
with the literary figure Faust, Reich early on projected himself onto a figure who could serve as a point of both conscious and unconscious self-
identification. In his case it was Ibsen's Peer Gynt, the protagonist of the
1867 play of that title. Reich also developed identification with Christ in
his later years and wrote a book that unfolded a unique and compelling
Christology, which served as a not-so-well-concealing mask for himself.[10]
Reich's Christology has very little in common with those of the Christian
churches. It is more of a model for a fully emancipated, sexually complete
human being than for a divine man or an exclusive son of God.

Of the two myths or archetypes Reich identified with (Peer Gynt and
Christ), that of the suffering servant of humankind is especially important
for this psychobiography. In his last decades he became persuaded that
he was called to bear the burdens for a sexually starved and sadistic human race and that he could point the way toward a new humanity if only
his healing message could be heard. He sensed that a great emotional
plague, or a psychic virus, was eating away at the collective psyche and
that only the right use of sexuality and cosmic orgone energy could counteract it. His desire to augment electromagnetic theory by grounding it in
orgone theory was part and parcel of this drive to conquer the emotional
plague. In the early 1940s he tried to convince Albert Einstein of the reality of orgone but was unsuccessful.[11]

Enriching the two tasks of a more generic philosophical anthropology and a psychobiography, I want to unfold what can be called the "unsaid" that lies in the written work of any great thinker—namely, the hidden but powerful conceptual structure that must be freed from its own distortion in order to be seen clearly. One uses the good aspects of a thinker against the weaker aspects. Needless to say, there is something both arrogant and dangerous in such an enterprise, but I am persuaded that, especially in Reich's case, it is important. So I shall engage in an *emancipatory reenactment* of his categorial array in such a way as to make his contributions more pertinent to the ongoing work of psychoanalytic theory.[12] I strongly believe that psychoanalysis is something at least *like* a science and that it will flourish in the twenty-first century if it gets the right conceptual foundation (as it already has an astonishing wealth of clinical material at its disposal). Much more work remains to be done in gender analysis, in race and class deconstruction, and in the area of metaphysics. This last claim may jar many readers for whom the word *metaphysics* connotes a pseudo-discipline that speculates into some realm beyond the physical. But that is almost never what philosophers mean by the term. In the strictest sense, the term denotes the analysis of the broadest categories we use to describe the world that we encounter. In this sense, Reich was always doing classical metaphysics, even though he strongly shied away from the term. My job, as I see it, is to make his nascent metaphysical categories stronger and clearer so they might be applied in psychoanalysis and so that my fellow metaphysicians might learn the utter necessity of psychoanalysis for *their* work.[13]

It is fairly rare for any theorist outside of mathematics or physics to do so much foundational work in her or his early to mid-twenties, but Reich had supreme confidence both in his destiny and in his clinical powers. In addition, he had greater theoretical power, as I will argue, than even Freud himself, whose writings, while often better stylistically, seem rather tame when compared to Reich's. This claim may startle readers new to Reich, but I hope to provide enough evidence in the elaborate story to follow to vindicate it.

As will become clear, his views on sexuality were already being formed in the fiery crucible of his chaotic home life before he found the technical language to give them voice. He was a sexually conflicted being who had very little of the Freudian superego in his *adult* psychic makeup.

His overarching concern was to free all of humankind from the personal and social superego so that what he thought of as healthy genitality could liberate the psyche from its many forms of muscular and emotional armoring. In some senses his message was a simple one, yet its expression required an elaborate conceptual structure that would incorporate nonorthodox psychoanalysis with nonorthodox Marxism (what he later called "work-democracy"). Like G.W.F. Hegel, whom he in many respects resembles, he wove together seemingly incompatible systems into an overarching synthesis that is unique in the psychoanalytic literature. In our emancipatory reenactment we will celebrate this synthesis while struggling to weed out any of its misconceived elements. The mystical Marxist philosopher Ernst Bloch often spoke of the "bursting front of the new." This is precisely what we will seek in the life and work of Reich, namely, that creative momentum in which his work continues to drive forward into the future and that can carry a robust psychoanalysis past and through its own occasional backward-looking tendencies.

WILHELM REICH

Family Tragedy, Sexual Awakening,

and World War I

Wilhelm Reich was born on March 24, 1897, on the outer reaches of the Austro-Hungarian Empire, on a fairly wealthy farm estate in Bukovina, in what is now Ukraine. His mother, Cecilie (or Cäcilie) Roniger Reich, was nineteen, his father, Leon Reich, at least ten years older. A sister was born the next year, but she died almost immediately. His one surviving sibling, Robert, was born three years later. Their fraternal relationship would be vexed for a number of reasons, especially those surrounding sexual rivalry and the competition for paternal affection, which was extremely hard to obtain.

Willy, as he was called, developed an attitude toward his mother that was deeply sexual and colored all of his subsequent almost frenetic relationships with women, compelling him to focus on their (maternal) breasts as their most important and soothing attributes. Indeed, one can say that he had an ongoing fascination for the female breast as the ground of all protection, healing, and safety. As he puts it in his early journals in 1919–22:

> Breasts which are round, full, supple, do not sag, and have a rosy-white hue are the most beautiful part of a woman. That is why I like poems that extol women's breasts with chaste but sensuous desire, for no yearning within me will ever be as strong as that for a woman's breast upon which to rest my head. Later I experienced many a night in which I abstained from intercourse but found a complete substitute for it by resting my head on a girl's breast and pressing close to her body.[1]

It is clear from other references in his autobiography that the source for this later breast obsession was his ongoing desire for his mother's breasts, a fascination that his mother seemed to encourage, as if to deepen their somewhat unhealthy Oedipal bond, which would prove to be so tragic in its consequences.

Willy's attitude toward his father was deeply ambivalent, ranging from extreme rage (certainly an appropriate response in his affection-starved youth) to a form of sentimental imitation. Leon was a brutal and sadistic man, given to constant psychosexual flirtation with staff, relatives, and wives of friends. He frequently beat the peasants on his estate and ruled everyone there with an iron fist, including his wife. Projecting his own desires, he regularly accused her of infidelity and made life profoundly difficult for the family, especially the two young sons, who adored their mother. Yet he was also a scholar of sorts and strongly supported his sons' education, hiring private tutors to prepare them for the rigorous examinations at the Gymnasium.

The farm life into which Reich was born was self-consciously aristocratic and assimilationist. The family was Jewish, but the Yiddish language was absolutely forbidden, and the children would be beaten for using it. High German was the language of the empire and thus the language of anyone wishing to climb the social ladder, while the lower classes spoke either Yiddish or Hungarian. Thus Reich's lifelong ambivalence about his own Judaism had its beginnings in Bukovina and his father's social pretensions. In later years Reich studied French, Latin, ancient Greek, and English and had a bit of Swedish, Danish, Norwegian, and Polish.

The family farm was located in a beautiful natural setting, and Reich early on developed a love of nature and of flora and fauna. He took to hunting and fishing and amassed an outstanding butterfly collection. His attention to naturalistic detail started in his adolescence and was reinforced by a series of fairly adept tutors from local universities. His refined observational and experimental eye later served him well in clinical settings, where he was able to size up a patient's muscular body armor in a matter of seconds, a skill not unlike that of taxonomic identification in the field. Reich was a *born* naturalist, and his later discovery of psychoanalysis has to be located in this prior biological and naturalistic background, a pre-thematic background that later became more clearly defined and shaped.

Willy was extremely precocious sexually. At the age of four he had his first noncoital sexual experience, with a maid; he lay on top of her and played with her pubic hair, intimating to her that he had already divined most things about the sexual act. He had also begun to watch the farm animals mating and found that he could artificially stimulate mares by inserting whip handles in their vaginas (an activity that later came to disgust him). His real sexual life started with the cook when he was eleven and a half. As he puts it in his autobiography: "She was the first to teach me the thrusting motion necessary for ejaculation, and at that time it had been an accident. From then on I had intercourse almost every day for years—it was always in the afternoon, when my parents were napping."[2] In his autobiography he states that his libidinal drive was quite powerful and that in his teens he frequented brothels. Often he would see his professors there, further teaching him about the deceits involved in "enforced monogamy." He masturbated compulsively during his early and late teen years, leading him, so he thought, into depression and despair over ever finding an ideal (maternal) woman who could rescue him from the abyss of his raging desires. From his fifteenth year until the war years (ages seventeen to twenty-one), he oscillated wildly between intense sexual episodes and severe suicidal depressions.

Reich gives a stunning description of one of his brothel visits when he was fifteen that shows both his capacity for frank honesty and his then-out-of-control libido:

Was it the atmosphere, the clothing, the red light, the provocative nakedness, the smell of whores—I don't know! I was pure sensual lust; *I* had ceased to be—I was all penis! I bit, scratched, thrust, and the girl had quite a time with me! I thought I would have to crawl inside her.[3]

His need to "crawl inside her" had at least two psychological sources, one being the suicide of his mother, which occurred in 1910, and the other being some probable borderline tendencies that drove him toward fusion with the Other rather than distance from her. In the former scenario there is an ongoing need to return to the paradise that has now been closed forever, in a quite literal sense. The body of the prostitute, which can be controlled by the patriarchal structure where money equals power over female flesh, is always available; always ready to provide an entrance

point into the dark taciturn world of the divine mysteries where generation takes place. Perhaps Reich saw the womb as being something like
Paul Tillich's great "ground of being," the source of all beings and the
sustaining ground of all life energy.[4] This fascination for prostitutes remained long after he stopped frequenting brothels.

In probing into the origins and trajectory of the family drama, we have
four sources that we can use to challenge one another. The first is the fascinating disguised case study, written in 1920, when Reich was twenty-
two or twenty-three—that is, about the same age when he wrote the first
part of his autobiography. The second is Reich's memoir *Passion of Youth*,
to which Sharaf did not have access (as it was published in 1988). The
third is Sharaf's biography, which first came out in 1983. The fourth is
Ilse Ollendorff's book *Wilhelm Reich: A Personal Biography*.[5] To add some
poignancy to the analysis of Reich's case study, it should be noted that
when Sharaf interviewed Reich's daughter Eva in 1971, she informed him
that Reich had admitted to her that the case study was a self-analysis.
What will become clear is that Reich's two depictions contain strong elements of denial, specifically surrounding his complicity leading to his
mother's ingestion of several poisons.

We will start with the disguised case study, published in 1920, when
Reich was a working analyst. It is entitled "A Case of Pubertal Breaching
of the Incest Taboo."[6] In English it is a brief nine-page document, but it
contains a wealth of material about the deep guilt structures that permeated Reich's partially unresolved Oedipal conflicts. The narrative's special urgency removes it from the usual genre of the clinical case study,
and Reich resorts to the interesting tactic of quoting a "letter" that he received from the "patient" that describes the family tragedy.

Reich introduces us to a student in his twenties who comes to him "all
choked up" and who cannot seem to function in the external world. He
states: "From our short, superficial conversation I could only surmise that
I was dealing with a compulsive symptom (a brooding mania)."[7] The
really interesting material begins to emerge when he starts unfolding the
patient's childhood Oedipal conflicts:

> From earliest childhood a deep tenderness bound him to his
> mother, and it was she who often protected him from the violent
> excesses of his father. His parents' marriage was not a happy one;

his mother "suffered terribly" because of his father's jealousy. At five or six, he had already witnessed horrible scenes of jealousy. Often his father had become violent. The boy had always been "on his mother's side." This is easily understandable since he himself was terrorized and loved his mother fervently. Because he had matured sexually at an early age sex was not a mystery to him . . . At age fifteen, the first slight feelings of inferiority found expression.[8]

The main features fall into line with his autobiography and with Sharaf's research, namely, the brooding, intense sexual fixation on the mother (he often engaged in a kind of sexual play with her with her consent), his very early sexual maturing, and his father's extreme physical violence.

Things became more complex when a series of tutors arrived in the household to prepare Willy and Robert for the Gymnasium. Perhaps in revenge for her older husband's constant brutality and flirtatious ways, Cecilie, never quite as beautiful as Reich liked to remember in his later idealizations, took a strong fancy to a tutor (called N in the case study) who had developed a special bond of trust with Willy. Reich watched with growing horror as they had sex whenever Leon was napping or away on business. In the letter that forms the heart of the case study, Reich describes how the patient slowly comes to realize that the primal scene is taking place right under his and Leon's noses, in his own house, with his own beloved mother and his own beloved tutor:

> Then, when Mother (oh, what a terrible ring that word now has!) came out of the room, which I could see was completely darkened, with flushed cheeks and a wild darting look in her eyes, I knew for sure; it had happened, although I had no way of telling whether or not for the first time. I stood in a corner, cowering behind a cabinet with tears streaming down my face. I wanted to run to her. But it didn't happen that way, to the great misfortune of us all. I am still deeply convinced that seeing me would have brought her to her senses, even though late, and saved us our mother and Father his wife. This would have been the only possible salvation.[9]

It is clear that Reich blamed himself for causing his mother's suicide by not confronting her straight away with her double betrayal. He was also afraid that if he had rushed in on the lovers, he might have been killed, a strange fantasy mixed with a desire to join the lovers in a threesome. Thus in one stroke he lost both his tutor and his mother, and he knew he was on the verge of a great paternal outburst that would shatter his home once and for all, which is in fact what happened.

He says nothing in the case study about how the father came to discover the infidelity, a very interesting omission, but merely asserts that it somehow happened. After his mother poisoned herself, "the patient's relationship to his father showed marked improvement. Gradually he became 'my best friend and advisor.'"[10] This is certainly a strange statement to make in a disguised self-analysis. Could Reich have been so blind to his real Oedipal feelings, or is he simply closing off the case study as quickly as possible so he can make his final comments on masturbation fantasies and the role of the "horrible secret" in adulthood? Indeed, he lightly passes over by far the most important question of the subsequent postsuicide family relationship—namely, how to deal with the violent father who is partially to blame for all that happened. Fortunately, we find a much more honest and revealing Reich in the (then unpublished) autobiography.

In the journal account of his discovery of the primal scene between S (not N) and his mother, he presents the narrative in roughly the same way. It is filled with a pained awareness that two of the most important people in his life have torn his world asunder:

> I heard them kissing, whispering, and the horrible creaking of the bed in which my mother lay. Ten feet away stood her own child, a witness to her disgrace. Suddenly there was quiet. Probably I had made some noise in my excitement. Then his soothing voice, and then, then again—oh!
>
> Oh, composure, peace! What a superhuman effort it takes to write this shattering tragedy "objectively"! What mockery! What an undertaking! All I remember of that catastrophic night is that I wanted to rush into the room, but was held back by the thought: they might kill you! I recalled having read that a lover will kill anyone who disturbs him. With a head full of bizarre fantasies I crept back to bed, without hope of consolation, my youthful spirit

broken! For the first time, a deep feeling of misfortune and of having been abandoned overcame me.[11]

He reports that he repeated his spying behavior night after night and even thought (as noted above) of "breaking in on them and demanding that she have intercourse with me too (shame!), threatening that otherwise I would tell Father."[12] Thus we see emerging a combination of guilt, lust, inferiority, rage, fear, need for betrayal, a feeling of being betrayed, and a sense of the woman (the "ideal" woman) as the most unreliable creature on earth.

Thus, the Reich of the secret journals is a Reich able to be candid about the Oedipal struggles among himself, Leon, Cecilie, and the tutor whom he identifies as S. At the same time he unburdens his "dual guilt" that lay behind what he thought of as his complicity in his mother's suicide. In the autobiography he seems unsure of the truth and presents the case as if his father forced the truth out of him by direct threats, but the evidence points more in the direction of an Oedipal revenge tragedy in which Willy gets back at his mother by willingly setting forth a series of strong hints so that Leon will be compelled to draw the inevitable conclusions. Sharaf interviewed several people close to Reich, who claimed that Reich had admitted that he had told his father of the betrayal (contrary to the accounts in the case study and the autobiography).[13]

The revelation came about after Willy, on a dare from a farmhand, stole some tobacco from his father's locked desk drawer. While rummaging through the drawer, he happened upon a picture book of naked women and a sexually explicit marriage manual. He devoured both books and quickly returned them to the safety of the locked interior of the desk (the paternal realm of secrets). But Leon discovered the theft of the tobacco soon enough and called for an immediate search of all the farmhands. Unfortunately for Willy, his mother found a "cigarette-rolling device" in one of his pockets and told Leon about it. So his mother in effect betrayed him to the paternal castrating power. Leon's response was swift and violent:

That settled it. I received a good beating and slinked off into the garden, without shedding a tear. The beating didn't bother me, I was used to that, but being betrayed by Mother confused me com-

pletely. She had delivered me into Father's clutches! I could not
get over it, nor did I ever forgive her.[14]

Interestingly, S was away for summer break at the time and was not one of
the innumerable sexual suspects on Leon's list. When Leon found out that
S was indeed the culprit, he started shouting, at which point a scream
could be heard from Cecilie's bedroom. She had swallowed a common
house cleaner such as Lysol, an act that was itself almost pathetic in its
combination of utter despair and its guarantee of excruciating suffering.
She swallowed one poison after another, while Leon continued to beat her
as she died. In Sharaf's account, Cecilie dies a few days later, while in
Reich's account, she lingers on for months.[15]

Cecilie's mother, who had a strong dislike for Leon, had tried to intervene after the marital estrangement by having Cecilie and her two children
move into town to get away from the daily beatings, but to no avail. Between
the poisons and the beatings, Cecilie's body could no longer hold out, and
she died in 1910, when Reich was, as noted, thirteen. It is unclear
whether her death was caused by an intentional suicide or came about as
the result of a cumulative series of self-destructive acts. In 1944 Reich
appended a self-lacerating note to his autobiography that shows how he
had continued to struggle with his Oedipal guilt (and sense of betrayal):

> How logical and rational! How mistaken my ideas were in 1919
> [that is, in his earlier journals]. The situation has now become
> clear to me: what Mother did was perfectly all right! My betrayal,
> which cost her her life, was an act of revenge: she had betrayed me
> to Father when I stole the tobacco for the Cartwright, and in return
> I then betrayed *her*! What a tragedy! I wish my mother were alive
> today so that I could make good for the crime I committed in those
> days, thirty-five years ago. I have set up a picture of that noble
> woman so that I can look at it over and over again. What a noble
> creature, this woman—my mother! May my life's work make good
> for my misdeed. In view of my father's brutality, she was perfectly
> right![16]

Here we see the idealization process really taking hold, part of the
Oedipal struggle and perhaps an element of borderline-like fusion. In the

early journal accounts there is a strong dose of devaluation, combined with a deeply conflicted idealization. Reich's account of uncovering his mother's body in front of her mourners the day after her death shows a callow disregard for everyone's feelings, and he responds to her corpse as if it were a scientific object for detached study.[17] He does observe, however, that this experience taught him that he had the character trait of "emotional masochism" and that he later came to enjoy the role of the martyr.

His father began to feel guilt over Cecilie's death, but it may have been tied to a kind of wounded narcissism rather than to any sense of genuine complicity in the tragic suicide. Yet he did begin to act out in a way that, at least unconsciously (according to Reich), showed that he took on the guilt burden of Cecilie's suicide (as it was understood) and sought a means of atonement. Leon took out a life insurance policy for his two sons and then, according to Ollendorff, exposed himself to the elements while pretending to be fishing. Already weakened by the family events, he contracted tuberculosis. He was able, after Reich's frantic efforts, to borrow enough money to travel to the Alps for convalescence, but the disease won out, and he died in 1914.

Thus, at the age of seventeen Willy had lost both of his parents, one to a suicide he dimly felt he had caused and the other to a carelessly contracted illness that was directly tied to the first. Meanwhile he was acting out sexually in ways entwined with the Oedipal triangle (or square if you include S) that he was forced to enter into in an abnormal way.

Willy and Robert remained on the estate, trying to maintain as much as possible of its previous successful operation. On July 31, 1914, news of the war and the general mobilization reached them. Reich responded almost indifferently to the idea of war at first. But when Russian soldiers arrived and briefly took over the estate, he began to understand its implications, especially since the locals soon took sides, choosing between their Russian liberators or their protectors from Vienna.

Reich was taken prisoner by the Russian army and ordered to join a horse column that was to be taken back to Russia for an uncertain fate. He was able to persuade his guard to allow him to use his own horses and sleigh rather than immediately climb into the army sleigh that was waiting for him. This diversion bought him enough time to get a farmhand to round up some bribe money to give to his Russian guard. As the column moved out of town (Reich had cleverly managed to be the last sleigh in the group) and Reich began to despair, several farm workers rode up to the back of the entourage and handed a large envelope to the guard. Reich slowed down very cautiously and at the right moment, with a wink to the guard, pulled away from the group and returned to his estate.

But the estate did not prove to be a refuge, as the Russians were active in a military charge against the Austrians and Germans. Chaos was raining down on the valley as the Austrian cavalry fled from the battlefield. Reich had only one choice, to whip up his horses, join the full retreat, and hope for safety behind the lines. By a stroke of luck he escaped with the routed troops, whereupon he joined the Austrian army. In his autobiography he recalled:

> I reported for military service half a year earlier than I was due to, legally, and was assigned to a division which built roads and simultaneously practiced with weapons. As a volunteer, I did not yet have the right to a commission, because I had not got my secondary-school diploma. But twelfth-grade pupils could get a *Notabitur*, or emergency diploma. You had to make up the courses of the final year and pass a somewhat leniently judged examination . . . By this time [summer 1915], I was in officer's school. We were eighteen-year-old boys, as were some thousands in the Eastern Army. With six weeks of infantry training behind us, we were being instructed in extended and platoon company leadership. The schooling was strict and difficult . . . I returned to the regiment a full corporal.[18]

Before too long he was assigned to the front lines to fight against the Italians. He seemed to have had little difficulty adjusting to life under fire, and he slowly began to probe into the psychological and sociological aspects of what he quickly came to see as an absurd war. In his view, the much older men under him did not much understand or care to know the reasons for the war. They simply were in no position to think in terms of class struggle, or of the dissolution of the empire, or of nationalism. He soon found out that food, sex, and survival were uppermost on his troops' minds, and he took every opportunity to provide his men access to these goods.

Of course, sex is especially brutalized during wartime, and the issues of patriarchy become intensified: men are causing the war, and men force women to offer them "relaxation" during brief moments of escape from battle. Reich expressed his moral indignation at the sexism of war in his account of brothel life on the front:

> The Italian prisoners brought their brothels with them: an older woman with four or five girls. Our people when on reserve were given "brothel leave." In Fiume and Trieste this business flowered in a ghastly way. The soldiers were lined up alphabetically to go to one girl. The Italian women were quartered in our camp. By day, some of the batmen [officers' servants] and some of the men slept with them. The following night, the officers took them into their rooms. Three days later, a whole column marched back to the rear with gonorrhea. Among them, our captain. So much for morality.[19]

This brief morality tale, of course, comes from a young man for whom prostitutes were his lifeblood after the death of his mother. Was he projecting his own fear of infection?[20] Or was his outrage tied to the shock of seeing a whole mass of men descending on four or five women in such a "military" fashion? At least in his brothel experiences the relationships had had the semblance of being one on one and had some foreplay and conversation. Here, perhaps, the depersonalization was too much to bear and would leave its mark on his later reflections on the need for total *social* sexual reconstruction, not just personal. Even so, his sense of the personal remained strong and rather elitist in the 1920s, centered on a kind of self-actualization and model tied to Germanic ideals of spirit and autonomy.

Reich was promoted to the rank of lieutenant and company commander. But his control over his troops diminished, and partially owing to the general war malaise, he gave them greater and greater latitude. His commanders seemed not to care about this lax behavior, which was spreading throughout the ranks; Reich was more or less conforming to the norm. Finally, at age twenty-one, he applied for a furlough, which soon led to his full demobilization. His strong desire to enter university studies had been put on hold by the war, and he was keen to embark on a degree program of some kind. He went immediately to the University of Vienna, thinking that he would study law, but his inner drives soon dictated otherwise:

> But law was not for me. I undertook it because one could earn one's living more quickly here than elsewhere. There were three-month cram courses for the first state exam. I studied industriously, but without inner involvement. Two weeks before the examination, filled with hundreds of paragraphs of Roman and ecclesiastical law, I ran into an old school friend who was studying medicine. He reawakened my interest in natural science. I dropped jurisprudence, and transferred to the faculty of medicine. It was a good intuitive move; a few weeks later Austria fell, and with it, its administration of justice. I would have gone under, as I was without any material basis of existence.[21]

What had Reich gained from his more than four years of war service? He had received basic and then advanced military training and, at the age of eighteen, had been given command over peasant and bourgeois men in their thirties and forties. He started developing a deep sense of class-consciousness that flowered into socialism and later into communism and finally in his later years into what he called "work-democracy." He saw how patriarchy can misuse sex, especially in extreme conditions, and how human life can be utterly devalued. One of his commanders had his legs blown off a few feet in front of him, and he saw many men die because of mindless and stupid orders, orders that he often had to countermand to save lives. His sense of self-worth was hardened by the war and was propped up, as he clearly notes in his autobiography, by his officer status. This status was especially evident via his uniform (every insignia of which had meaning in a semiotic code that soldiers treated with great seriousness).

Sharaf gives his own summation of what the war might have meant to Reich, seeing it as a partial cure for the family traumas of 1910 and 1914, a means for looking back at the suicides and for preparing for the emergence of what Jung called the great "hero myth." Sharaf argues:

> In a life of danger, he could feel some relief from the inner pressures, some surcease from the guilt of the past. In time, he would

channel this "heroic" effort into a task that made sense, into a mission not of simply staying alive but repairing the conditions that had produced the early tragedies.[22]

The hero myth can inflate the ego and provide a goal and direction that can seem to overcome all obstacles. One of the emergent features of the postwar Reich was an intensely driven and laserlike focus concerning his mission in life, and anything connected with his myth was protected from internal and external criticism. This heroic myth can also be seen in Freud, Adler, Jung, Einstein (hardly the benign, wise old man of Princeton he pretended to be),[23] and many others. In fact, it may be a necessary condition for genius-level productivity. In the next chapter Reich's genius will measure itself against the university world and against the father of psychoanalysis. At the same time (in the 1920s) Reich will write a series of papers that show his immediate grasp of classical psychoanalysis and, in turn, the first unfolding of his own unique vision.

2

Medical School, Freud,

and the Early Papers

In switching from law to medicine, Reich reignited his youthful passion for the exploration of natural phenomena. But he was also to come into conflict, as Freud had decades earlier, with the rather crass materialistic reductionism in Vienna, whose leading thinkers remained profoundly unfriendly to theories of vitalism (which posited a unified life energy behind the seeming dualism of mind and matter) and to any hint of dark mysterious unconscious mechanisms that could somehow have somatic consequences. In its worst form, such reductionism recasts the status of the mind to that of a purely neurological event with no independent status in the body, no goals, no laws, no teleology. From this it followed, given the physicalist presupposition, that the mind had no independent causal or teleological sequences that would follow their own logic or require an alternative explanatory model. In the most famous analogy used by these mind/brain identity theorists, the thoughts that came out of the brain were likened to the bile that is secreted by the liver (or as a philosopher would have put it, thoughts were mere epiphenomena, not genuine self-standing phenomena in themselves). Consequently, the very idea of a *depth* psychology was ruled out of court in advance.

Freud in 1885 decided that he had to travel to Paris to find some help in escaping from the death-grip of this reductionism. He went to study with the two most famous neurologists outside of the Vienna school, Jean-Martin Charcot (1825–93) and Pierre Janet (1859–1947),[1] to gain access to the then emergent thinking on so-called conversion hysteria (partial bodily paralysis due to hidden unconscious conflicts) and hypnosis, both phenomena entailing an unconscious mechanism as their causal explanation. Both neurologists were on the staff of the Salpetrière, the famous mental hospital for insane women. To the Paris school, Viennese psychoanalysis owed such key insights as the role of psychic-to-somatic conversion of a mental conflict into a physical symptom. They also learned that there could be a hypnotic reversal of this conversion process in which suggestion would remove the symptom.

The gender issue of the relation of hysteria to women had yet to be thought through carefully, the idea then being maintained that hysteria was primarily a female pathology. Reich, of course, came on the scene two decades after the classical papers on hysteria were written, and psychoanalysis had moved in decisive new directions, leaving behind some of its more distasteful patriarchal conceptions, although it had a long way to go in its understanding of the role of sexual repression in woman vis-à-vis men (and still does, according to many). Strange as it may sound to some, the very Reich who violated some personal and professional sexual boundaries actually broke down many more of the patriarchal structures of his own discipline than did chaste analysts such as Freud. Whether there is a causal link between these twin and seemingly conflicting aspects of Reich's life and work is a question that we will keep very much in mind in all that follows.

Reich certainly had an astonishing ability to understand the unconscious sexual strategies and needs of both men and women and to understand their complex forms of entrapment in social and political forms of power. He understood the ways women were exploited in patriarchy and in capitalism, as Freud did not, and in his mature phase came to understand that there would be no genital liberation for men or women until these unjust power structures were conquered. But he was also very critical of personal forms of psychosexual manipulation even within these external patriarchal structures. In his journals of the early 1920s he remarks on the chaste women who use flirtation as a tool but do not take ownership of their own sexuality, calling them the true "whores." Of course, many women of that kind turned down his sexual overtures, and his sensitivity for rejection was acute.

Reich's powerful mind, combined with an occasional dose of psychic inflation, not to mention the energy that also came from his naturally intense libido, drove him into his studies with a seizing passion. He worked in warm cafés from the early hours of the morning, took breaks for classes, then returned to the cafés and worked until late at night. His own rooms were unheated during his first year at the University of Vienna, and he had to live off the charity of others. He was forced to wear his army uniform to class (as was not uncommon) and to share his fellow students' care packages. Fortunately, as a war veteran, he was put on an accelerated track whereby he could complete his degree with four years of extra-intense study rather than the customary six.

Already in 1919 he had heard of psychoanalysis through a student group on sexuality that could operate only outside of the classroom, since the university professors were generally hostile to Freud and his ideas and to any serious discussion of sexuality. He quickly rose to a leadership role in the student group and took the initiative of introducing himself to Freud, also in 1919. For Reich this was and remained *the* decisive personal encounter of his life. Even though he broke with almost all of the members of the Vienna group by the end of the 1920s, father Freud included, he never developed any personal rancor toward Freud, always putting him into a very special category. Here is how Reich describes Freud the person in the revised edition of *The Function of the Orgasm*:

> Freud was different. Whereas the others all played some kind of role, whether that of the professor, the great discerner of human character, or the distinguished scientist, Freud did not put on any airs. He spoke with me like a completely ordinary person. He had bright, intelligent eyes, which did not seek to penetrate another person's eyes in some sort of mantic pose, but simply looked at the world in an honest and truthful way. He inquired about our work in the seminar and found it very sensible. We were right, he said . . . Freud spoke rapidly, objectively, and animatedly. The movements of his hands were natural. There was a hint of irony in everything he said.[2]

Freud's nonmantic pose and noninvasive eyes were often noted by others, and of course Freudian irony is as well known as the ancient Socratic form.

By his second year, partially because of his outstanding grades and charismatic performances in the classroom and in student groups, Reich landed many tutoring jobs and bettered his living conditions. He also started taking on patients, referred to him by Freud, who had appreciated Reich's talents after meeting him and assessing his analytic abilities and after Reich, as required by the rules of the Vienna Psychoanalytic Society (of which he was now a member), underwent analysis himself. His early analysts (Isidor Sadger and Paul Federn), by the conclusion of their work with their young candidate, "came to dislike Reich bitterly."[3] Partially because of this early experience of his own aggressive negative transferences as an analysand (patient), I speculate that Reich was reluctant to undergo any long-term analysis. Perhaps this also led him to champion the short-term *character analysis* rather than the detailed retrospective *symptom analysis* practiced by most Vienna psychoanalysts.

Thus, between the time he started medical school in 1919 and his graduation in 1922, he had already been invited into the inner circle of psychoanalysis and started to write papers that show his vast knowledge of the current and past literature.[4] He was especially taken with Freud's *Interpretation of Dreams*[5] and started applying its model to his own dream material outside of the analytic sessions. It is a common misconception that Reich was not concerned with classical dream analysis, but in fact he occasionally took note of his own rather revealing dreams, and he recorded and analyzed the dreams of his patients to help him with his work on their muscular armoring.

I think that his dream interpretations often fell into Freudian ruts, and I propose to give them a more capacious reading, going beyond his analyses. In general, his personal dreams were less complex and multilayered than Jung's, as one can say that Jung was a true creative genius of the dreamscape in a way that neither Freud nor Reich ever was. I think that the deep flaws in Freud's dream theory stem largely from the fact that his own dream life was too linguistically oriented, seeing plays on words from the residue of the previous day's activities as being the main work of the dream economy. Consequently, Freud's dreams simply lacked the metaphoric density of Jung's (which were image focused), and the dreams that he wrote about were not as amenable to as much categorial or phenomenological probing as Jung's. Further, Freud's wish fulfillment and displacement model, based on an archaeological and resistance hermeneutic (theory of interpretation) places far too much power in the hands of the analyst (who must overcome the resistance), while Jung's model of circumambulation and amplification of symbols is teleological (goal-oriented) and lets symbols unfold according to their *own* multiform future. But Reich, more than Freud, revealed some of his anima fixations (the archetype of the "divine feminine") and the presence of his hypomanic characteristics when he wrote about his dreams.

In addition to his classwork and his budding work in psychoanalysis was his growing interest in politics and in the "Jewish problem." Central to this interest is a journal entry from February 25, 1919, when Reich reports on having gone, somewhat reluctantly, to hear a Dr. Bergmann from Prague talk about a new understanding of Judaism and of the role of Jews in the postwar world:

> There was no hatred for everything non-Jewish, but a meaningful receptiveness to others; no controversy over Jewish versus Hebrew, over blue-and-white versus red-and-green, but expansiveness in all directions, renewing itself in ever-widening circles. Down came the impenetrable barriers, and then—the word came to me—international cosmopolitanism in the broadest sense! I confess that, for the first time since hearing or experiencing similar speeches, something arose within me—an explanation! This was the reason why I hated—yes, hated—all those who endeavored to help the Jews attain happiness—not along with other human beings, but over their dead bodies; not with the consent of others, but against their will! Not "we are all together," but just "*we*"! And finally I was listening to a man who is both a Jew and a human being simultaneously, not a chauvinist! We shall see what kind of fruit his efforts will bear.[6]

Needless to say, this is a pre-Holocaust writing, and it ignores the growth of anti-Semitism in Vienna and throughout the former Austro-Hungarian Empire. It reminds one of another Jewish thinker who expressed international cosmopolitanism in his philosophical perspective: the philosopher Baruch Spinoza (1632–77), who was excommunicated from his religious congregation in Amsterdam for holding views that were outside of the Torah.[7] For both Spinoza and Reich, a religious community must bind itself to the power of universal reason and the cosmic power that can best be defined as "nature continually creating itself out of itself." Neither thinker required a paternalistic god who would somehow magically create the world out of nothingness and then rule it on the model of an earthly (and abusive) father. There are some surprising parallels between a psychoanalytic deconstruction of the patriarchal deity and the rationalistic elimination of classical theism. Both Reich and Spinoza, then, represent thinkers who could show a tradition how to become generic and emancipatory from within.

Reich's brilliant academic work, his sudden emergence as a young force within the Vienna Psychoanalytic Society, his slow political radicalization, and his unique form of cosmopolitan Judaism all still took place against the physical background of his libidinal surges, and he again found himself on the edges of Oedipal and professional boundaries. On December 22, 1919, he wrote in his diary, "Twice I masturbated while consciously fantasizing about my mother—saw and felt only her abdomen, never her face."[8] We have noted above that Cecilie had encouraged fairly serious erotic play with Willy, especially with her breasts, and that he came to regard such boundary transgressions as within the bounds of normal behavior, perhaps as part of a legitimate means of testing his male prowess against the abusive father. My speculation is that his later propensity for complex emotional triangles had its root in his mother's "permission" to invade forbidden territory. This evolved into his need to rescue the (lucky) chosen woman from a partner whom she may not even have suspected was unworthy of her devotion, compared, of course, to the great man himself, who was more than happy to provide an escape from a (secretly) unhappy situation.

On the professional side, Reich worked on a case that had profound implications for his personal life, even if he was to keep the immediate professional censure (this time) at bay. It should be remembered that in the early days of psychoanalysis, the rules for analyst/analysand behavior outside of the analytic situation were not as clearly set as they are today. For example, it was Jung's practice to tell his patients about any major dreams he had about *them*, thus revealing key pieces of his countertransference. This would be very much frowned upon today by most analysts. And of course Jung committed many sexual transgressions, indiscretions that he struggled to keep hidden, especially in the well-known cases of Sabina Spielrein and Toni Wolff.[9]

The case in point involved one of Reich's first patients, with whom he worked even before getting his M.D. The patient was a nineteen-year-old kindergarten teacher named Lore Kahn, who came to Reich in the winter of 1919–20. According to his account in his autobiography, which strikes me as a bit defensive, Lore declared her love for him after a few sessions, and he wrote it off as a classical father-transference. Yet he soon admitted to himself that he might be able to have her *after* their analysis was completed. After all, nothing was to prevent such a *post*-therapeutic relationship:

> In short, Lore declared one day that she was analyzed, and now she wanted me.
> I did not feel much desire for her. One should not sleep with one's patients; it is too complicated and dangerous. But Lore was at last "herself." She could wait, she said . . . After all, she was no longer a patient. And it was nobody's business. I loved her, and she grew very happy.
> On the 27th of October 1920, she wrote the last entry in her diary:
> I am happy, boundlessly happy, I would never have thought that I could be—but I am. The fullest, deepest fulfillment. To have a father and be a mother, both in the same person. Marriage! Monogamy! At last! Never was there coitus with such sensual pleasure, such gratification, and such a sense of oneness and interpenetration as now. Never such parallel attraction of the mind and body. And it is beautiful. And I have direction, clear, firm, and sure—I love myself this way. I am content as nature intended! Only one thing: *a child!*[10]

It is characteristic that Reich referred to the analyst/analysand sexual prospect as "too complicated and dangerous" rather than as unprofessional or unethical, even postanalysis. But people with borderline tendencies are often drawn to the complicated and dangerous, and for good or ill, this tendency makes for daring science, great art, charismatic leadership, and dynamic speaking.

The relationship flowered after the (premature?) termination of analysis, and Reich immediately encountered hostility from Kahn's family, who assumed that he was abusing his power as an analyst over their emotionally fragile daughter. Their position is understandable, given that Reich's personality was a dominating force in almost all of his relationships, even though he had, as he admitted, deeply seeded masochistic components derived from, I think, paternal abuse. In any case, their intense love affair was complicated by a typical Reichian triangle. He was also in love with a fellow medical student, Lia Laszky, and was unwilling to give up this "necessary" psychological lifeline:

> She knew that I loved Lia, differently from her. We understood that one can love two people simultaneously when one is young. She was not angry, any more than I was angry with Lia. All was well between us. But we had no room in which we could be together undisturbed. It was no longer possible at my place; the landlady had become hostile and a threat. So Lore got a room at a friend's. It was unheated and bitter cold. Lore became ill, ran a high fever, with dangerous articular rheumatism, and eight days later died of sepsis [toxic condition resulting from bacterial infection], in the bloom of her young life.[11]

One theme emerges here that became an important social issue for Reich, namely, the lack of access to private spaces for lovemaking for the urban youth of Vienna. His hatred for patriarchy had as one of its sources the ability of fathers to literally control their daughters' living spaces so that they could not begin the sexual experiments that he saw as so crucial to their full development as human beings. The issue of Lore's rather sudden death quickly started a series of accusations that could have brought Reich to complete ruin.

Lore's mother accused Reich of forcing Lore to have an illegal abortion, the botched effects of which caused her to die alone in her room. She further asserted that Reich used his "influence" to cover over the fact, and that this was more evidence of his callous and ruthless behavior. To be implicated in an illegal abortion, especially if one was a medical student who should know the law, was a very serious charge, but Reich met it head on. From his perspective, the mother was in love with him, and she was doing all in her power to damage him because he had not reciprocated her love. But she claimed to have evidence from reliable sources that the abortion had indeed taken place, that Reich was covering it up, and that she could, and would, use this evidence against him.

His tactic was simple: he took her with him to meet the people she named, and they simply denied any such knowledge of what she had been told. From Reich's autobiographical account, this closed the matter, although it did not cool off the mother's displaced romantic longings. To compound the tragedy, and to add irony to irony, Lore's mother committed suicide by gassing herself in December 1920. In his diary entry of December 10, Reich blamed himself: "But this time it's different [from *his* mother's suicide], for I am the cause—not a soul to help me! It's awful! Who will tell me how I should have behaved? I was the cause, but could I have helped it? Who will tell me what I am?"[12] In Sharaf's account, based upon 1971 interviews with Reich's fellow medical students Grete Bibring and Lia Laszky,[13] he accepts the validity of the abortion charge. What is one to make of this rather serious conflict in interpretation, where you have the word of Reich, which is clearly designed to present himself in the best possible light, in conflict with the accounts, taken down fifty years later, from one member of his love triangle (Lia) and from another woman (Grete) who spurned Reich's romantic interest at the time and later often spoke of Reich with distaste? Until more data appear, one can only hazard a guess.

Whether or not there was an abortion, Reich repeated the analyst/ analysand love relationship a year later with a patient named Annie Pink. On January 13, 1921, he wrote in his diary:

> It is becoming increasingly obvious that I am analyzing Annie Pink with intensions of later winning her for myself—as was the case with Lore . . . How do I feel about that? What must I do? Terminate the analysis? No, because afterwards there would be no contact! But she—what if she remains fixated on me as Lore did? Resolve the transference thoroughly! Yes, but is transference not love, or, better said, isn't all love a transference?
>
> A young man in his twenties should not treat female patients.[14]

The analysis lasted six months, and at its termination Reich was able, by his account, to declare his love to Annie, who had, interestingly enough, been a friend of Lore. By the middle of the summer they had become lovers. On March 17, 1922, they were married in a civil ceremony, although Reich insisted in his diary that it was a "forced marriage" due to intense pressure from Annie's parents. This, to me, is a striking and interesting pattern—namely, that Reich had to gain control of his future wife by analyzing her psychosexual Oedipal structures and cathecting them in his direction as the new Oedipal and transference object. He conflates the distinction between transference and love in a way that gives serious pause, precisely because the transference is unconscious and takes away autonomy and also involves the projection of complexes, whereas genuine love entails the opening of one integrated psyche to another integrated psyche. The marriage was not destined to survive; but the pattern that set it in motion was.

One of Reich's first recorded dreams sheds some light on his therapeutic and relational strategies as well as on the depth structures of his intense drive to connect with powerful female figures. This classical anima dream was recorded on January 3, 1921:

> A tall girl, with long, flowing hair, in a loose garment, spoke from a sweet little mouth; I kissed her hand, leaned against her—shoulder to shoulder, cheek to cheek—and far beyond, beyond the gray-gold city, the sky opened up. Two large, bony hands wave—you call out—why should that not be possible?
>
> No! Joyous, calling, singing—Leopoldsberg—the church rising from the old wall—below us the deep Danube valley—clothes off, and we danced, naked as our mothers bore us, danced, so close to the edge.
>
> *Scherzo (Allegro)*—we danced, danced naked as the children of God, in the long shadows of our bodies cast by a silent moon—peace drew us together again and I buried my heated brow in her tender thighs, covered my head with her long blond hair—so close to the edge—while we wound our arms around and around each other like serpents and my brow found her soft white breast.
>
> Oh, what a pitiable psychoanalyst I am! How well I know what all this means![15]

Unfortunately, Reich does not enlighten us as to "what all this means." But several aspects of his dream shed great light on his personality, both at the age of twenty-three and as it intensified in his later years: (1) the dreamlike quality of the landscape, showing its mythic and archetypal nature (in the prelude to the dream proper he states that he is "off in a cloud"); (2) the classic larger-than-life anima as divine figure with flowing hair who contains magical secrets and healing energies (especially between her thighs and on her breasts); (3) the magical gray-gold city that is unlike, yet like, any earthy city (a classic archetypal paradox); (4) Reich and his anima always dancing "so close to the edge"; (5) the lunar power that is another representation of the anima; and (6) the serpentlike entwining (a still-lingering patriarchal image in need of transformation).

The repeated image of dancing naked, close to the edge, is a perfect iconic representation of both hypomania and borderline/impulsive features, as both entail a rich transgressive energy that *must* find itself "on the boundaries," in the words of Paul Tillich. At the same time, because of the devouring quality of the abyss that lies just beyond the edge, the protective thighs and breasts of the anima must be available for the "heated brow" of the satyrlike creature who is as primal as the day he came out of his mother's womb. He dances the triple-time *Scherzo* and the brisk *Allegro* to express his mania and to divest himself of some of its fury. The healing anima becomes the divine Other who takes on his mania and cools its energy, especially with the voluminous in-taking power of her vagina and the cooling power of her "soft white breast." Here there is no hint of the *vagina dentata*, namely the devouring vagina that eviscerates the penis and leaves the man castrated and ruined. This dream anima is almost exclusively a positive energy, which shows that the dream is a compensatory dream for his strong negative/conflicted feelings toward woman, especially Cecilie and perhaps the deceased (murdered?) Lore. The anima is blond, which was the preferred hair color for all of Reich's fantasy women and many of his actual women.[16]

Serpent power is an interesting concept in its own right. From the patriarchal perspective, the serpent has been associated with feminine wiles and has thus been abjected as a form of life that should be distrusted and even destroyed. In a postpatriarchal world the serpent (perhaps no longer even called a "serpent") will be more properly seen as a symbol of constant renewal and regeneration, rather than as a source of evil and temptation. It is interesting that in Reich's dream the serpent symbol takes on the makings of a postpatriarchal image and functions in a more positive way, leading me to further suspect that he was moving beyond the kind of patriarchy that was so endemic to Vienna in the 1920s and later.

There is also a clear sign of his dominating presence, a key trait of his therapeutic relationships, which were anything but passive. He actively buries his head in the anima's thighs, not waiting for an invitation. He gathers her long blond hair around his head as if to hide from the gaze of the outside world. The image I have of his anima ideal is similar to that of a Pre-Raphaelite painting by Dante Gabriel Rossetti, namely, his 1849–50 *Ecce Ancilla Domini*, or *The Annunciation*, that shows Mary and the angel of the lord as two young and beautiful blond women with flowing hair and thin, lean, intense faces. They represent a combination of nineteenth-century northern European ideal womanhood and medieval iconography. Clearly, they could be the rescuers without parallel.

Dreams are not the *only* "royal road(s) to the unconscious," even though they are among the most important indicators of the inner dynamics of the personal and collective psyche. For the philosopher, theologian, or intellectual historian, *conceptual structures*, when looked at from a psychoanalytic perspective, also contain clues pointing to the inner life of their creator.[17] At this point enough has been presented of the early biographical and autobiographical work to prepare the way for a categorial analysis, remembering the promise in the preface that the issue of validity will be placed on the same level of importance as the issue of probing into the "unsaid," both psychological and conceptual, in the texts themselves.

My focus will be on ten of the twelve papers in the English edition of Reich's *Early Writings* (volume 1; volume 2 is titled: *Genitality*).[18] They cover the years from 1920, the first essay being Reich's inaugural paper to the Vienna Psychoanalytic Society on Ibsen's *Peer Gynt*, to the final essay (actually more like a book or monograph), namely his 1925 study of the impulsive character. We have already dealt with his so-called "case study" ("A Case of Pubertal Breaching of the Incest Taboo"). I will not deal with the *Peer Gynt* essay, as it would require an extensive literary background reconstruction.

Consequently, we will start with the third paper in the book, "Coition and the Sexes," which was first read before the Seminar for Sexuality in

Vienna in 1921, when Reich was around twenty-four.[19] Reich wrote the brief (thirteen-page) paper as a direct response to a paper in an earlier issue of the *Zeitschrift für Sexualwissenschaft* that had argued for a physiological and biological basis for the time differences between male and female orgasms. The author, one Urbach, had maintained that males ejaculate before females because their biology so dictated but that a second male orgasm would be most desirable for procreation. Reich argued that, quite to the contrary, nature would never have staked the future of the species on something as risky as a second male orgasm and that the differences in the timing between male and female orgasms must have a pathogenic and psychological cause. His arguments reveal a great deal about his own sexual splits, his Oedipal struggles, and the lingering power of patriarchal thinking, even over someone as liberated as Reich. But they also reveal that he had an understanding of healthy sexuality and mature relationality, even if the issue of monogamy continued to puzzle him.

He first attacked the problem of the time differential between male and female climaxes by focusing on the pathology of male premature ejaculation and its internal psychological causes, again sidestepping any biological causal agency:

> Beginning with the mildest disturbance of potency—ejaculatio praecox—there is every imaginable intermediary stage up to the most severe cases of total incapability of having an erection. Psychoanalytic treatment of such illnesses regularly reveals one characteristic common to all patients suffering from impotence . . . This one characteristic is the split of all libidinous drives into a tender and a sensual component. This split is most obvious in cases of facultative impotence, where, for example, the patient is always unable to have intercourse with his own wife but never fails with a prostitute.[20]

He fails to mention that the man could be consciously or unconsciously afraid of infecting his wife with syphilis (which was incurable, although partially treatable, in the 1920s and in its tertiary stages could produce severe brain and central nervous system disorders).[21] But in any event, a facultative impotence was person specific and clearly psychological rather than biological. It was a direct manifestation of the "tender" and "sensual" split that harked back to conflicted feelings connected with the mother/whore.

Reich probed deeper into another aspect of male premature ejaculation and of personal and even class-specific impotence. He brought in the tried-and-true theory of castration anxiety to beef up his concept of the dynamism behind the tender/sensual split, in turn shedding light, unwittingly, on his own anima fixation and his own unresolved relationship to the powerful father who forced the mother to submit to his will, thus making her a *de facto* whore:

> Ejaculatio praecox and facultative impotence usually occur together, but the former also occurs separately and in relation to all women. It is the expression of a certain unconscious fear, usually that of castration. The patient may also have inhibiting ideas, e.g., that a woman has teeth in her vagina, or that something exists at the end of the woman's "tube" that snaps at the penis, etc. However, when ejaculatio praecox is also a symptom of facultative impotence, these fears are augmented by an express antipathy toward coitus with a woman of the patient's own social class, even his own wife. The reasons for this antipathy and for the curiously undisturbed potency with prostitutes can be found, on close investigation, in a split of the first love object desired as a child (usually the mother, the nurse, or an older sister) into two opposing figures; first, the prostitute and second, the unattainable, idealized, "sacred" woman, to be approached with the utmost reverence.[22]

In retrospect it seems plain that Reich adopted the conventional Madonna/whore split, in which the presence/absence of the paternal force makes the maternal vagina the source for potential death rather than rebirth. Of course, he was trying to illuminate the pathological extreme of the already damaged psyche that has been forced into and out of the Oedipal struggle in a pathological fashion, only to revisit it without the requisite psychological tools. But his psychopathological theory drew too strongly on his own experience to have the status of objective psychoanalytic science. And the tender/sensual dyad was standard conceptual issue in the Vienna of his day, a Continental Victorianism that simply impaled women on one or both poles of the dyad. Yet in spite of his traditionalism and his unwitting autobiographical betrayal, Reich was moving toward a conceptual reconstruction (remember that he was only around twenty-four) that boded well for the future.

He wanted to provide a convincing alternative to the biological and physiological arguments that attempted to explain the different time ratios between male and female climaxes. Simultaneously he wanted to free himself, and his patients, from the eternal hell of the tender/sensual split and the impotence and problems associated with premature ejaculation that the split caused. He was also aware that one dimension of this (patriarchal) split was found in the class system, which he later came to see as a class war in the classical Marxist sense. While he did not make use of the concept of narcissism in *this* paper, especially where it could be most useful in deconstructing the male patriarchal psyche and its inability to respond to female sexual needs, he did argue that healthy sexuality entails that a man learn to adjust his climax to that of his partner (thus solving, in part, the evolutionary problem of continuing the survival of the species). His solution is surprisingly simple and quite convincing: *"What nature demands is therefore not a second ejaculation but that both tender and sensual impulses coincide."*[23]

A sexually healthy woman and a sexually healthy man would adjust the rhythms of their preclimactic states so that they would enter into the same upward curve, slowing down or accelerating as required. A mutual orgasm would ensure the best possibility of impregnation, should that be the desideratum. Even if procreation were not the desired goal, maximizing pleasure, what Reich called "pleasure premium," would be attained when the split between the tender and the sensual was overcome in a psychological Hegelian synthesis where the tender was the sensual and the sensual was the tender, and where in the new *Aufgehoben* (higher synthesis in which the earlier finite forms would become transfigured into a new, more complete form) one could not tell them apart.

So we can ask ourselves: what is valid and what is invalid in this youthful paper, in which Reich struggles to replace a biological argument with a psychoanalytic one? Let me list what I think are Reich's valid points: (1) pathological splits do exist in males between the sensual and the tender, but only under the conditions of patriarchy; (2) healthy sexuality does indeed require the mutual adjusting of climactic timing to attain simultaneous orgasms; (3) males do often fear being enveloped by females, generating castration anxiety; and (4) women have equally complex reasons for clitoral or vaginal anesthesia as do males for facultative impotence.

On the obverse side, I would argue that (1) the pleasure principle, or "pleasure premium," is a reductive concept that sounds materialistic and is but one explanandum in a larger categorial synthesis; (2) the argument that women have a diffuse sensuality while men have a penis-focused sensuality is not true, as Reich's own later experiments on body armor made clear; (3) sexual triggers can be extremely complex and multi-causal, often overriding such things as class-consciousness (which are, of course, still very important); and (4) Reich downplays the very important role of psychological and linguistic foreplay (which were *very* important in his life) in weaving together the so-called tender and sensual, which can take innumerable forms, not just that of the wife versus the paid prostitute.

But as an initial foray into the terrain where the psychoanalytic does battle with the biological, this early paper is a commendable piece of work. He entered into more capacious territory when he next tackled the concepts of drive (*Trieb*, sometimes less adequately translated as "instinct," which is *Instinkt*) and libido as they had evolved from within the psychoanalytic movement. In this rather long paper (of thirty-nine pages), Reich prepared for his reconstruction of the energy theory, which would eventually flower into the orgasm and orgone theories. The paper is "Drive and Libido Concepts from Forel to Jung."[24] The heart of the paper, which will be the focus, was a crash course of Freud's understanding of the structure and dynamics of pathology and childhood development up to puberty and beyond, ending with a Freudian-based misreading of Jung.[25]

Again, Reich attacked the idea that the sole purpose of sexuality was procreation and, following Freud, argued that there were at least four groups or forms of sexuality that had been isolated by psychoanalytic science. They were: (1) procreation (the normal form, which is still pertinent in a limited sphere), (2) perversions, (3) infantile sexuality, and (4) most neurotic symptoms (based on repression and substitution).[26] He went on to argue again that the procreative drive had been replaced, especially for modern persons, by the goal of "sexual pleasure," which was the end goal in itself (*an sich*) and not the means to something other than itself. That is, nature does not "use" pleasure in order to make babies. Of course, the pleasure drive is vulnerable to numerous forms of displacement and distortion; hence the need for psychoanalytic intervention.

In this 1922 paper Reich remained the faithful lieutenant by uncritically describing Freud's theory of the death drive, as Freud had presented it in his *Beyond the Pleasure Principle* two years earlier. Soon Reich took very strong, one could say almost vitriolic, exception to the whole idea of dualism between an erotic and a death drive, preferring to see only one eternal drive at play in nature: the life drive. Consequently, in his later writings (at least until the 1950s), Reich always distinguished between the largely correct early Freud (pre–1920) and the conceptually confused later Freud. This is one of the many actions that led to his ouster from the Vienna Psychoanalytic Society, an expulsion that Freud quietly approved of from behind the scenes but left to his loyal lieutenants to carry out.

Focusing on the form of sexuality, Reich gave his summary of the Freudian perspective on the nature and origin of the neurotic type: "The neurotic is a sexual hyperaesthete, or a pervert with a negative symbol, namely, an individual who was forced to repress his sexual desire because it was too strong or not compatible with the reality principle, but did not succeed in doing this, so that the repressed libido is released in symptoms."[27] The neurotic individual has a greater degree of sexual energy than other people, or has libido objects in the outside world (such as his mother or father or close family members) who are inappropriate ("negative symbols"), and thus has to repress this libido through a strong act of will. This act cannot go without some compensatory response by the psyche and returns via the unconscious in the form of a specific symptom or series of symptoms that can often be decoded by the psychoanalyst. Suppose, for example, that a sister wants to sleep with her brother but on some level realizes that she must repress the longing for this libidinal object. Further suppose that her brother is an award-winning swimmer. The repression can do its necessary work, but pushing the desire underground may transform it into a phobia concerning water, making it difficult for the sister to be near large bodies of water or to drink water. From the Freudian/Reichian perspective, all neuroses have their origin in such sexual conflicts, and all cures must delve into the origins of these conflicts, although Reich later moved strongly away from the idea that each symptom had to be traced back to one or more childhood traumas or libidinal connections.

The third conception of sexuality, the theory of infant sexual development—one of the crown jewels of psychoanalysis—goes through the now-well-known phases of oral, anal, and genital, with a latency period lasting generally between the ages of five and twelve, in which the organism is gathering up its sexual energies so that they can emerge in a more unified form at puberty. Also, the latency period is enforced through the external superego, which imposes notions of guilt, especially over masturbation and sexual experimentation. Reich described this external aspect of the superego as it correlates to the latency period:

> Between the ages of five and twelve, psychic dams and reaction formations are constructed against culturally unacceptable partial drives [i.e., oral, anal/sadistic, and genital]; disgust counters anal eroticism, shame counters exhibitionism, and, in general, every morally pertinent concept begins here. These reaction formations are aided and accelerated by training at home and in school, as well as by the general coercion exerted at the child's first introduction into a social community (kindergarten, school, etc.) . . . Furthermore, the incest barrier is erected during this stage, probably by sexual intimidation by the father.[28]

So the child's pleasure at sucking, derived from the mucous membranes in its mouth, has to be suppressed so that substitute objects can be found. By the same cultural logic, its pleasure at retaining its feces, or with playing with its feces (when it was an infant), has to be transformed into a social channel (perhaps of a sadomasochistic form). And genital expression, the most socially dangerous of all, has to be fully suppressed because of the towering figure of the intimidating father, a father who also becomes the ultimate symbol of castration anxiety.

The castration complex is a central concept for both Freud and Reich (far less so for Jung), but Reich modified the concept, fully aware of some key ideas of Alfred Adler with his concept of "inferiority" (as well as some of the stranger ideas of the then-very-popular Otto Weininger as presented in his 1903 *Sex and Character* [*Geschlecht und Charakter*]).[29]

Reich moved from the Oedipal complex to the notion of the inferiority feeling:

> The Oedipus complex results in castration fear in boys due to slighting by the father, or frequently even to a direct threat of penis amputation. In girls, the result is envy at the sight of the boy's penis. The notion that the penis was cut off, or is simply very small and still to grow, plays an important part. Both are combined under the heading "castration complex." However, we must warn against taking the concept of castration too literally and interpreting it only as penis amputation. Actually every inferiority feeling [here is where Reich refers to Weininger] in whatever area it falls, belongs in the category of a castration complex.[30]

So every inferiority feeling, for the son, derived from the threat of the father, however literal vis-à-vis his penis, is a form of the latent castration complex. Women as well can feel this anxiety insofar as their clitoris is seen as the promise of a penis or as a reminder of a penis that once was. Within the latency period the hint of castration, broiling just beneath the surface of the family drama, keeps any emergent genital expression at bay and emerges into a more generalized anxiety that will produce a constant feeling of inferiority in the young adolescent. As if to add insult to internal injury, when caught in the act of masturbation, the child is often brutally suppressed by the parental superego, and another layer of guilt-consciousness is added to the hypervigilant social superego.

Reich's gender analyses do not give one much hope at *this* stage. As we just saw, he burdened us with the standard psychoanalytic line that women by nature had penis envy. Or consider this piece of wisdom: "The majority of women love because they are loved, and to the degree to which they are loved."[31] He further argues that homosexuality in men was tied to a dim memory of their mother's once having what they now have: "Perversion can also arise from unsuccessful repression, for example, the homosexual love of effeminate boys caused by a return of the repressed idea of the mother having a penis."[32] Homosexuality is never, for Reich, a legitimate libidinal object choice but a regression to an Oedipal longing for a maternal penis that can be found only in the substitute object of an "effeminate" male. In this way the castration anxiety of paternal competition is cunningly outwitted, while at least some modicum of sexual pleasure is attained, but never, of course, that great "pleasure premium." Reich does not have as much to say about perversions (a second form of sexuality) as he does about neuroses. For women, who must become passive during the latency period, it is important that clitoral sexuality be repressed in favor of vaginal sexuality, a distinction that is not widely championed today. In general, Reich subscribed to the view (certainly in the 1920s) that women preferred to be passive and to let men be the sexual aggressors, while also arguing, as noted in the previous paper, that men should become sensitive to the orgasm curve of their female partners.

The last piece of Freudian doctrine in this essay is Reich's analysis of the contrast between the ego drives and the sexual drives. His underlying point is that the organism is a battleground between the two directions in which energy, which is always psychosexual, must flow, with the reality principle (that is, what is and is not possible in the external world vis-à-vis both the superego and empirical fact) serving as the court of final appeal for the ego:

> Ego drives are characterized by (1) susceptibility to being acquired through ontogeny [i.e., *personal* development]; (2) the change of objects according to time and place; (3) the fact that they are subject to the reality principle, i.e., they proceed toward postponed, modified, and decreased pleasure gains.
>
> Sexual drives are characterized by (1) definite phylogenetic [i.e., species] development (restriction takes place during ontogeny); (2) permanent objects or autoeroticism; (3) unintelligibility, unsusceptibility to influence, and the fact that they are subject to the pleasure principle, i.e., they are directed toward achieving rapid, intense pleasure.[33]

Thus the ego drives emerge only for the specific individual in a definite time and place (are part of an ontogeny). The objects of the ego are subject to constant change, and the reality principle compels the ego to continually modify and transform its goals if it is to attain any pleasure. Thus the ego is constantly scanning the outer environment as well as listening to the inner voice of the superego (which is part of the unconscious) in order to gauge its possibilities of success for any given goal. However, like the stronger and deeper sexual drives, the ego drives are governed by the pleasure principle (*Lust*).

The sexual drives are much more intense than the ego drives, and even during the latency period they can surface when they are least expected. They have their roots in the phylogenetic evolution of our species. The ontogenetic structure of the individual, which is finite, must shape and craft this infinite energy into some kind of workable and finite configuration. In the state of narcissism, the sexual drives are reversed and return toward the self, often literally through excessive masturbation or a kind of exhibitionism. Or the sexual drives seek a permanent external object (which the ego knows is impossible, hence the eternal conflict). The sexual drives remain a mystery; they cannot speak, they are pre-intelligible (I would say pre-semiotic) and have no assignable meaning; that is, they simply are. They, like the ego drives, are subject to the pleasure principle. But unlike the ego drives, which have learned the "virtue" of displacement and delay, the sexual drives demand immediate and constant gratification. This basic warfare model, with its underlying philosophical dualism, is one that Reich broke through less than a decade later, coming to the conclusion that life would not fight against life, that nature would not create against itself.

In the last few pages of the article, Reich took issue with Jung on how far one can stretch the concept of libido beyond the purely sexual sphere. He accused Jung of introducing philosophy into the sovereign sphere of psychoanalytic science rather than staying within the orbit of objective research (as if one could have a philosophically neutral perspective once one used a human language). What Reich failed to recognize was that Jung broke with Freud by 1912 because he was convinced that psychic energy was not of one and only one quality but was more neutral in constitution and that its sexual manifestation was but one of its myriad forms. Thus the psychic quest for meaning became the touchstone of Jung's later research. The Jungian text to which Reich refers is *Psychology of the Unconscious: A Study of the Transformations and Symbolism of the Libido.*[34] When Freud read the book, he concluded that Jung had broken away from him in a final and, as he thought, rather brutal fashion (making Freud the sacrifice and Jung the hero—two great themes of the book). The castration complex, it seems, cut both ways.

Reich did not open up much new ground in this essay, although he

was able to position himself at the heart of the psychoanalytic movement
and to line up his perspective on sexual development with classical theory. What is interesting is that he had already begun to think in what
might be called (ironically) generic philosophical terms. He lifted the
concept of the drives (both ego and sexual) out of the narrow framework of
the biophysical organism and started to analyze them in terms of their relationships to the species, social life, evolution, the role of inferiority (depression), what might be called the dialectic of finite and infinite, and
their continual movement in and around the genitals (which soon became
his major focus). We witness the slightest hints of the cosmic-poet-in-the-
making who personifies the great drives and writes them across the face
of the deep. Rather than provide a list of what is living and dead in this
essay, I will move on to the next set of essays, with the recognition that the
previous essay was more of a historical reconstruction designed to show
that the lieutenant had truly earned his stripes. In the seven much shorter
articles to follow, we see Reich return to more of his own distinctive thinking around such issues as masturbation, narcissism, genitality, tics, and
hysterical psychosis.

Reich showed his sensitivity for detail as a taxonomist and naturalist
when he probed into the specific features associated with masturbation in
the 1922 essay "Concerning Specific Forms of Masturbation."[35] He accepted the basic thinking on the roles of unconscious fantasy and the consequent guilt that emerged from the act itself, but he wanted to go further
than his colleagues had gone in their theoretical work and look into the
immense variations he had encountered among his female and male patients: "The difficulties encountered in the treatment of impotence have
taught me to pay special attention to the manner in which the patient
masturbates."[36] He asked himself such basic questions as: (1) where do
they masturbate? (2) when do they masturbate? (3) with what materials do
they masturbate? (4) with what fantasies do they masturbate? (5) how often do they masturbate? (6) in what bodily posture do they masturbate,
and is that posture related to any childhood event or events? and (7) with
what furniture do they masturbate, and what associations does the act
have with that furniture? This set of questions placed the masturbation issue on new ground and helped Reich to ramify his query by probing into
undisclosed background sources. After all, he was a seasoned journey-
man of the art himself and often wondered how it might be related to

Oedipal and castration issues. Now he was to turn his searchlight onto the structural issues in the psyche that could tell him how to separate out healthy from nonhealthy forms of masturbation, remembering that the issue of narcissism was already pacing hungrily in the wings.

One of his case studies was a young man who could masturbate only by placing his penis between his thighs and then gently tickling his thighs (not his penis) from behind. Reich was able to uncover two childhood circumstances that led to this unusual form of masturbation. The first was that the child was a bed-wetter and was beaten by his father for his "crime." He always covered his genitals by hiding them between his legs in defense against the lash. The second event occurred when he was older: he broke in on the maid and her lover near climax and grabbed the lover's erect penis. This led to a reaction formation in which he dissociated his hand from his own penis, so he had to masturbate by a different means; the "resulting guilt feelings had placed a taboo on the hand."[37]

His second case study involved a thirty-two-year-old "psychosexual hermaphrodite" male who would bend over backward to masturbate in his bed, which was located in his mother's room. In analysis he remembered a picture in his home of the bound Isaac being towered over by Abraham about to slay him at the patriarchal god's command. His masturbatory position turned out to be identical to that of the bound Isaac. Reich uncovered some deep castration anxieties in the patient and remarked, "His form of masturbation coincided with his masochistic submission to castration by his father, whom he loved and hated intensely."[38] The connection between masochism and the maternal room (Reich strongly urged him to vacate the room as soon as possible) governed the ways in which he could climax. It must be remembered that neither of these two patients had a healthy sexual life at the time and that each lived only in the realm of masturbation.

As a good taxonomist, Reich concluded this short article (seven and a half pages in English) with several categories of normal and deviant forms of masturbation that could help the clinician decide what the prognosis might be for healthy genitality. These suggest that already (he was around twenty-four or twenty-five at this stage) Reich could think in both particular and general terms, provided that the particular facts always served the still-emerging generic theory. The categories are (quoting Reich):

1. Masturbation against the sheet or an improvised vulva (shirt, pillow, etc.), lying on the stomach, by means of active movement of the pelvis and without manual assistance. In this case the masculine adjustment seems to be assured and the fantasy directed toward the opposite sex (even if unconsciously incestuous). Alloerotism is the motivating force here.

2. In manual masturbation, lying on the side or in a bathtub, the autoerotic element is much stronger. In my experience, this form of masturbation is by far the most frequently employed.

3. When the individual masturbates lying on his back with all activity localized in his hand, the prognosis is not very favorable. My experience has shown that this mode of masturbation is primarily practiced by males with female attitudes . . .

4. Masturbation in front of a mirror (narcissistic); while reading rape scenes (this is very frequent); on the toilet; in public parks, even though well hidden behind bushes; mutual masturbation with friends; etc, etc. All these indicated pathological processes in the unconscious.[39]

His conclusion seems to be a sound one, namely, that the act of masturbation is at least as complex as its innumerable unconscious causes, which often involve Oedipal and castration issues. Again, however, he brings in some of the reigning gender prejudices, as when he argues that some pathological women are guilty of "masturbation by tugging at the clitoris (desire for a penis)."[40] As a putative logical sequence in which an argument attempts to assert that proposition B follows from proposition A, Reich falls into a fallacy. Proposition A asserts, "A subject S (woman) is doing X (tugging at her clitoris)." Proposition B asserts, "A subject S (woman) desires Y (a penis)." A simply does not entail B, as the A proposition is about an observed state of affairs, while the B proposition is a counterfactual about an alleged state of affairs, which may or may not be the case.

In psychoanalysis, at least according to some narrowly focused philosophers, one is dealing *primarily* with counterfactuals (claims contrary to empirical observation or claims lost in the indefinite long run, as in Peirce's theory of the evolution of science), but I think that there is very strong cumulative and indirect evidence for a high percentage of psychoanalytic claims and that they have cashed out or will cash out. The gender "analyses" from the early and middle decades of the twentieth century, however, are on shaky ground and must be put in a special category. Typical Reichian terms such as *passive-feminine* and *aggressive-masculine* do not have much phenomenological warrant—that is, they do not reveal any data or experiential field that is amenable to sustained and direct observation. These are (negatively inscripted) *normative* terms, not (generically neutral) *descriptive* phenomenological designators.

Let's bring narcissism out of the wings and see how Reich treated it in 1922. He accepted the general Freudian view that narcissism was basically a movement of libido back into the internal realms of the self after its failure to secure proper object cathexes (releases of energy or drives) into the outer world. The article is "Two Narcissistic Types"[41] and was published in the *Internationale Zeitschrift für Psychoanalyse*. In it Reich employs the emerging distinction between what he calls the "neurosis" and the "neurotic character," arguing that in the end one must move analysis in the direction of the whole character structure rather than toward specific neurotic symptoms (the backbone of his argument in his 1933 *Character Analysis*). He states, "Actually there is no neurosis, no matter how clearly defined, without traces of a disturbance of the entire personality. Feelings of inferiority, an accompanying symptom of all neuroses—the 'narcissistic scar' (Marcinowsky)—are the ever present expression of this disturbance."[42]

Reich also started referring to the concept of armor, which, of course, became one of his lasting contributions to theory and therapy. This concept got implicitly linked with his new interest, the concept of the negative transference (certainly not invented by him), which later became the *latent* negative transference, as if to deepen its relationship to the phenomenon of resistance. Hence the armor became the outer cover of the negative transference, and it had to be penetrated (Reich was never afraid of aggressive language) if the negative transference was to be pried loose. He stated, "The neurotic character perceives analysis (which involves the rendering of associations and the relinquishing of tangible means of satisfaction) as castration itself, because of his castration complex. Sooner or later he will construct a negative transference in which the analyst is the natural enemy to him, in much greater measure than he is to the neurotic."[43] The neurotic character, compared to the person with neurotic symptoms, has deeper defects and a more damaged personality structure that will require far more analytic work, and there is a far slighter chance of success.

Reich delineated two types of narcissist who had come to lie on his analytic couch. (He still used the standard Freudian passive couch therapy but was slowly beginning to make exceptions with the occasional face-to-face interaction.) One type was relatively latent with her or his narcissism, while the other was far more manifest and harder to treat:

> This first narcissistic type, with manifest feelings of inferiority and latent narcissism, may be contrasted to a second type with, as analysis shows, manifest and compensatory narcissism and latent feelings of inferiority. This type is more sparsely represented than the first, less transparent, and offers a poorer prognosis for treatment. Here we have the obtrusive, conspicuously self-secure individual, always thrusting himself forward in an attempt to gain the center of attention, thinking he knows it all, and showing not the slightest trace of any critical perspective of himself. Transference in treatment is minimal since what actually keeps him in analysis is his mania to boast about his experiences, intellect, wit, and to find an obliging listener in the analyst. All transference is based on identification; he wants to solve everything himself and knows everything better than the analyst. Whereas exhibitionist tendencies are repressed in the first type and reappear only as neurotic modesty and complexity, in this type they are fully manifest; the large and powerful penis is exhibited—symbolically—time and time again.[44]

So the first type of narcissist will present with manifest feelings of inferiority while the second will have suppressed those feelings and present with strong bravado. If the first type is a masochist, the second is a sadist. The first lives through an impossible ego ideal (which must be deconstructed), while the second has an "overvaluation of real ego" (a form of manic inflation). It is very interesting that the transference relationships are so different, with the first, more "passive-feminine" type being open to a deep transference, while the second, more aggressive type withholds the transference out of both a fear of castration (source of the negative transference) and for sadistic purposes (desire to hurt and control the analyst/father).

Returning to the concept of the drives (*Trieben*), one sees that within the space of a year Reich had moved to place the concept of the pleasure principle underneath the concept of the drives (all the while claiming that this was consistent with Freud's perspective). The article, which appeared in 1923, was "Concerning the Energy of the Drives."[45] What was clearly not consistent with psychoanalytic doctrine was Reich's softening of the strong Freudian distinction between pleasure (*Lust*) and unpleasure (*Unlust*). Again, Reich had a basic philosophical distrust of any idea that would split nature into two contrasting *primary* principles, and he appealed to the thought of the (then highly influential) French philosopher Henri Bergson to shore up his vitalistic and monistic arguments. Bergson insisted that all of nature was linked by a surging primal energy that could not be quantified at its source: the élan vital, or vitalistic component, which remained central to Reich. The monistic component worked against any mind/brain dualism that would either impose a mysterious psychophysical parallelism or derive the conscious or unconscious mind from the brain in a reductive manner. For Reich, mind and brain were of one piece.

Unlust, or so-called unpleasure, became a form of semipleasurable tension within the sexual arc. As Reich put it, one took five pleasure steps forward and three back, but the three back were not forms of unpleasure, merely a different kind of pleasure. He was developing his excitation climax release formula in a more primitive form, but the underlying intent was to outflank the unpleasure principle (and any hint of a death drive). So the loyal lieutenant had started his own Jungian-style sacrifice of the father, what he, of course, would have seen as a narcissistic defense against the castration complex (using the classical psychoanalytic concepts). What is interesting is that he was smart enough (or self-deluded enough) to mask his deeper intent behind a promise of loyalty to the psychoanalytic tribe. But by 1923 any serious observer could see that a break was in the offing.

Let me give an example of what analytically trained philosophers would call "fudging," namely, the blurring of boundaries so as to avoid making distinctions where distinctions are (allegedly) required. Reich states, "However, the nuances between pleasure and unpleasure are so vague, and the various phases intermesh so finely, that one feels justified in speaking of 'pleasurable tension.'"[46] Freud was more inclined to link tension with unpleasure (*Unlust*), while Reich wanted the pleasure principle (the generic expansion of *Lust*) to envelop unpleasure as a mere subspecies of the genus. All tension serves to enhance the higher pleasure. So the role of unpleasure and the death drive were slowly being erased. Later, in yet another move away from the classical Freudian framework, the so-called aggressive drive would be relegated to the status of a mere secondary drive (a drive based not on nature but solely in human pathology). Of course, for less narrow philosophers, such subordination of one category under another would in no way be an instance of "fudging" but would mirror the innate encompassing structures of nature itself.

Even though he knew that the primal life energy could not be strictly quantified, Reich, a fairly sophisticated amateur mathematician, sought a formula that would give some shape to the tensions and currents that moved within the tensional streams of sexual energy (the true foundation of the various drives). In this 1923 article he started his lifelong practice of using visual diagrams to augment his categorial analyses. He was beginning to feel more and more comfortable with mathematical terms and metaphors:

It is characteristic of sexual pleasure that partial reduction acts as a stimulus for the building up or increase of tension. However, this is valid only in forepleasure. In end pleasure, tension differences become increasingly great; the increase and reduction pass through larger ascending and descending phases, until finally the descending component reaches the desired zero point and the ascending component cancels itself because both originated at the zero point.[47]

The "desired zero point" is no longer seen in negative terms (as a point of unpleasure) but as an organic goal that is felt throughout both forepleasure and end pleasure (coitus). The fluctuations in the tensional system all serve to enhance sexual pleasure, not to fight against it. The sought-for mathematical formula would trace the energy movements from the zero point to the tension and relaxation points and back again to the zero point. As always, for Reich, nature does not fight against itself. His perspective grew more and more optimistic (perhaps in compensation) concerning the ability of primal life energy to overcome any so-called death drive or aggressive drive. Whatever may seem like death or aggression is actually sexual tension reaching the bursting point, ready to spring forth and free the organism from extreme internal pressure, a sensation that merely *feels* like death or depression, or makes one have aggressive fantasies; this bursting sensation is still strictly libidinal in a healthy sense.

When Freud published *Civilization and Its Discontents* seven or eight years later, Reich was appalled. In this hundred-page monograph Freud presented his pessimistic evaluation of the eternal conflicts among the libido, ego, and superego within the self and between the self and its community.[48] Eros and death remained the same major players they were nine years earlier (in *Beyond the Pleasure Principle*), and the aggressive drive assumed center stage. Needless to say, none of this sat well with the antidualist Reich, who thought that there was no death drive and that the so-called drive for aggression was the result of bodily armoring rather than an innate piece of nature. Freud concluded his jeremiad on human frailty with a blunt query: "The fateful question for the human species seems to me to be whether and to what extent their cultural development will succeed in mastering the disturbance of their communal life by the human instinct of aggression and self-destruction."[49] By 1930, of course, Reich and Freud were in different worlds, and the breach between them (held open with great intensity by Freud's inner circle) could in no way be healed. But the astute interpreter can see the cracks opening in 1923. Reich thought that all so-called discontents were eminently curable once their emotional and bodily armor were opened up (past the latent negative transference, of course) and their life-enhancing libido could surge forth. Reich's optimism on this issue had already emerged by 1924 and came to full flower in 1927, as we shall see in the next chapter.

Of the next four papers, Reich devoted two to the issue of genitality, one to a very specific pathology related to masturbation, and the last to a problem in psychosis. The two papers on the issue of genitality are "On Genitality"[50] and "Further Remarks on the Therapeutic Significance of Genital Libido."[51] Both of them were based on Reich's growing clinical experience, derived from his private practice and from his work in the Vienna Psychoanalytic Outpatient Clinic (in 1923 and the spring of 1924). In the second paper he employed the concept of "orgastic potency" for the first time, as far as I can tell, and also finally came out against Freud fairly directly.

In the first paper, Reich cited seven case studies in which the partial drives (oral, anal, and "phallic/clitoral"—this last pairing is my choice of terms to add some clarity) all produced neuroses unless gathered up under the more powerful forces of genital sexuality (which was more diffuse and primary than all of the partial drives added together). Any partial drive will *always* cathect to an inadequate object and thus run afoul of the reality principle. The oral drive is incestuous, while the anal/sadistic drive might be related to a paternal castration complex, and so on. Reich also reiterated his view that the focus of therapy was character neurosis, not the concentration, via free association, on individual neurotic symptoms, which he likened to the peaks of mountains rather than mountains proper. Reich's optimism concerning the power of primary genitality to overcome the resistances tied to the partial drives was very concisely expressed:

> In other analyses I perceive our task to be the use of flexible, unrepressed drive impulses against those, which are repressed, rigid, and fixed (Freud). Further, we can observe how genital libido aids recovery tendencies (cases 1 through 3) and how other rigid drive impulses become more flexible and reconcilable in the transference struggle or in recent conflicts, finally either yielding to the main genital impulses or achieving sublimation through other means.[52]

Genital libido is seen as global and was not limited to the phallus, clitoris, or vagina, although again Reich, following Freud, emphasized vaginal sexuality over the clitoral form. Most patients do not know that there is even a difference between the object cathexes of the three partial erogenous zones and the primal genital libido. Reich actually has a logically tight argument here, namely, that there is a direct correlation between a neurotic symptom and a given erogenous zone. The dissolution of the symptom may or may not affect the underlying character neurosis, but in any event the object cathexis could simply move elsewhere. But if the entire *character* neurosis is reconstructed, and with it (by definition) the free movement of the primary drive (*Trieb*) of the genital libido, then it follows that the repressed partial drives can be freed and properly woven into the genital drive until they cease to thwart healthy sexuality.

Here the argument would go like this: in its failed form (the rejected Freudian version) we have "Subject S dissolves neurotic cathexis X." "Therefore it (falsely) follows that S has freed the genital libido G." The only thing that does follow here would be: "Subject S may have freed him/ herself from one object cathexis at time T." G is simply not entailed in any way. What Reich is asserting, contra Freud, is: "Subject S has now become subject S1." "Any subject S that becomes an S1 also becomes G." Therefore it follows that: "Our initial subject S in becoming S1 is now G." That is, with character analysis, a subject becomes transformed into what is in essence a new person (S1) and in doing so frees the natural energy of genital libido (G) to transform the partial drives from below, not in a piecemeal fashion and one at a time but in a great transfiguration. Or to put it ironically, $S \rightarrow S1$ and $S1 \longleftrightarrow G$. This argument remains one of Reich's most lasting conceptual achievements and reinforces his move from symptom to character analysis.

To be even more specific, there will still be traits that separate the genital libido from the partial erogenous zones, and these traits can be mapped with reasonable psychoanalytic precision, "namely, erection, active entrance into an opening, longing for the womb, and rhythmic ejaculation."[53] Alas, these male-specific traits do not help us understand genital libido in women, except that the clitoris is but a mere shadow of the great penis and that the vagina has to take over its role in any event.

The second paper, "Further Remarks on the Therapeutic Significance of Genital Libido," is slightly more interesting than the first and has a stronger focus on issues in therapy. Here we see the twenty-eight-year-old analyst combining his growing restlessness with the classical psychoanalytic doctrine with his sensibilities as a healer. He is now willing to fire his shots across Freud's bow and to stir up the waters of the Danube in order to stake out his own post-Oedipal terrain. I sense that this essay is a kind of coming-out event for Reich, an event on which Reich's movement toward identity turned, although it is always dangerous to identify any one such magical text as the locus where an "identity crisis" can be seen in the making. But he does come out swinging and pulls few punches—that is, he is sure of his ground and is ready to start building his own school of psychoanalysis.

In general this paper probes into the theoretical structures underlying the general theory of libido as developed by Freud and Karl Abraham. Thinking that his own work was incomplete, Reich specifically tackled the issues of libidinal repression, the nature and movement of pregenital libido, the problems of regression in libidinal fixations, and the issues surrounding the "curative function of genital libido." His earlier clinical observations needed a stronger theoretical structure, in his mind, and he also wanted to find out how his new theory of orgastic potency could shed light on the processes of neurosis and healing.

Under the subheading "Genital Potency" Reich makes one of his ex cathedra pronouncements: "Virtually no neurosis without disturbance of the genital function."[54] So whether you are engaged in old-fashioned symptom analysis or in character analysis, you are obligated to recognize the correlation between frozen libido and improper object cathexis. But Reich recognized that at the other extreme (was he holding up a mirror to himself?) were those who could not control the outward flow of their libido. How genuine were they? Did they have true orgastic potency?:

> We may assume that all so-called Don Juan types who pride themselves on possessing a great many women or on proving their potency by consuming the greatest possible number of acts in one night are attempting to compensate for an inordinate fear of impotence, among other motives—for example, seeking the mother (Rank). Such men manifest limited potency.[55]

I think that most readers will feel comfortable with the conceptual link between Don Juanism and the lack of genuine orgastic potency, although Reich's thought had to evolve further before he was able to work out *all* of the details as to what made real potency different from sexual excess. My own sense is that he reached a truly workable solution only in his later writings, when his naturalistic and ecstatic religion grounded his sexual program. After all, he was his own best case study on this issue, and many of his sexual encounters had almost nothing to do with genuine love or with the mystery of Otherness in the fullest sense. Like Paul Tillich, the great Protestant theologian who acted out sexually in a similar way, Reich seems to have had a deeply fragmented personality that could not relax enough to let any woman get fully inside his shell.

One of the more interesting, but slightly vexing, aspects of this essay is Reich's privileging of the reality principle. The vexing aspect has to do with the question of who controls the meaning of "reality" in the analyst/analysand relationship. Reich took a fairly hard line by insisting that the analyst knows better than the analysand how best to free up orgastic potency, for example, around the issue of homosexuality, where he insisted that the patient must always be cured of this neurosis rather than try to integrate himself into a welcoming subcommunity. Here is one of his shots across the bow: "If I were to rigidly maintain Freud's position, I would not be allowed to conduct an analysis at all, as my postulate is to 'guide' the patient away from the pleasure principle to the reality principle."[56] Hence the pleasure principle might not call for a heterosexual lifestyle, while the reality principle will (under the conditions of patriarchy).

Reich insisted that the pregenital drives are not based on reality: "All pregenital drives as such, to the extent that they claim exclusiveness [which seems inevitable], are counter to reality and can be partially disposed of through sublimation if the ego structure is suitable."[57] So any part of the pleasure principle that is still trapped in the pregenital sphere (as a homosexual fixation would be in the anal zone) has no connection to the reality principle. Consequently, if the analyst is to do her or his work, then she or he must be able to separate out the partial drives and their ersatz realities from the truer reality that can be known only by the genital libido. Obviously, the analysand cannot have access to this deeper reality. In a sense, this is not an objectionable theory, assuming that the underlying theory of the unfolding of the partial erogenous zones is correct and further assuming that the genital libido is "meant" to be the higher synthesis of zones and genital libido by the momentum of the life drive, and finally assuming that the highly trained (and analyzed) analyst has the second sight to see all of this as of a piece (past and through the latent negative transference). But a more democratic and goal-oriented sensibility would want a creative dialectic in which the reality principle itself, not to mention the contours of the ego, was probed mutually (by analyst/analysand) as well as socially and politically. We are certainly more accustomed to seeing alternative lifestyles as possible forms of liberation per se rather than as regressions to pregenital fixations.

More compelling is Reich's move to open up his orgasm theory to cover the entire body and to free the depth energy of the psyche to become coextensive with its entire musculature. In today's language we would say that he was starting to think in terms of field theory and leaving behind a more corpuscular and classical language:

> The libido of the entire body flows outward through the genitals. The orgasm may not be considered completely successful if it is experienced only in the genitals; convulsive movements of the entire musculature and a slight clouding of consciousness are its normal attributes and are an indication that the entire organism has participated.[58]

In Reich's view neither the nymphomaniac nor the Don Juan ever felt the clouding of consciousness or the "convulsive movements of the entire musculature" that marked the truly potent. Elsewhere he argued that the orgastically potent want to go to sleep after climax, almost always with their partner, and that they were never visited with the immediate guilt and disgust that suddenly descended upon the impotent but sexually active. It became obvious that the transition from the partial sexual drives to orgastic potency required a complex shifting of the unconscious. True orgastic potency entails a remaking of the self, and Reich's position on sexual liberation was never a simple libertarian rejection of all restraints—far from it. The necessary psychological antecedents for full sexual health that had to be in place *before* genital expression could unfold were strenuous indeed, and Reich never shied away from placing these demands on his patients. It should be added that these requirements were not superego requirements but internal libidinal requirements, which were in turn tied to the reality principle, however construed.

Focusing on issues of masturbation and the cunning of the unconscious and its shape-shifting ability to remove the object of repression from one location to another, Reich presented the case study of a forty-seven-year-old embroidery worker named A.F. who had been referred to him by a colleague in the Vienna Psychoanalytic Outpatient Clinic. Her case was considered to be almost hopeless. The case study appeared in the 1925 article "Psychogenic Tic as a Masturbation Equivalent."[59] The patient presented with the following symptoms: "sudden convulsive exhalations accompanied by violent spasms of the entire body, especially the neck and head, and a cramping of the shoulders. At times there were only a slight clearing of the throat and a sudden forward and upward jerking of the head."[60] From her perspective, the worst symptom was her constant whooping cough, which made it difficult for her to appear in public.

Reich was unclear as to how to proceed. First he tried the Freud/Breuer technique of hypnosis but found that her resistances were too great—she reacted to any hypnotic suggestion with further whooping. Then he took a more aggressive approach, which he called the "palimnestic method," borrowed from a psychoanalyst named Kohlstamm, which involved giving the patient specific dream assignments so that she or he would report back the results (if any) at the next analytic hour. Again we see Reich deciding to intervene directly into the analysand's resistances to frustrate the passive/aggressive behavior of the unconscious. This proved to be a very successful approach for him and dramatically shortened the course of therapy, but at the same time it risked neglecting the teleological dimension of the drive for meaning that unfolds after the emotional armor is reconfigured. But Reich was always a pragmatist who took neurotic and psychotic suffering seriously. Because the unconscious would use everything in its arsenal to thwart the process, the energetic flow of repression to symptom and back again had to be rooted out by the most direct means possible.

This formula of "repression to symptom and back again" is tricky, however, because the symptom (projected onto a cathected object) must change if the first object/symptom is found out by the analysand. Reich gives a wonderfully clear presentation of the psychoanalytic wisdom on this point:

> Unreleased impulses seek escape in a symptom and, if one channel is blocked, will search for another. Proof of this can be found in all psychotherapeutic treatment of symptoms; if a regnant symptom is eliminated through suggestion, another will take its place, either immediately or somewhat later, according to the strength of the rapport with the physician.[61]

Symptom analysis is neither a necessary nor a sufficient condition for successful therapy, although it may have some strategic value in the short run, especially insofar as it helps the analyst gain access to the inner workings of the analysand's psyche. But Reich (unlike Jung) always held to the absolute necessity of the transference, the "strength of the rapport with the physician." He insisted that this rapport made psychoanalysis superior to all other forms of therapy, because it compelled the unconscious to become fully engaged by forcing it to reenact the Oedipal struggle, the castration complex, and its various erotic fixations. Finally, it compelled the unconscious to give some priority to the reality principle.

Reich's use of the invasive "palimnestic method" had limitations, as he soon discovered, but it did enable him to uncover some vital dream material. He quickly divined that A.F. had some deep sexual conflicts related to her dominating mother and aggressive sisters (who were a decade older than she was). Further, he found out that her father had died when she was thirty-eight and that she had broken off her brief relationship with a fiancé. She blamed her mother's aggression on herself, she blamed her father's death on herself (because she had "allowed" him to be hospitalized rather than treating him herself), and she thought her sisters were right to mistreat her. At one point he proposed that she had converted her guilt into the lung disorder of pleurisy and suffered intensely. Reich ordered her to dream of pleurisy and come to the next session to report any possible dream material. Instead she presented with all of the classic symptoms of the illness itself, including a fever of 100.4°F, a perfect example of conversion hysteria at work.

Reich continued to order A.F. to go more deeply into her dream world and soon found the thread he was looking for, namely, that she had a deep fear of masturbation combined with an equally strong desire to masturbate. The strength of her repression was so great, in his view, that she converted her resistance into her whooping cough, which manifested itself whenever the threat of autoeroticism appeared in her unconscious. Reich coaxed her into at least a partial recognition of this deadly neurotic logic, and she became capable of some minimal form of self-pleasure, during which periods her coughing stopped and she could get a full night's sleep. But there was no full cure, and Reich ends the essay with the admission that her age (forty-seven) worked against her and that the severity of her repression was too great. But he had shed great light on how sexual repression can manifest itself in somatic tics and that such tics can almost always (he would say *always*) be traced back to the eternal battle between a partial drive and a malevolent superego.

The final short paper to be analyzed before we look at the monograph on the impulsive character takes us into even deeper waters and shows how young the psychoanalytic study of psychosis was in the 1920s. The distinctions among the various psychoses that we now take mostly for granted were still quite murky, and it is a good object lesson to listen in on how psychoanalysts were struggling to deal with unusual cases that presented a variety of complex symptoms that spilled over the categories that were *themselves* not yet fully formed. They were unsure how to tell the differences among such disorders as schizophrenia, hysteria, autism, mania, depression, mutism, catatonia, and the schizoid type, among others. Reich, of course, plunged in and started to cut up the categorial pie in his own way. The 1925 article was "A Hysterical Psychosis in Statu Nascendi" (the Latin means "in the state of being born").[62]

Reich, now twenty-eight, inherited the case of a "nineteen-year-old female hysteric" who was undergoing "the emergence of an unchanging psychotic split. The patient had suffered from insomnia for more than five years and from a hysterical conversion in the form of abdominal pain for one year."[63] This case gave Reich the chance to witness the process by which a psychosis was "in the state of being born" out of previous neurotic abreactions to traumatic events. Reich believed this put him into terrain where Freud could no longer be a guide (precisely the conclusion that Jung had drawn over a decade earlier when working in a mental hospital dealing with psychotics, not neurotics).

The patient, Eva S., presented with a variety of symptoms: crying, twilight states, so-called hysterical symptoms (what we might call exuberant extraverted behavior), deep depression, mild catatonia, and quick intuitive flashes of insight. She was fluent in several languages, including ancient Hebrew, and during one session she suddenly mumbled a few Hebrew words, though she claimed that she had not spoken the language in thirteen years. Reich, realizing he had at least one key to something crucial in Eva S.'s neurotic etiology, probed further during their next session until

the repressed traumatic situation she had re-enacted in her semiconscious state erupted with all the characteristics of a cathartic explosion. Between the ages of five and seven she had studied Hebrew with a young tutor. One day he had gotten her intoxicated with liquor. She awoke with a stabbing pain in her genitals, naked

in his bed. He was kneeling next to the bed at her right side, resting his head on her abdomen just above her right groin (the locale
of the later pain) with his finger in her vagina (hence the pain when
she awoke). As he saw her awakening, he threw himself on top
of her; she no longer knew what had happened then. Later she
thought she vaguely remembered his pressing his penis to her
mouth.[64]

Imagine Reich's fascination with yet another trusted tutor who had betrayed his pupil in the sexual sphere. Eva S. had also presented with a
sharp abdominal pain that always appeared in the afternoon and subsided
by the evening (perhaps mimicking the time period of the Hebrew
lessons). Clearly her "hysterical" conversion had its roots in her rape
episode. Further, Eva S. developed a strong oral fixation in her partial
drives, which derived from her unwitting and forced fellatio. Unable to
reveal this horrid story to anyone, she and her unconscious had to deal
with it by displacements, thus fixating on the oral stage and thwarting the
emergence of her full genital libido. Reich argued that she orally fixated
on her father and developed an oral resistance to her mother by refusing
to answer any of her questions. She also developed an eating disorder, as
if to refuse the demands of her orality.

The psychosis proper emerged on the anniversary of her sister's death.
Eva S. suddenly refused to use her native German and would communi-
cate only in written French. She was beginning to develop a split-off self.
Today we could refer to this as an example of Dissociative Identity Disorder (300.14 in DSM IV), formerly called multiple personality disorder. It
should be noted, of course, that there is no unanimity, either among legal
theorists or among psychiatrists, as to whether this disorder actually exists. But it is certainly the case that people do dissociate under conditions
of stress, whether or not a genuine autonomous part self emerges with its
own history, personality, behavior, and memories. From Reich's perspective, Eva S. was in the process of becoming someone other than Eva S.,
and for many contemporary theorists there is a strong link between severe
sexual abuse and Dissociative Identity Disorder.

Eva S. made some progress once her traumatic memory came to the
surface, but the progress was short-lived. She slowly sank into a more depressed state. Reich reported, "The patient does not leave the house,

speaks little, and sits in her room still firmly believing she is not Eva S."[65] He concluded that her ego was not strong enough to withstand the power of the psychosis and that all therapists must gauge the analysand's ego strength before initiating therapy. Again, he insisted on the importance of the reality principle in any psychoanalytic technique, especially one that involved a potential psychosis *in statu nascendi.* He provided some ground rules for fellow analysts, which were almost a mirror image of what Jung was then saying in Zürich:

It is already known that "latent" schizophrenics may, through analysis, become manifest schizophrenics, and this may be un-mistakably traced to ego, or rather superego defects. In such cases it is necessary to prevent associations, memories, and above all in-cestuous conflicts from becoming conscious too rapidly, as they did in the case of Eva S. The reader will have noticed how much taboo material emerged in the short span of three and a half months. The inundation of the conscious with the repressed mate-rial must then work disadvantageously, as it cannot be sufficiently processed. The ego lacks time to assimilate it bit by bit.[66]

Reich had at least learned that his invasive technique had some real dan-gers. His hypomanic drive to pry loose the great secrets came into conflict with fragile structures of Eva S.'s psyche, which had built up highly de-fensive mechanisms for the sake of sheer survival.

Reich's final diagnosis (and he was not as clear as he ought to have been) was that Eva S. suffered from a cluster of symptoms, all contribut-ing to a schizoid or split personality. Among these symptoms were autism, mutism (connected with her refusal to speak German), regression to an oral stage (partial drive fixation and limited object cathexis), castration anxiety (of course), conversion hysteria (displacement of rape experience into abdominal pain), submania, and melancholia. But he had not come up with a single designator for this symptom complex, merely hinting that schizophrenia might be the culprit. Still, as always, he did show that he was a brilliant taxonomist on the details, even if he was groping for a generic category that might pull all of the discriminanda together.

To conclude, Reich took another shot across Freud's bow, arguing that Freud's theories, while pertinent to the sphere of neurosis, had little or no application to the sphere of psychoses. And since Reich was far more interested in the psychotic structures of the self and society than the more pliable neurotic ones, this became a further place where his negative Oedipal struggle with father Freud could break out into the open. Reich said:

> I am convinced that Freud's classic rules are sufficient in all cases of mild neurosis, but the analysis of impulsive characters [borderline personality disorder] and severe character neuroses has shown that purposeful inroads can be made only through continuous analysis of transference. I count this case among the most severe neuroses and suspect that here too daily transference analysis may have been necessary.[67]

Philosophically, Reich is implicitly arguing here that "theory B has greater scope than theory A because it can account for everything that theory A accounts for but can also account for other even more encompassing phenomena as well." The most famous example of this line of argument is Einstein's theory of general relativity, which explains all of Newton's classical mechanics but then goes on to give an explanation of space and time in a richer and truer sense that does not negate Newton so much as relocate Newton within a much narrower sphere of legitimacy.

We are now ready to examine Reich's long monograph on the impulsive character. This subject should have been close to his heart, had he enough self-insight to see himself in this portrayal. My argument is that his concept of the impulsive character has the same phenomenological contour as the contemporary concept of borderline personality disorder. For many Reichians this analysis of impulsivity is Reich's first lasting achievement (although I think that the other short essays are *very* important in their own right) and it propelled him forward to his first significant book, *The Function of the Orgasm*. The 1925 monograph is entitled "The Impulsive Character: A Psychoanalytic Study of Ego Pathology" and was published as the book *Der triebhafte Charakter*.[68]

Reich began by reiterating his conviction that character analysis must replace symptom analysis if lasting cures are to be possible. In analyzing the impulsive character, where the neurotic individual does not have enough self-control or superego restraint to keep from acting out sexually or in other ways, Reich wanted to know why:

> In the analysis of impulsive characters, one encounters cases of amnesia, which have all the symptoms present in typical hysterical amnesia. Other mechanisms of repression, such as fragmentation of genetically connected experiences, displaced guilt feelings, and defense in reaction to destructive tendencies, are at least as intense in the impulsive character as in the compulsive neurotic . . . Hence one cannot speak of weakness in particular repressions but of what causes a lack of defense. This will be the central issue of the discussion. We shall examine the mechanisms of repression for defects enabling actions to take place which would never attain motility in a simple symptom neurosis.[69]

That is quite clear and precise, especially concerning the difference between particular repressions as they work in "simple symptom neurosis" and the more global defects in repression (ego and superego restraints) that allow for certain "actions to take place" that manifest a clear transgression of boundaries and show an inability to control impulses. The impulsive character (or borderline individual) cannot control his or her impulses, whether they are sexual, aggressive, financial, or verbal. There has been some recent informed speculation that neurological structures are involved, which are perhaps also related to forms of addictive behavior, which in consequence complicate the problems involved with impulsivity. The big issue for Reich was with finding out what caused the *total* "lack of defense" for the psyche as a whole, namely, what made the impulsive character so vulnerable to unconscious or conscious impulses that, when acted out, they had negative consequences from the standpoint of the reality principle.

The strength of his character-analytic technique is well evident in his ability to probe into the global issue of the character defects of the entire impulsive character and thus move the analysis into the entire structure of the defense apparatus rather than get bogged down in piecemeal analyses of fragmented repressions of particular cathected objects. Even Reich's many detractors allow that this theoretical move puts him in the canon, at least until he became "schizophrenic" sometime in the 1930s. What his detractors do not acknowledge is that the character-analytic technique continued to evolve throughout Reich's career and that its later transmutations (in the forms of armor work and orgone work) were natural and consistent growths of his work in 1925.

Interestingly, Reich insisted that "repetition compulsion" behavior was part of the impulsive character when that character acts out vis-à-vis the external world. Today DSM IV has a separate category for what it calls Obsessive Compulsive Personality Disorder (301.4), but it *is* still a personality disorder like the borderline/impulsive form (301.83). So there is what the philosopher Ludwig Wittgenstein would call a "family resemblance" between these axis-two designations. But obsessive-compulsive behavior is somewhat treatable with medication, while borderline personality disorder is still highly recalcitrant, very hard to define, and often the bane of many therapists. It need not entail repetition, but it does entail the continual transgression of personal and social boundaries or a desire for fusion with the Other.

Let us listen in on the gifted taxonomist as he continues to work and rework his definitions so as to position himself within and against orthodox psychoanalysis. He used his mountain-peak-to-mountain-peak metaphor again (suggesting that it had great power for him—he was a dedicated amateur mountain climber) and found a place for the partial drives in character analysis:

> Thus every neurotic symptom is founded on a neurotic character and may speak in terms of a hysterical or compulsive (and possibly schizoid) character being topped by its symptoms as a mountain by its peaks. Both the neurotic character and the neurotic symptom are determined in their specific qualities by the phase in which development was arrested. The compulsion neurotic who seeks treatment because of an impulse to stab his friends in the back (a compulsive symptom) will inevitably exhibit the compulsive traits of pedantic cleanliness, orderliness, and exaggerated conscientiousness. Both the specific symptom and the character traits display typical features of the anal-sadistic phase. In this light the term "impulsive character" can allude to only one specific form of the neurotic character, namely, to a disturbance of the

personality as a whole, marked by more or less uninhibited behavior.[70]

The entire character structure of the impulsive character, like those of
other neurotics, is frozen at a particular level of development; the stress,
however, is less on how a partial drive (oral, anal, phallic/clitoral) cath-
ects outward than on how the inhibition structures are derailed by incomplete ego and superego development. The transaction from impulse to act
is almost like a simple reflex arc with the desired object serving as stimulus, the pregenital libido as the nerve track, and the act as the muscular
response. Nowhere is there an intervening process that would inhibit this
arc from going through an almost automatic firing.

For Reich, the childhood of the impulsive character was usually tragic
and filled with intense sexuality combined with profound love/hate ambivalence toward the love object. Such impulsives had a great deal of difficulty negotiating with the dialectic of connection and denial that was
an inevitable part of the transition among the external erogenous zones.
Foreshadowing the work of Julia Kristeva,[71] Reich acknowledged the
pain of denial: "Even the first phase of this significant [upbringing]
process, however is accompanied by denial: the mother's breast is with-
drawn. But denial and gratification stand in contrast to one another in
every phase of development, and indeed progress from stage to stage is
only ensured by denial."[72] For the nonborderline individual, this dialectic of denial and gratification can be negotiated successfully if painfully,
while for the impulsive, it soon becomes the source of a strong sense of
abandonment, a raging gap that needs to be filled by mother or father sub-
stitutes again and again, perhaps throughout life. Suppose the child has
an inconsistent or even brutal upbringing, and further suppose that she or
he has an underlying fragility in the nascent ego structure. The consequences are all too clear: "Inconsistent upbringing and insufficient drive
inhibition, on the one hand, and isolated, concentrated, or sudden denial
(which often comes too late), on the other hand, are common features in
the development of the impulsive character."[73] The breast is truly lost,
and the drives will not be thwarted in their drive to find replacements or,
where pertinent, oral or anal replacements and so forth.

What happens to the latency period for the impulsive character? Reich
perhaps came closest to writing about himself in the following passage, in

which he argues that the impulsive character is extremely sexual in early childhood and does not undergo the kind of superego suppression during the latency period (ages five to twelve) that others undergo. This is another contributing factor leading to the lack of impulse control:

> The childhood games of such individuals will be found to be typically polymorphous-perverse [involving diverse and "disgusting" fantasies, such as the ingestion of feces as a sexual act]. Due to neglect in their environment, they have witnessed and understood far more of adult sexual life than is generally the case in simple neurosis. Hence the latency period is either not activated at all or only very inadequately. If one considers the important role the latency period plays in human ego development in regard to sublimation and reaction formation, one will best be able to estimate the damage done during this phase. Because the impulsive character does not experience this latency, the onset of puberty is accompanied by a drastic breakthrough of sexuality for which neither masturbation nor sexual intercourse is due compensation, as the entire libidinal organization is torn between disappointment and guilt feelings.[74]

Here as in his previous essays Reich goes on to argue that the latency period unfolds when the pregenital drives are suppressed by the social and parental superegos, thus forcing the libido to learn of compromise formations in which object cathexes can be idealized and sexual energies can be transformed into less dangerous forms. But for some reason, usually related to deeply wounding sexual parental transgressions, the impulsive character cannot find the right ego and superego structures during the unfolding of the latency period that would control the hyperintense sexual and conscious incestuous impulses that remain unfulfilled.

As Reich discovered in his own acting out, all of the masturbating and all of the brothel visits in the world would not still the "disappointment and guilt feelings." His feelings of abandonment, related to his mother's suicide, drove him into the arms of innumerable substitute mothers, and he never fully learned the psychological "wisdom" of latency as a necessary condition for moving past the pregenital phase into full genital sexuality. He learned of sexuality by the age of four and used his status as a privileged son of the estate to gain access to the bedchambers of his cook and one of his maids. Boundary transgression and lack of impulse control were a way of life for him, a way learned very early on in Cecilie's all-too-inviting lap.

Reich listed the necessary features found in impulsive characters. Presented with slight modifications for clarity, they were: (1) manifest ambivalence (love/hate), (2) no reactive transformation or dominant hate, (3) isolated superego, (4) defective repression, (5) sadistic impulses without guilt feelings, (6) no conscience, manifest sexuality, and (7) ego trapped between pleasure ego and superego with ambivalence toward both and obedience toward both.[75] We can add to this list other traits that Reich spoke of in the text to this point, namely: (a) fear of abandonment, (b) emotional instability, (c) impulsive acting-out behavior ("numerous affairs" and "smashes dishes when she is angry"), (d) destructive interpersonal relationships ("inability to love"), (e) suicidal ideation ("Finally, she grew incapable of work and decided to kill herself and her children"), and (f) feelings of meaninglessness ("extensive depersonalization" and "sensing of alienation").

In bringing his analysis of the impulsive character to a conclusion, Reich explained the three steps that must be gone through in the analyst/ analysand relationship if there is to be a movement toward a restoration of both superego and ego—both being necessary if the analyst is to gain control of the impulses. As always, Reich saw the transference to the analyst as the key in helping the patient find a healthy superego that was not a neurotic version of her or his parental projection. The three stages are:

1. No insight. Pathological reactions are in perfect accord with the effective superego, or the isolation of the superego from the ego enables submission of the latter to drive-dominated impulses.
2. Increasing positive transference. The analyst is made the object of the patient's libido. This suppresses the old ideal to the object level. Insofar as narcissistic libido was attached to the old ideal, it is now converted into object libido. The new object, the analyst, may function as the basis of a new superego formation, to the extent that he assumes the standpoint of the reality principle and explains that attitudes not understood until now are opposed to reality.

3. Effective recognition of illness (insight). A part of the new, and
   furthermore thoroughly incestuously assessed, object (the analyst) is introjected, constituting a new ego ideal. The old, complete with its course, is condemned. Only now can the actual
   analysis begin.[76]

The superego is never secure in the impulsive/borderline character. It is
isolated and unrooted, resting in a nebulous sphere where it is propped
up by neurotic incestuous projections, hammered at by the pleasure ego
and the libido. The analyst has one supreme tool at her or his disposal,
namely, the transference, whereby the analysand can learn to suppress
the old ego ideal (and weak and misguided superego) and begin to trans-
fer the old projection onto the analyst. Again we see Reich taking what
could be called the "strong intervention" position that the analyst is the
gatekeeper to the reality principle and is the model for the appropriate
new superego formation. The analysand comes to see that the old ego and
superego were loaded with incestuous content and that the new projection
onto the analyst could be the path to a postincestuous world where the libido would learn to negotiate with a more self-controlled pleasure ego and
a more reality-oriented superego. Out of this transformation she or he
would find the impulse control that would end the world of guilt, acting
out, mania, and extreme melancholia.

What, then, were the main theoretical and therapeutic accomplishments of this monograph and of Reich's earlier papers? He had reached
the age of twenty-eight and was now three years out of medical school; he
was still a member of the Vienna Psychoanalytic Society and was working
with a growing list of patients. He had survived the "abortion" crisis over
Lore Kahn and the trenches of the Great War. But had he fully grasped his
own borderline tendencies? In two years his world was to close in on him,
and he was to find himself convalescing from tuberculosis in the Swiss
Alps. Yet by 1925 he had also proven himself to be a theorist of the highest order; he had moved past the inner circle with his nascent system of
character analysis and had dared to push beyond the theories of neurosis
into the terrain of new psychotic and personality disorders (a distinction
that would be more sharply drawn by the 1990s—that is, an axis-one
versus an axis-two designation).

My sense is that Reich had shown himself to be a sensitive and intuitive taxonomist of individual symptoms and their corollary antecedent sexual etiologies, tied to pregenital fixations. But this symptom-specific taxonomy was soon woven into a more generic anthropology of the character structure as a whole, and he was beginning to deal with the whole self-in-process. While fellow psychoanalysts were still working with a model of conflicting and antagonistic drive forces, Reich was probing into the psychic structure that housed all of these forces. He went beneath the drive theory itself into the domain of genital sexuality that would become his *summum bonum*, or highest good.

He had an uncanny ability to unmask sexual intrigues and to spot the analysand's tricks well in advance. But he was also especially vulnerable to his own many countertransferences, often romanticizing them in the terminology of love. He worked with classical Freudian dream analysis, which used the model of the hidden and repressed latent dream wish as it was translated by the dream work into the more acceptable manifest dream content, which then had to be decoded by the omniscient analyst who could peer past the latent negative transference. When he applied this model to his *own* dream material, he rarely came up with any startling insights, which suggests as much about the limitations of the model as it does about the power of his resistance.

Reich's work on facultative impotence was, I think, insightful, and certainly resembles a frustration that many people are familiar with in their own sexual histories, even if he clothed it with Victorian mythology. He reworked the theory of conversion hysteria into a broader theory of sexuality and narcissism, as well as one of deeper character defects that made it possible for him to leave the neurotic sphere behind and to probe the impulsive/borderline character. By separating out this special category of impulsivity from other forms of pathology, he was able to rethink the roles of the superego and what he called the "pleasure ego" within the abusive family dynamic, especially against the background of the dialectic of denial and gratification that every infant and child must negotiate. His rethinking of the latency period is, I think, especially illuminating and sheds light on how the impulsive character comes to lack all impulse control (and, of course, shows us indirectly how he came to be who he was).

His stress on the centrality of the transference (a view he certainly shared with others, such as Otto Rank) does, however, give one some pause. Theoretically it sounds like a perfect model for moving the impulsive character past her or his incestuous fixation into a healthier object cathexis toward the "safe" and "neutral" analyst. But what if the analyst has not learned how to deal with the countertransference or simply likes to stir up the transference pot to satisfy her or his own narcissistic needs? And if this is the case, how many of these analysts are fully aware of these needs on their part? Reich, after all, could not live without romantic triangles (or rectangles) and needed to have some kind of energized transference field in his life to derive support for his ego structures. Yet I think that it would be a mistake to put this in purely moral terms, as there is always much to be gained in the transference/countertransference currents, provided that the full integrity of the Other is always respected (which is very hard if one partner is wrestling with borderline traits).

As we move on to the next phase in Reich's life and career, we will see how his internal struggles deepened. We will see him being abruptly pushed out of the Vienna Psychoanalytic Society (in September 1930) and will find Freud growing cooler to him, both as a person and as a writer. His marriage was shaky, and his self-image was undergoing seismic tremors. But he also managed to write the book that put him on the map and that emancipated him from Freud once and for all.

3

The Function of the Orgasm,

and Late Reflections on Father Freud

Already by the mid-1920s Reich be-
gan to feel tensions within his marriage to Annie, but she was less aware
of these tensions than he was. Of course, Reich would never become a
friend of "enforced monogamy," and in each of his three marriages he
soon came to chafe under the bonds of sexual exclusivity. He and Annie
had "agreed" (always a dubious notion in such cases) to allow each other
extramarital affairs, but Reich was too jealous by nature for such an
arrangement to work out in practice. My sense is that he wanted a constellation that worked in one direction, namely, as solely directed toward
the patriarch.

Compounding his marital difficulties were his growing but repressed
frustrations with Freud. He approached Freud from the very vulnerable
position of the young son who was asking to be one of his analysands. He
could hardly have been in a psychologically more exposed position, especially given his overwhelming need to find a replacement for his own
dead father. Freud turned down his request, citing the alleged precedent
that he did not take on young analysts as patients. This was not quite true,
however, as he had made exceptions for young analysts before.

Also in 1926 Reich's younger brother, Robert, toward whom he had
always harbored ambivalent (love/hate) feelings, died in a sanatorium in
Italy. Like their father, Robert died of tuberculosis, and Reich had failed
to visit him in Italy, perhaps because of a fear of literal and psychological
contamination. Surprisingly, perhaps in an unconscious act of conversion
hysteria—not unlike the pleurisy case of the patient A.F., whom he had
discussed in "Psychogenic Tic as a Masturbation Equivalent"—Reich

went to the Davos sanatorium because he had contracted tuberculosis on his own, although in a milder form.

Finally, there was the precipitating cause of Freud's growing coldness toward Reich's theory of genital sexuality. This was manifested in Freud's terse comments on the manuscript of *The Function of the Orgasm* and in Freud's step back from his earlier sponsorship of Reich. Combined with the growing jealousy of the older analysts toward the usurping young hero, this led toward a public castration ritual that was, unfortunately, drawn out too long. The cumulative effect of all of these events made it psychologically impossible for Reich to remain in Vienna.

Thus at least five trigger events led to the move to Switzerland: (1) marital problems, (2) Freud's rejection of the twenty-nine-year-old's request for private analysis, (3) the premature death of Reich's twenty-six-year-old brother, Robert, from the very disease that had killed their father, (4) Reich's own tuberculosis, and (5) Freud's rejection of his fundamental theory of genital sexuality (with a little help from his loyal lieutenants).

Ilse Ollendorff Reich, his third wife, writing in 1969, struggled to give her own account of what had happened to her husband (they were separated in 1954) during the period that led up to his tuberculosis and convalescence in 1926–27. She was persuaded that the rejection by Freud was the major trigger event:

> But on the basis of my personal understanding of Reich, and the observations I have been able to make about his reactions in somewhat similar situations, I would tend to accept Annie Reich's version of the conflict. Freud had become, as I see it in simple terms, a father substitute for Reich. The rejection, as Reich felt it, was intolerable. Reich reacted to rejection with deep depression.[1]

My own sense (highly speculative, of course) is that Reich wanted to be analyzed by Freud because he had found that the other analysts were inadequate and that Freud had the brilliance and insight to work with the deep conflicts and sheer energetic powers within his psyche. Further, he felt a strong bond with Freud because of their mutual affirmation of a kind of naturalism concerning the psyche and its place within the world. Freud would give him a strong dose of the reality principle and help to root out any strong countercathexes on Reich's part. Perhaps most importantly, this therapeutic relationship would enable Reich to come to grips with the deep castration anxiety that stemmed from Leon.

Ilse accepted the view that the convalescent time in Davos was *the* turning point in Reich's life, but she did not accept the view of his many detractors that it marked his descent into madness (an absurdly vague and useless term in *any* context). Rather, she saw it as a regathering of his remarkably intense energies as he prepared for the great work ahead:

> Annie Reich [who had been in analysis with Anna Freud], and with her other Freudian analysts, believed that a "deteriorating process" began in Reich during his stay at the sanitarium, that he was not the same person after his return, that he must have gained new insights into some of his own problems and been disturbed by them. This theory has been advanced again and again by those attacking theories developed by Reich at this time and later. I feel that this is a mistaken viewpoint in general and on the part of Annie Reich specifically a rationalization of her personal difficulties in living with Reich because he was an unusual person with unusual energy. Reich had a driving force that made it very hard for anyone to follow him, or to live with him for any length of time. He was violent of temperament, taxing people around him to the utmost, but he was at the same time terribly exciting to be with, and it was a privilege to participate in his enthusiasm and to share his insights.[2]

Like Annie, Ilse jumped ship because Reich *was* almost impossible to live with in an intimate way for any length of time. Ilse understood, in my perspective at least, those borderline traits that almost always evoked strong positive or negative responses to Reich: his immediate plunge into intimacy, his equally intense rejection of the intimacy he had already established, and his emotional volatility. These, combined with his sheer energy, made Reich not so much a "fury on earth" as a catalyst for others' powerful projections and for both positive and negative transferences.

Sharaf, in his biography of Reich, argues that Reich's stay in Davos marked an intensification of his psychic inflation, a trait that had emerged during his time in the trenches of World War I. Sharaf had some deeply personal reasons to project some strongly negative complexes onto Reich (especially his sexual jealousy), but that did not prevent him from being insightful about a few of the more basic psychic dynamics that drove Reich. If the precipitating triggers leading Reich to withdraw to Davos produced a severe clinical depression (partially caused by his battle against tuberculosis), his stay there nursed a growing hypomania:

> There is no doubt that at Davos Reich was taking himself more seriously than ever. From that time on, he saw himself as living or wanting to live a heroic destiny. And from that time on, he had a sense of his remarkable powers. He recorded his life in voluminous detail, keeping careful notes and diaries of his intellectual development. To a high degree he had that "fierce love of one's own personality" that Isak Dinesen noted as a hallmark of the creative individual.
>
> The sense of himself as a remarkable person, perhaps a historic figure, was heightened—I am suggesting—during Reich's stay at Davos. His daughter Eva thought that this was the time he "found out who he was."[3]

From a Jungian perspective, the symbolic setting is striking. Reich moved from the conflictual Oedipal world of Vienna to the heights of the Swiss Alps, far away from the nagging superego and the reminders of his sinking powers in the land of the castrating fathers. Like Nietzsche, he found the Swiss mountains to be a place of release, a place where he could let his psyche and soma rebuild themselves without having to pay continual homage to the forces that seemed, in his anxiety, bent on thwarting him.

Reich's text shows how his slow but steady emancipation from classical psychoanalysis had unfolded by 1927. The problem that we are *sometimes* faced with, and it can be a substantial one, is that Reich rewrote several of his early books many years later with no regard for the difference between the old and new material. That is why a *critical edition* is so important in which each text is presented in its original form and in proper sequence.[4] We are lucky that the Wilhelm Reich Infant Trust Fund, which is responsible for keeping Reich's books in print and for contracting for new translations of his hard-to-find books, has issued a translation of the 1927 edition of *The Function of the Orgasm*. Wisely, in order to avoid any confusion between this edition and his American 1942 revised text with the same title, the first edition has a different title in English, *Genitality in the Theory and Therapy of Neurosis,* volume 2 of *Early Writings.*[5]

Reich, as he was correcting the page proofs of this book, deeply ensconced in the Swiss Alps, must have been pondering the upshot of this translation in his life. Being speculative and a bit fanciful, we can almost picture him, like Thomas Mann's character Hans Castorp, lying on his balcony, smoking a cigar or cigarette in the high thin crisp air, wondering about castration and Oedipal longing and betrayal, asking himself at age thirty if he had at last written a masterpiece (*Meisterstück* or *Meisterwerk*). And like many male authors, he looked at his words, now in printer's text, with that love/hate ambivalence that the new cathected object takes on, namely, the book as mother/lover/breast/divine anima. We cannot know exactly what he saw and felt at Davos in that winter and late spring of 1927, but we can reconstruct his thinking and perhaps a small piece of his psychobiographical *unsaid.* Annie Reich said that he came back from Davos a changed man, having undergone a "deteriorating process." And yet he would continue to come out with almost a book a year from 1929 through the 1930s, with many articles besides, in spite of numerous physical dislocations. So I suspect that the concept of "deterioration," especially from an estranged wife, has many meanings in different contexts.

In his 1947 preface to the second edition of *The Function of the Orgasm,* Reich looked back to the years surrounding the writing of the 1927 book and to the reactions that immediately came from the inner Freudian circle, which were not friendly. He pulled out his hidden possibilities in their nascent form and was able to see their incomplete and partially distorted emergence in the 1920s, thus acknowledging how the book might have triggered the negative responses that, at the time, puzzled him:

Even less were, or are, psychoanalysts ready to confront the ramifications of this theory [genital potency]. But it is out of this theory that those methods and conclusions which have brought me into serious conflict with the official position of psychoanalysis have gradually evolved: the sexual economy of psychic life; the technique of character analysis; my views on infantile and pubertal genital functioning; my critique of the ruinous sexual regulation of our society; and, above all, the clinical criticism of the direction in which psychoanalysis has developed since the hypothesis of the "death instinct" was adopted. The orgasm theory leads quite logically into the fields of physiology and biology, and to experiments on the vegetative nervous system. Sex economy and psychoanalysis are today totally separate disciplines, both in method and content; they have only their historical origins in common.[6]

He again contrasted the implied "good" early, more biological Freud with the "bad" post-1920 Freud of the "death instinct," who left his biological foundation behind for some fool's gold in the psychic sphere. Reich further implied that the psychoanalytic establishment of the 1920s did not have the courage to follow out the simple logic of its *own* discoveries and to acknowledge that genital primacy and genital potency were the touchstones of all analysis of neurosis and the foundation of all potential cures (a point on which Freud really balked). Reich assumed that the psychoanalytic circle had failed to follow *him*, rather than that he had failed to honor their hard-won wisdom. My sense is that he was more right than wrong in this belief, especially in his brilliant move to connect genital potency (the power to experience orgasm) to the entire vegetative bodily system (the electrical-chemical energy system) and the character structure (the whole depth personality that underlies given symptoms).

Reich was far more of a poet in his German text than sometimes comes through in English. This is not surprising, given that his philosophical vision is rooted in what I might call the German ecstatic naturalist tradition from Meister Eckhart, to Goethe, to Schiller, to Hölderlin, to Beethoven (his favorite composer). He was not a serious scholar of these thinkers (although he knew most of them), but an "elective affinity" clearly bound him to them. In his continual affirmation of the "life energy or life function" that would never allow for a contrary death instinct or death drive, he showed affinity for Beethoven's expression of the primacy of life-infused tonal harmony and contrast over dissolution and the loss of forward momentum. Like Goethe, he sensed the power of natural energy in all things, causing them to evolve and transform themselves around central patterns that can be discerned by the artist and thinker. And life and sex go together: "The sexual function is the core of the life function per se."[7] His view of the cosmos was that it was a place of swirling life-forms, all surging forward into new creation and structures, never allowing destruction to have the final word. Even the great "emotional plague," one of his most valuable insights, can be overcome with the right use of depth psychology and a new kind of energetics.

Reich distinguished between the Don Juan character (a sex addict) and the genuinely orgastically potent person. By 1927 there were some striking signs of conceptual growth, especially around the issue of so-called male aggression versus female passivity. For a male to be genitally potent, in Reich's view, he must learn to experience true surrender in the act of making love:

> With the exception of tender utterances, orgastically potent men and women never laugh or talk during the sexual act. Both talking and laughing indicate severe disturbances in the ability to surrender oneself, which demands undivided absorption in the pleasure sensations. Men who regard surrender as "feminine" are usually orgastically disturbed.[8]

This emphasis on *surrender* became a necessary ingredient in all of Reich's later work on emotional and bodily armoring. To surrender to the flow of the life function and genital libido meant to let the underlying knots behind each symptom untie on their own, with the consequent release of the grip of the symptom and its object cathexis. Reich placed less emphasis on symptom analysis and the talking cure than on the physical blockages that, once removed, would allow the core of the symptom to express itself with full emotional intensity.

Reich, still struggling, hope against hope, to be something of the loyal lieutenant, tried to rescue elements of the pregenital theory of Freud, but he pushed into his own domain by stressing the primacy of the orgasm. As if to drive home the Oedipal challenge against father Freud, he put his key point in italics:

> This summary will explain why the following proposition encountered strong resistance when I introduced it to the Psychoanalytic Clinic. I maintained that *disturbance of the genital function always plays the principal dynamic role in establishing the neurotic-reaction basis upon which the neurotic conflict is then built. Because*

of its relation to the neurotic process, its removal is crucial to the treatment of the neurosis.
The primary proof of the validity of this view is the fact that *there is no neurosis or psychosis without disturbances of the genital function* . . . In concluding this summary, the cases of addiction and other forms of impulsive behavior, which always manifest grossly disturbed genitality, should also be mentioned.[9]

We have seen the argument of the first paragraph before and have commented favorably on its logical structure insofar as it is linked to the concept of character analysis (S → S1 entails S1 → G). The self (S) must become a new self (S1), thereby becoming open to the deeper genital structures (G) that can flush away the less deep neurotic symptoms. What is interesting and added to Reich's arsenal at this stage is the last sentence, where he brought in "addiction and other forms of impulsive behavior." Jung would call the state produced by the warm breast, or by the presence of alcohol, the "lowering of the threshold of consciousness." For Reich, of course, this would be the "clouded consciousness" of the postcoital moment. Yet for many, the quest for this special state of consciousness takes on intense pathological forms, especially when there is lack of impulse control, or where there is no true surrender to a genuine transference object, or when the partial drives, rather than the full genital libido, are activated.

Can we be ambivalent toward the most important and liberating part of our lives? It seems strange that we could abject something that has such obvious curative powers and that could give us the "pleasure premium" right here on earth. But as with virtually everything else, something about our own genital potency frightens us and produces guilt-consciousness. Looking at his female patients, Reich asserted, "The most frequent cause of orgastic impotence in women is *fear of orgastic excitation.*"[10] One of his patients could not achieve orgasm after her husband had laughed at her during climax, forcing her to regress to a pregenital state. And for many of his female patients, climax was unconsciously associated with urination or defecation or a general sensation of bursting. Also, an intense falling anxiety was often reported to him: "*If the organism is disturbed by anxiety, orgastic release of tension is experienced as falling.* This may be one of the reasons why dreams of falling so frequently represent genital anxiety and impotence."[11] As he would come to put it by 1933, the sensation of bursting through rigid body armor is like the sensation of falling off a high cliff, and there is a tremendous fear of loss of control. So along with many other factors (the superego, the Oedipal prescriptions, fear of disease, patriarchy, and so on) there is the fear of one's *own* energy as it batters against internal structures that at the time seem to be there to protect the organism against falling, either into chaos or almost literally into pieces.

Reich set his sights on the problem of sexual stasis and how the loss of the flow of sexual energy led to the emergence of neurotic symptoms. He moved away from what one could call a hermeneutic or interpretive model of therapy, in which the analyst struggles to find the causal meanings behind each symptom complex so that they can be decoded like a great text. While Freud stayed within a version of the decoding model and Jung developed a very strong version of a *teleological* or goal-oriented model, Reich took the opposite tactic of moving into an analysis of vegetative biological energies that were more basic than any conceptual structures.

My point is that the ideal synthesis (to be laid out in the final chapter) requires both a vegetative framework *and* an archetypal depth psychology, which are both in turn encompassed within a semiotic anthropology. And finally, in a last philosophical construction, akin to the one that Reich *did* make, all of this would ultimately be enveloped within an ecstatic naturalist religion that is truly universal and antitribal. The two pieces that Reich did not have, and they are absolutely central, are the archetypal and the semiotic. He did not avail himself of Jung's archetypal model because of the Vienna prejudices against the Zürich school (after the 1912–14 break) and because of his strong extraversion (which was *compensatory* against his highly intuitive and anxious introverted probes of the inner life). The semiotic model was not yet available to him, at least in its most rigorous Peircean form (which, while first created in the 1860s, did not really come into extensive use until the 1960s or so). The French/ Swiss model of Ferdinand de Saussure, which would have been available, lacks philosophic power and is based on a fairly trivial linguistic model. Unfortunately, it continues to hobble a number of postmodern thinkers who should know better.

So we must look at his own abjection of the "meaning question" as an abjection of his own guilt structures about his mother's suicide, the death of Lore, his rejection by father Freud, and his passion for total cures without the tedium of piecemeal analysis of each symptom and its etiology. On the positive side, however, was his longtime interest in natural science, his genuine breakthroughs in finding the depth structures of the total neurotic character, his link between the orgasm and the life energy, and his discovery of the drive of the organism as a whole toward overcoming its own pathology. Jung put this last insight in a slightly different way, namely, that a neurosis was an attempt at a cure rather than a manifestation of a mere random breakdown of the psyche.

Which brings us back to the issue of "sexual stasis" and the central role it plays for Reich as the source of bodily ills. Once again he started with Freud, only to move very quickly beyond him into his own sphere of the vegetative and the realm of energy regulation. His language sounds more and more like that of a biology or physics textbook and less and less like that of a classical psychology book:

> *Psychic meaning.* Since Freud, this has meant, in the simplest terms, those repressed ideas, experiences, desires, satisfactions, self-punitive acts, and so forth, that achieve disguised expressions in the symptom. But these psychic elements would not be able to create symptoms if they were not charged with dammed-up drive energy. Most of the repressed ideas that emerge as significant components in the analysis of a neurotic symptom are secondary additions to an already established symptom . . . This activity is subject to biological laws and is predominantly rooted in physiological processes occurring in the realm of vegetative energy regulation.[12]

We have a pyramid in which the neurotic fantasy is at the top, supported by the neurotic symptom, which is in turn supported by dammed-up drive energy. The analysis of this dammed-up energy is no longer a proper subject for psychoanalysis but belongs in a new science, still emerging, that deals with the vegetative currents that flow through the body. What value does symptom analysis now have when the real problem has to do with blocked energy, which, by Reichian definition, is sexual? Isn't the issue now one of finding a way to break the dam that is holding back this genital libido, which will in turn, by another Reichian presupposition, wash away the debris that has been allowed to gather because there has been no water to wash them away in the normal course of affairs? After all, Reich had established that there can be no neurosis if there is genital potency—that is, the two states of affairs are in the disjunctive category. Put iconically, we can only have a negative formulation: $\sim N = G$, that is, only *not* neurosis ($\sim N$) can equal genital potency (G), or put the other way, $N = \sim G$. The transition from N to $\sim N$ is through a reconfiguration of the vegetative energies.

Actually, Reich's system can be surprisingly simple at times, even if he was quite rightly compelled to wrestle with other systems and use appropriate technical terminology. On one level, he was unfolding a simple hydrology, with an analysis of how vegetative currents are like mountain streams moving under gravitational pressures, flowing downward toward "expression." He put this correlation as simply as possible: "Instead of inflow, we must refer to energy build-up or tension; instead of outflow, energy discharge, release, or satisfaction."[13] So he translated the hydrological terms into sexual and energetic terms. The inflow—say, into a reservoir—becomes the increase of sexual tension, while the outflow—say, through the floodgates—becomes the climax or at least the partial drive satisfactions. His by-now-indispensable diagrams depict the nature of an unbalanced sex economy in which the ratio between tension and release will always produce a neurotic split until the proper discharge takes place. For Reich, it is as simple as can be: "Orgastic disturbance is thus the key to an understanding of the energy economy of every such illness. Neuroses are nothing but the attempts of the organism to compensate for the disturbance in the energy equilibrium."[14] Sexual stasis, then, is what results from the inhibition of the genital libido when its outflow/discharge is blocked by a reason or reasons known or unknown. But what are the symptoms of genuine sexual stasis?

It is another mark of Reich's post-Davos extraverted turn that he started his symptom analysis by looking at how the *body* presented itself to the analyst as the most telling location for catching the sexual stasis out of its hiding place. So he listed fairly clear external signs that need not have internal psychic *meaning*: "The typical symptoms of illness caused by sexual stasis are heart ailments (asystole, tachycardia, arrhythmias, extrasystoles, etc.), dizziness, diarrhea, and, occasionally, increased sali-vation."[15] One element that thickened the plot is that anxiety seemed to Reich to produce the same symptoms in his patients as genital excitation. This link became very important to Reich and led him to modify Freud's theory of anxiety (as we shall see later) in important respects. For Reich, "Genital excitation and the anticipation of sexual pleasure produce the same phenomena in the heart and the vasomotor system as does anxiety. This most certainly cannot be considered irrelevant for comprehension of the relationship between anxiety and sexuality."[16]

In the blockage of genital libido one can observe the pounding of the heart combined with a sensation of warmth and an increased pulse rate. Further, the patient will experience irritability, anxiety, nervousness, ill humor, sudden sweats, or conversion hysteria. For example, "Hot flashes are very frequently revealed in analysis to be the expression of physical genital excitation which is not allowed to become conscious; diarrhea may be an expression of anxiety or sexual excitation."[17] And of course, the entire character structure can be involved, spawning one neurotic symptom after another in an endless cycle with no relief. But I do not want to give the impression that Reich had *entirely* abandoned the psy-choanalytic case study approach, with its focus on Oedipal conflicts or the pregenital stages of fixation; rather, it had been removed from its foundational role and placed in a subaltern position where it was now meant to serve the allegedly more encompassing vegetative energetic framework. *Genitality* was still laced with fascinating case studies, some of which bear our examination.

Reich presented a very detailed case study (running almost eight pages) of a twenty-six-year-old woman who presented with "nightly spells of anxiety, pounding of the heart, trembling, hot flashes, and tearing of the eyes."[18] She was frigid and had very great difficulty having sex with her husband. Around nine each evening she would start developing these symptoms so as to avoid sex. She also developed the idea that sex itself was "animalistic and dirty." Reich was able to trace her original negative sexual feelings (within the context of the marriage) to an abortion her hus-band had forced her to undergo years earlier, when he felt that he was not in a strong enough financial position to raise a child. She deeply resented both the loss of her child and what she thought of as a "bloody genital in-tervention." This second sensibility rendered her genital zone anesthetic, and she certainly felt that she could not place it at the disposal of her husband.

For good or ill, Reich once again brought up his gender analysis, in which he contrasted the patient's masculine traits with her husband's feminine traits. The patient was disappointed that her husband was not aggressive enough in the marriage (other than when he demanded the abortion) and that she had to resort to the fantasy of being a "tender wife loved by a strong and extremely rough husband." This was, of course, part of her unconscious reason for withholding sex from her "feminized" husband.

But of course, this was hardly the end of the story. After several months of analysis, Reich was able to probe more deeply into the patient's life history and to discover that she had had a profoundly wounding experience of adult sexuality. Her parents had had a bad marriage, due for the most part to her father's alcoholism. He would come home late every night and force himself on his wife. The primal scene (*Urszene*) was always noisy and brutal. The patient was at first struck with fear, as if a catastrophe were about to take place. In adolescence she learned to masturbate "during parental coitus," drawing the conclusion that her father's behavior might not be so bad after all. She developed the fantasy of becoming a prostitute so that she could use money "to put her father in a gentler frame of mind and win him for herself." This in turn developed into sadistic fantasies in which she would get sexually excited whenever she saw a dog or a child being beaten in public. All of this early material laid the groundwork for a whole series of repressions that would be reactivated by the abortion trauma many years later. In her mind, she made a connection between her father's aggressive sexuality and the failed sexuality of her husband, and between pleasure and procreation.

To free the patient from her genital insensitivity, Reich worked to allow the traumatic material to become conscious and to help her understand how her physical symptoms (anxiety, hot flashes, crying, and trembling) could be ameliorated if she let loose the flow of deeper genital libido. She was able to regain some pleasure in masturbation, but Reich considered this to be only a halfway measure at best; her marriage had built-in problems that perhaps thwarted a full cure. Yet she did move some way down the road toward true genital satisfaction; to put it differently, her vegetative energy flow was freed up enough to ease some of her neurotic symptoms. Reich concluded: "The success achieved was due solely to the mobilization of previously bound anxiety, which included a quantum of sexual energy."[19]

But what of the ever-vexing problem of relapses? Most patients are prone to return to old neurotic patterns, old vegetative energy pathways in between their full genital discharges (orgasms). What makes patients so vulnerable? Reich presented a very straightforward energetic model:

> *In a symptom-free patient the propensity to relapse depends primar-*
> *ily on the amount of dammed-up sexual energy resulting from the*
> *as-yet-unresolved inner inhibitions and external difficulties that*
> *hinder the establishment of an orderly sex life.*[20]

The two things working against full liberation are "external difficulties" (which the analyst knows about better than does the analysand) and inner inhibitions (namely, social and parental superegos). The dammed-up sexual energy (which has now encompassed the pleasure ego) will be more or less intense depending upon the twin powers of the superegos (acting as one) and the reality principle. In the case study of this patient, her husband, with his insistence on the unwanted abortion, functioned as a negative reality principle. At the same time, the abortion reactivated her childhood trauma of the primal scene, which reawakened the Oedipal prescriptions (part of the parental superego). Her genital libido was trapped behind an energy dam composed of the reality principle and the parental superego, whereupon it announced its hidden presence through physical symptoms.

In this case study, Reich blended his earlier psychoanalytic categories, which he had already reconstructed from the classical model by 1923, with his new energetic system in a highly original and highly successful way (even if the hint of an imminent cure was far too optimistic). Here is how he summarized the blend:

1. The Oedipus complex provides the basic material (content, fantasies), and the sexual stasis, the energy, for the creation of the neurosis.
2. Sexual stasis transforms the Oedipus complex from an historical fact into a topical one; this then causes the acute sexual stasis to become chronic by inhibiting the genital function.

Thus the ring of the two etiologies closes to form a continuous cycle: fantasy, disturbance of the genital function, sexual stasis, anxiety; fantasy, disturbance of the genital function, etc.[21]

In this account the Oedipus complex (the stage of life between two and
a half to about six—a period that ends when the latency period begins)
goes from being a historical structure per se to becoming a topical structure, a lasting but transformed constituent of all consequent behavior and
ideation. Even though past the Oedipal and latent stages, the neurotic
character will have Oedipal *structures* that will be activated whenever the
historical material is reawakened. Dammed-up genital libido will be produced whenever an Oedipal structure in the present touches upon a traumatic Oedipal event in the past—as when this patient's recent abortion
awakened her childhood response to her father's brutal sexual behavior.
When the topical Oedipal conflict entwines with the historical Oedipal
trauma, the sexual stasis becomes "chronic."

Reich further developed this blend of the historical and the topical/
structural in a second case study involving a thirty-two-year-old married
woman with an eight-year-old son. This woman was convinced that she
and her son were both destined to die of tuberculosis, even after doctors
assured her that neither of them had any symptoms of the disease. Her
general hypochondria deepened into "crying states and acute anxiety
states." After just a few weeks of analysis Reich discovered (1) that the
patient had witnessed her thirteen-year-old daughter masturbate, (2) that
she was afraid that her daughter would teach her son to masturbate, (3)
that the patient had witnessed her husband flirt with and kiss a young girl,
(4) that after witnessing her husband kiss this girl, the patient had an "ir-
resistible urge to masturbate," and (5) that on the night after witnessing
her husband, she had a dream of having sexual intercourse with her father
in which she experienced far greater sexual pleasure than she had ever
experienced with her husband. In Reich's view this made her even more
anxious about the "inevitability" of she and her son dying soon of tuberculosis. In her unconscious she had made the connection between masturbation and its punishment by disease, tuberculosis (as her cathected
choice) being the disease that killed her father.

Masturbation guilt, especially strong in the early decades of the twentieth century in European culture (where, for example, the patient had

read that she would get syphilis if she masturbated), manifested itself in neurotic symptoms and strange object cathexes. Reich concluded: "In keeping with her old attitudes, she saw death or ruination as the inevitable consequence of masturbation. Masturbation desire, as well as fear of punishment, was projected onto the boy."[22] Told then, it is a wonderfully complex tale. First the mother transfers her masturbation guilt onto her son. Then she grows fearful that her daughter will teach her son the secret art. Her father appears suddenly out of the unconscious in classical Oedipal fashion, showing that he is a better lover than the pale shadow whom she foolishly married, and she must struggle with newly freed libidinal energy.

In a form of conversion hysteria, the patient now developed large blisters on her legs, arms, and face whenever the combination of sexual excitation and guilt became too strong. In analysis with Reich she traced this to a childhood memory of being slightly fondled by a young boy who pulled up her dress when she was about ten. From that point on she felt extremely shy about being partially undressed in public situations—for example, on a beach—and often the blisters would appear during crises or during periods of decreased sexual satisfaction, as in her marriage. But during puberty she blamed the blisters on her "excessive masturbation." Significantly, the blisters reappeared during her analysis with Reich, and he obviously concluded, "It was genital anxiety that was, after all, primarily responsible for excitation being diverted from the genitals to the skin."[23] This gives some indication of how powerful Reich considered thwarted genital libido to be in shaping the mind/body relationship.

But this accords with Reich's view of the "dammed-up" libido. What else can the unconscious do but let out this dammed-up libido by any means possible? It cannot achieve coital satisfaction, except in dream material (which serves this function indirectly), so it must unleash its drive through pathological physical symptoms. This is a process that Peirce called "secondness," that is, brute dyadicity in which one thing collides with another without any synthesizing meaning (which Peirce called "thirdness"). You are simply hit over the head with a *second*, a brute fact that as yet has no meaning. It is a pre-intelligible something-yet-to-be-named that needs meaning, that needs a name. And it is at this juncture, where secondness yearns to become thirdness, that the analyst intervenes, attempting to name the complex or the process whereby energy is manifested as a symptom, as part of character analysis.

For Reich the symptom as *second* (say, blisters on the skin) will become the symptom as *third*, as always (the symptom as blocked genital libido) in and through the interpretive act of the analyst, who works through and past the latent negative transference (another form of secondness). What Reich failed to grasp and Jung *did* grasp is that the unconscious is also a birthing-ground for thirdness (meaning) in itself, and that it is far more than just streaming libidinal energy awaiting some kind of external reality principle to *give* it meaning—such as the principle supplied by the analyst.

In Chapter 5 I will explore how Peirce's categories of secondness and thirdness, as well as his category of firstness (a kind of pre-semiotic floating ground of absolute immediacy), can help us to understand Reich's work on character analysis. But at this point we can already see how these categories describe the way meaning emerges from a pre-semiotic background of nonmeaning. Conversion hysteria, for example, is a semiotic process in which the unconscious maneuvers to convert a blocked drive into a physical symptom, which is clearly manifest to both the analysand and the analyst. Secondness is the category that pertains to a simple causal relationship that does not involve a third meaning-filled category that would confer meaning to the dyad. So in the hidden translation from blocked drive to manifest symptom, there is a causal link that gets meaning only when it is seen to *have* meaning by the analyst, who acts as the third term. Yet on a deeper level the unconscious "chooses" a symptom that already has some meaning (thirdness) that is personally relevant to the analysand. Therefore it must follow that there is in fact thirdness in the unconscious itself. That is why it makes perfect sense to assert that the unconscious has a form of consciousness (as for Peirce, consciousness and thirdness, quite rightly, entail each other), but the form is different in nature from that of ego consciousness. At the appropriate juncture I will differentiate between two kinds of thirdness and their corresponding types of consciousness, but in such a way as to help transfigure Reich's position.

We have seen how Reich applied his insights into genital libido to issues in conversion hysteria and to such problems as premature ejaculation

and genital anesthesia. Further, we have seen how he brilliantly connected
a historical Oedipal model with a topical model to show how a contemporary event in the life of the analysand would reactivate the historical part
of the Oedipal drama, thus creating a kind of continuous feedback loop
that could only deepen in intensity without intervention (or in the rare
case, sheer good luck). But what did Reich have to say about some of the
other classical issues in psychoanalysis—for example, the dialectic between sadism and masochism? What did Reich's model of genital libido,
which undergirded the drives, have to say about the formation and expression of these twin antisocial forces? In working out the inner mechanisms of sadism and masochism, he wrote:

> *Sadism* is always ultimately destructive and cruel. Arising from
> dammed-up sexual excitation, its purpose is sexual gratification.
> In this sense, sadism is always pathological, a sure sign of a dis-
> turbed sexual economy, wherever and whatever the context.
> (*Masochism*, according to sex-economic investigations, is not the
> opposite of sadism; that is, it is not the expression of a striving
> for pleasure through pain [as it is claimed by psychoanalysts].
> Masochism, whether erotic or moral, is an act of aggression against
> the other person, an act that makes use of suffering as its means.
> Physiologically it corresponds to the drive for guiltless release of
> tension, or satisfaction, through the other person. However,
> masochism is not a drive in the biological sense. It does not exist
> in the animal world any more than does sadism. Both are symp-
> toms of social pathology.)[24]

Several points are especially striking here. Reich rejects the view of his
fellow psychoanalysts, noting that for them masochism is "a striving for
pleasure through pain." He links masochism to sadism, in that it is also an
act of aggression directed outward toward an Other. He sees both sadism
and masochism as involving the struggle to release blocked sexual tension.
And in his view, neither "drive" is biologically primary; both are culturally
inscripted (secondness) and hence amenable to treatment that will unleash
genital potency. Once potency breaks through the dam holding it back,
sadism and masochism disappear since sexual tension is overcome and
there is no longer any need to be cruel or to use the Other as a cathected

object. Implied in the entire argument is that Freud's model of the so-called aggressive instincts or drives is based upon a conflation between the primary (biological) and the secondary (cultural) drives.

Reich makes this argument even more emphatically in his next chapter, entitled "The Social Significance of Genital Strivings." This chapter is a clear transition between his classical (but renegade) psychoanalysis and his emerging left-wing thought, in which he sees social structures as shaping and damaging genital libido in ways that the Vienna analysts failed to recognize. In his view, patients could not be cured without a reconstruction of the entire social order; healing was not a matter of adjustment but would require a revolution in sexual attitudes. The first step was for the old Viennese guard to acknowledge this reality:

> In the preceding chapter we established that aggressive attitudes toward the world increase when genital strivings meet with internal or external obstacles. In compulsion neurosis the penis becomes a fantasized instrument of hate, and genital eroticism is enlisted in the service of the destructive drive. We found that genital satisfaction relieves destructiveness, that a lack or deficiency of satisfaction precipitates it, and that a removal of the source of sexual impulses causes destructiveness to become permanently inactive. We are able to confirm this with examples from the animal kingdom.[25]

Reich learned from his war experiences that the lack of genital satisfaction turned the penis (certainly in the symbolic and fantasy orders) into an "instrument of hate" that could be cathected onto other objects.

Reich insisted that genital satisfaction would dissolve the destructive drive and end war and patriarchy. His horrible experience with the almost mechanized prostitution of the war, in which an entire company contracted gonorrhea, doubtless convinced him that a mere sexual climax with a stranger under war conditions had absolutely nothing to do with genital potency (any more than did the life of the Don Juan or the nymphomaniac). As we have noted, the necessary conditions for genital potency were fairly complex for Reich, involving far more than the ability to climax; now, in 1927, they came to involve some complex social elements as well. Clearly this was terrain that *had* to be explored. The fact that his fellow analysts failed to follow him says far more about their conceptual and experiential inadequacies than about Reich's alleged heresies. Ironically, his very daring in moving psychoanalysis in a social direction would in turn alienate the social theorists with whom he would soon work, as they had very strong personal and ideological reasons for rejecting sexuality and its role in the class struggle.

Reich made it absolutely clear in *Genitality* that he saw sadism as a result of the "cultural negation of sexuality"[26] and not part of an innate aggressive drive. So from Reich's perspective, there were no biological drives that could be labeled "destructive" in the human and pathological/cultural sense. The core biological drives were tied to the expression of life, and destructive aggression was a secondary by-product of repression, sublimation, and social control.

Sadism has one of its strongest supports in the realm of religion, where a rage against the body and genital potency assumes cosmic proportions. By projecting castration anxiety onto an otherworldly male figure, the individual was in effect castrated already and his or her powers of resistance were checked. Consequently, organized religion came in for a fair flogging in Reich's analysis. This remained a consistent theme for the thoroughly humanistic Jew who had become as fully distant from his own religion as he possibly could. But again I will insist that Reich was, in his own unique way, a deeply religious person, who found his particular religious language only by the late 1940s. Here in *Genitality* he came out against both the Hebrew scriptures and Roman Catholicism:

> Let us recall, for instance, the austerity of Catholic dogma and especially the cruelty of the Inquisition, which accompanied religious hypermorality and pretended to protect it. The religious demand for and observance of asceticism itself resulted from deep-seated guilt feelings; the original sin in the myth of Adam and Eve was a genital act forbidden by God the Father. The external denial developed into an internal prohibition, exactly as in compulsion neurosis. Furthermore, Freud and [Theodor] Reik have proven that religious ceremonies obey exactly the same laws as compulsion-neurotic ceremonials. However, to the best of my knowledge, the fact that it was the suppression of genital impulses

which produced brutality has not yet been given due recognition. Sadism developed first and was subsequently perverted to religious masochism. Thus medieval masochistic orgies and the excessive brutality of the Inquisition were essentially discharge manifestations of libidinal energies.[27]

Patriarchal religion was founded on an asymmetrical power relationship between the human subject and a male quasi-human deity with some form of consciousness who "must" shape finite and human autonomous consciousness to his capricious will. The power flows in only one direction, so as to humble any human efforts to become self-directed or autonomous. Reich correctly concluded that this model mapped out an already-blocked genital libido and turned it into (1) an external prohibition by an invented deity (Yahweh), (2) which was internalized into a compulsion neurosis, (3) became a systematic sadism through religious hypermoralism, and (4) deepened into masochism through medieval Catholicism, which had its "finest" flower in the Inquisition, which (5) enabled the medieval Inquisitors to discharge their repressed genital libido, through the systematic torture of so-called heretics.

Reich was struggling to deconstruct the patriarchal myths of the 1920s in central Europe, but many of these same myths are being revived in the present. Reich listed four prohibitions or taboos that he linked to a social compulsion-neurotic ideology:

1. Extramarital sexual intercourse is generally portrayed as animalistic (sadistic) and dirty (anal).
2. With no consideration for physiological and biological facts, premarital and extramarital asceticism is promulgated often by physicians.
3. Masturbation is viewed as the evil of evils, even by physicians, although it is factually irrefutable that masturbation normally dominates a certain phase of development.
4. Love impulses are fragmented: young, unmarried men are allowed intercourse, but since the girls of the same class are to be protected, prostitution is tolerated as a "filthy" but necessary evil.[28]

Obviously the first point, prohibiting adultery, is one that most people will still affirm, even if it is widely practiced by many of these very same people. The second point, however, at least in the form of premarital asceticism, has come to be questioned by most people, as it is seen to be damaging to psychic growth and well-being. Reich was very concerned that women of his Victorian generation should avoid the horrors of the "first night" deflowering because it would set the sexual tone for the rest of the marriage: "The wife confronts this new experience, tabooed from childhood, with fear; and where fear presides, there can be no pleasurable experience."[29] Their mothers would have burdened them with the idea that this moment had to be endured with stoic fortitude and that it was going to be physically painful.

Masturbation is less demonized today, and it is certainly accepted by many as a positive alternative to promiscuous acting out. And virtually everyone, from the libertarian to the religious puritan (with the exception of the self-privileging patriarch), would agree with Reich's deep distaste for the dual standard over gender rights and privileges in the sexual sphere. Remember that Reich's views on the third point of masturbation were quite interesting and multilayered. Initially he struggled with his own guilt during his latency and puberty periods in which masturbation alternated with sex (with the cook and with prostitutes). In his technical writings he saw masturbation as both partially liberating and as related to pathology but never as an end in itself. If the analysand could masturbate after a long period of genital anesthesia, that was a positive good, but if masturbation became the sole form of object cathexis or became a pregenital fixation, then it would mark a regression away form the path toward genital potency. Ultimately, the vagina/clitoris and the penis served the entire vegetative muscular system of streaming energy rather than the other way around.

Reich asked whether men and women are polygamous by nature, and if so, whether this is a neurosis. Since he was himself conflicted about monogamy, he fudged the issues quite a bit, coming up with the following loose argument: (1) polygamy is somewhat neurotic in itself; (2) most marriages are intrinsically neurotic; therefore (3) polygamy is virtually inevitable and (4) should be seen not as immoral but simply as a reality of human life. Plato, via Socrates, might call this a bit of sophistry—that is, a bit of "reasoning" that is outside of the *Logos* (the true structure of things). But is it? Statistically it seems clear that polygamy is almost universal (despite its being well hidden) and that either neurosis or full genital potency brings it on and makes it fascinating.

Reich was reasonably fair in his gender analyses in this section of *Genitality*. He refuses, for example, to blame wives for their husbands' straying. In fact, he traces the frustrations in the wife's psyche back to her parental (especially paternal) upbringing and shows exactly why the husband cannot provide full genital satisfaction to his mate no matter how hard he tries, because he can never fulfill the paternal ideal, which is simultaneously sexual and asexual. By the same token, he argued that both husband and wife would convert their genital frustration into neurotic symptoms (such as gambling or drinking) in order to avoid adultery. He distinguished between psychoanalytic *science* and the philosophy of *values*, insisting that neither should intrude upon the other. Reich concluded that sometimes the married analysand must commit adultery to free up genital libido, but that the affair should be conducted openly, not secretly. Obviously, Reich was in part justifying his own behavior; even so, it was courageous to bring this common problem out into the open and struggle with it, theoretically and clinically applying his psychoanalytic and biological/energetic tools to it.

Reich brought *Genitality* to a conclusion by reiterating his theme that the erotic drives, now almost cosmic in scope, were the link to the social reality principle, primarily because eros must move outward from private genital satisfaction to social work libido, which has its own pleasure principle. Reich argued that sexual frustration is the source not only of personal unhappiness but of widespread social disorder:

In social terms, satisfied genitality, as the primary basis of a well-ordered psychic economy, is also the prerequisite for the ability to work, which is the only satisfaction-seeking tendency which society permits and, to some extent, condones. From the biological standpoint, genitality is the only one of all the drives that also serves the preservation of the species.[30]

True work takes place when the power of genital sexuality unfolds in the social and economic environment. The Freudian superego is actually overcome, and a thorough critique of the sexual mores of the society takes place. For Reich this helps the individual to distinguish between external commands (with their internalized unconscious quilt) and genuine sex economic (that is, social/sexual energy dynamics) requirements.

The coda to the entire argument of *Genitality* was sounded in two striking sentences: "Satisfied genital object love is thus the most powerful opponent of the destructive drive, of pre-genital masochism, of yearning for the womb, and of the punitive superego. This superiority of sexuality over the destructive drive is the objective justification of our therapeutic efforts."[31] It is fascinating that Reich included the "yearning for the womb" here—a yearning that might be thought of as a longing to return to the ground of being; namely, to the dangerous realm of pure immediacy (which we will discuss vis-à-vis Peirce's category of firstness). The womb, for Reich, was the ever-inviting and ever-treacherous place of death that would envelop autonomous consciousness as it separated itself from the divine maternal—the suicidal mother. Genital sexuality is the pathway away from suicide and the alleged death drive. And ultimately genitality is the magical potency that melts away all destructive (and merely secondary) drives from the self-in-process as it birthed itself from out of its dark ground.

Whatever one makes of Reich's blend of renegade psychoanalysis and a nascent vegetative science (that is, a science of bodily energies) in *Genitality*, the book's underlying mythological structures are fascinating in their own right. Reich may not have been aware of his mythic identifications, but they are, so I would argue, operative within the more explicit text. First there is the *hero myth*, which posits a young bearer of light who must conquer the forces of maternal darkness by the power of solar consciousness. This hero is constantly being seduced by those dark powers and their uncanny ways, especially in the form of the devouring anima, which wants to pull the hero back into the Oedipal womb. This is, of course, a patriarchal myth, although with some effort it might be made more gender inclusive if in fact a myth can be *created* by an act of will.

Secondly, there is what might be called the *pan nature myth*, in which forces of nature act as some kind of sexual energy field that is most profoundly embodied in the human genital organs. Nature is more than a mechanism that reiterates its own archetypal patterns. Rather, nature is a self-expression of the expansion of life energy that breaks through static boundaries, especially in the human order. This expansion never fully returns to its antecedent states and always adds new pathways to the release of blocked libido.

Finally, there is the *myth of the ecstasies*, which sees energy as leaping outward from a partially frozen position. In the Greek philosophical tradition, the concept of *ecstasy* refers to that "which stood outside of itself." An ecstatic experience is one in which the religious worshiper is drawn out of himself or herself into another realm entirely, perhaps infusing the hero with the power of a god or goddess. One could be infused with Zeus or Aphrodite and cease to be, for the moment, a mere citizen of Athens or Corinth. Thus, from a Jungian perspective, Reich unconsciously framed *Genitality* with three very rich mythological structures: (1) the hero myth, (2) the pan nature myth, and (3) the myth of the ecstasies. The hero brings the fitful light of consciousness into the realm of the unconscious, fighting against the temptations of the womb and the various pregenital attachments, while feeling the genuine pull of nature's sexual energetics. The sexual pull of nature is felt in the vegetative currents in the body, as focused in the genitals, but is not confined to them, and it is then released in the outward ecstasy in which the body stands outside of itself and becomes not so much "god or goddess infused" as nature infused.

Genitality was an amazing achievement for a thirty-year-old medical school graduate and practicing psychoanalyst. But now Reich had to come down from the mountains and return to Vienna for the denouement of his conflict with the great father over the issue of autonomy. Once there he witnessed firsthand the slaughter of one hundred socialist workers on the streets of Vienna on July 15, 1927; he and Annie watched the "senseless machine" police systematically shoot workers within the swirling crowd. This experience prompted his turn to social issues.

In 1952 Reich looked back on this period and his close work with Freud. Three themes from his interview with Dr. Kurt Eissler (which took place in English on October 18 and 19 in Rangeley, Maine) emerge: (1) his assessment of Freud's and his own attitude toward Judaism; (2) how he, Freud, and Freud's loyal lieutenants came to differ on the libido theory (where Reich used mostly ad hominem arguments); and (3) his ability to find his own way back to an appreciation of a modified form of the death drive.

We have seen how ambivalent Reich was about his own Judaism, from the prohibition of the use of Yiddish in his parental home to his determination to shy away from Jewish groups at the University of Vienna. He argued that Freud remained trapped in his own form of patriarchal Judaism and that this contributed to Freud's general sexual unhappiness (that is, his genital impotence from the mid-1920s on):

> "He suffered, just plain suffered from it," Reich told Eissler. "He didn't want to be a Jew. Never. He wasn't Jewish. I never felt he was Jewish. Neither did I feel Anna Freud as Jewish. They had nothing Jewish in them, either characterologically, religiously, or nationally. That doesn't mean I'm anti-Semitic . . . On the other hand, he was a German. He liked Goethe's *Faust*. His language was German. His style was the wounded, German style of Thomas Mann—the rounded, harmonic, but very complicated expression, in contradistinction to the English, which is straight and simple.[32]

Freud's dilemma, in Reich's eyes, was that Judaism trapped him in a patriarchal marriage and therefore wouldn't allow him to get a divorce and free up his blocked genital libido. Reich blamed Freud's jaw cancer on his characterological armoring, not on his twenty-cigars-a-day habit (for example, Reich says, "Bite—a biting-down impulse, swallow something down, never to express it").[33] This armoring, in consort with his impotence, showed the effects of the constrictions caused by his ensnarement in patriarchal Judaism. Clearly, Reich's understanding of Judaism remained narrow, and he focused on only a few traits manifest in its diverse traditions.

Reich was determined that Judaism should never be his own "downfall" or the hidden side of an internal contradiction. It is as if he sailed right over it, or that it never entered into his bloodstream, thus bypassing the suicidal mother from whom he could have "contracted" it. I feel as if I am insulting the reader to use the word *denial* here, as it is so obvious in this context, but clearly he was running away from the parental tragedy—and perhaps from anti-Semitism emerging in the Austro-Hungarian Empire. Here is how he dealt with his own relationship to Judaism in 1952 and adumbrated his own antitribal Christology:

> Now, while Freud was caught in Judaism, I was free of it. I'm much more in sympathy with the Christian world of thought and the

Catholic realm. Not that I condone it, or that I believe in it. I don't
believe in these things. But I understand them well. The Chris-
tians have the deepest point of view, the cosmic one. The American Jew has it, too, but not the European. I don't know whether we
should go into that. But I am very much interested in the history of
Christianity. Do you know what Christ knew? He knew about the
Life Energy. I don't know if you get me now. In a simple way, he
knew about the fields and the grass and growth and babies.[34]

So the Christ that we get is not the Jewish rabbi but the nature mystic. In
the past several decades there has been a great deal of effort on the part
of Christian theologians to overcome Christian anti-Semitism by *stressing* the Jewish nature and culture of Jesus. Consequently, we have to
be careful not to fly right away in the Reichian direction of making Jesus
or Christ into a new Goethe or an ecstatic Hölderlin. One of the still-
standard readings of Jesus in theological schools (at least of the more liberal persuasion) derives from Albert Schweitzer, who argued that Jesus
was an apocalyptic Jew who simply was wrong about the impending end
of the world and thus died a lonely and broken death on the cross.

What about the libido theory? Reich linked Freud's so-called entrapment in Judaism with his failure to carry the libido theory forward, for the
straightforward reason that patriarchal Judaism kept him from freeing
himself from the misery of his family life, in which he was forced to give
up sex altogether. Sublimation, not surprisingly, became Freud's theoretical hobby horse in his abstinent years, and Reich pounced upon this explanation for why Freud could not endorse his concept of genital potency.

Further, Reich argued that the other loyal lieutenants around Freud
started attacking Reich's own extension of the libido theory because of
their own unconscious sexual envy at his seeming sexual potency (a false
projection on their part), while they themselves were carrying on clan-
destine affairs. Reich cunningly pretended to find such gossip distasteful,
yet he was more than willing to use strong ad hominem arguments against
those who had accused him of schizophrenia and sexual indiscretion:

You know what happens when somebody lives too long in abstinence. He gets dirty, dirty-minded, pornographic, neurotic, and so
on. I never permitted that to happen to me. *One only shrinks if one*

lives against nature. One shrinks, gets sick, ill, in one way or another. I never permitted that to happen. My life was an open secret, or, should I say, quite in the open. On the other hand, the private lives of the analysts were very much hidden. However, through analysis, and so on, we knew what was going on . . . There were instances where psychoanalysts, under the pretext of a genital examination, of a medical examination, put their fingers into the vaginas of their patients . . . They would pretend there was nothing there and would masturbate the patient during the sessions.[35]

So Freud stayed within a narrowly defined libido theory because of the constrictions of his patriarchal Judaism, which operated unconsciously, compelling him to live a celibate life. The lieutenants rejected Reich's more robust genital theory because they were in denial of their own mischief and could not face the implications of their repression and its displacement into unethical and neurotic behavior. Reich's tactic was to argue that the rejection of his breakthrough theory was based on neurotic denial rather than scientific evidence. So they simply projected onto him what they were doing (or secretly wanted to do), and that ended the matter in their eyes.

I am persuaded that Reich's extension of the libido theory is warranted and that he was probably right that Freud's sexual abstinence had a causal relation to his privileging of the sublimation theory. I am less certain what to do with his theory of the correlation between Freud's Judaism (about which he seems inconsistent) and his lack of courage to get a divorce (if that is even what he wanted), but Reich was at least consistent about his *own* relationship to Judaism, not that he understood much about the religion itself.

In the 1952 interview, Reich seemed intent on setting the record straight and correcting what he saw as an ongoing stream of vilification that had hampered his work. His deep ambivalence toward Freud came out with some force, especially around the issue of the social transformation of psychoanalysis. He was not bitter toward Freud, merely disappointed that Freud did not have the courage to follow the best and brightest of his sons into the true heartland of psychoanalysis. It was as if he saw himself as the true non-Jewish Moses, who had found the promised land that Freud had pointed toward but lacked the (genital) energy to enter. He was bitter toward almost everyone else in the inner circle, especially toward his early analyst Paul Federn and toward Anna Freud (who was Annie Reich's analyst for a period). He was proud of his early achievements but wanted to distance himself from psychoanalysis entirely, dismissing the entire movement as once a necessary, but now a superfluous, antechamber to orgone therapy, even though its insights are still pertinent when transformed into the terms of orgone therapy. And last, we see a Reich who was willing to admit that he had made some theoretical and even political mistakes in the 1920s and that all of his troubles might not have come from outside evil forces but from some of his own inner demons.

4

The Sexual Is the Social,

and *The Mass Psychology of Fascism*

Reich came down from the mountains to find Vienna in turmoil. His party, the Social Democrats, was in conflict with both the Communists on their left and the Christian Socialists and nationalists on their right. Reich felt that the Social Democrats, who were in the majority in Austria, were actually too weak structurally and psychologically to take strong political action against the rightist forces, which were psychologically astute enough to appeal to deep Oedipal and patriarchal desires in the masses. So Reich felt compelled to join with the Communists while remaining a Social Democrat in order to find a power base, with international ties, from which he could also carry out his growing commitment to his sexual-political program (*Sexpol*). That is, he wanted to combine his work in the sex clinics in Vienna with an effort to combat what he saw as the rise of fascism (an illness coming from the genitally impotent). He felt that the Communists were at least able to address some of the correlations among economics, consciousness, and desire that the Social Democrats, as bourgeois status quo thinkers, could not.

By locating himself in this way, it is easy for us to predict in hindsight what would have inevitably resulted. The Social Democrats grew uneasy with his many public appearances on behalf of Communist organizations, while the psychoanalytic establishment, which was often more comfortable with the conservative Christian Socialist position, was deeply suspicious of Reich's synthesis of Freud and Marx (especially since it was a Freud who was growing more and more unrecognizable to them). Eventually, the authorities in Moscow forbade Reich to publish his *Sexpol* articles under their banner, and he had to launch out with his own publishing house. This was also made necessary when the press of the Vienna Psychoanalytic Society reneged on its contract to publish his *Character Analysis*. Consequently, after 1932 his publications came out from his own printing house, Verlag für Sexualpolitik. Thereafter a large part of his time was spent in finding funds to publish his works.

The singular event that radicalized Reich—and that made him forever suspicious of the Social Democrats and of any notion of political compromise or, further, of any notion that having a sheer majority in the electorate was sufficient protection against a black fascist (Italian and German) or red fascist (Soviet) takeover—was the "slaughter of the innocents" on the streets of Vienna on July 15 and 16, 1927, a few weeks after he had returned from Davos. On July 15 workers held a mass rally in the heart of the city, only to be met with well-armed police, who turned their rifles on the crowd and opened fire at will. Approximately one hundred civilians were killed, and another thousand were wounded. Yet the police and the civilians were both members of the Social Democratic Party, and even more distressing, the armed wing of the party, completely separate from the "official" city police, did not come to the assistance of its fellow workers (which it had been created to do in the first place).

Reich and his wife Annie were in the streets and observed some of the slaughter at close range, hiding behind a tree so as not to be shot themselves. Reich came to some new conclusions about mass pathology, partly based on his earlier war experience, and about the mechanization of nongenitally potent humans:

> Again I had the feeling of watching a "senseless machine," nothing more. A stupid, idiotic automaton lacking reason and judgment, which sometimes goes into action and sometimes does not. And this was what governed us and was termed "civil order." It ruled and prescribed whom I was allowed or not allowed to love, and when. *Machine Men!* This thought was clear and irrefutable. Since then it has never left me; it became the nucleus for all my later investigations of man as a political being. I had been part of just such a machine during the war and had fired just as blindly on command, without thinking. "Lackeys of the bourgeoisie"? "Paid executioners"? Wrong! Merely Machines![1]

Before too long, certainly by the mid-1930s, Reich abandoned the classical Marxist concept of class warfare and the myth of the emancipation of an isolatable proletarian class (which he held to be nineteenth-century ideas unsuitable for the twentieth-century economic situation). The betrayal of human rights by the Social Democrats, a party that cut across class lines, convinced him that all classes are subject to the same underlying psychological and vegetative bioelectrical dynamics and that economic variables, in the end, have very little to do with anything but the *form* that sexual and economic suffering takes. That is, even the ruling classes suffer sexually but in a different way from the underclasses, while economic variables in a patriarchy hurt everyone but obviously women more than men.

By 1933 some wealthy people opposed Hitler just as some poor workers did, while many poor workers adored Hitler and many wealthy people disguised their contempt for him and went along for the beneficial financial ride. Reich learned far more quickly than his colleagues that the masses were capable of sustaining astonishing unconscious contradictions, chief among them a desire for freedom combined with an even stronger fear of freedom combined with a need for patriarchal punishment for sexual cravings. And if the Jews could become the locus for the projection of sexual craving, then the formula was in place for a near-perfect system of *internal* control over the rest of the population.

Reich had, I think, a genius for grasping psychic contradictions in the making, especially as manipulated by Hitler and others of "lesser" stature. And he was absolutely right that the Communists in Austria and Germany failed against the fascists because they had no depth-psychological insight, primarily due to Marx's simple-minded philosophical anthropology of the self as the maker of its material world through instrumental and material reason. There is no question but that the correlation of some notion of material and class consciousness, if regrounded, must be worked through a powerful genital and archetypal depth psychology if there is to be *any* long-lasting chance of deconstructing red and black neofascism (which are, once again, a growing threat, in Asia, for example).

Reich's marriage was floundering, to some extent due to his intense involvement in the *Sexpol* movement, which took much of his time and energy away from his intimate relations. Annie was involved in a lesser professional way in psychoanalysis but was never as politically active as Reich, a fact that grieved him. In September 1930 he moved from Vienna to Berlin in the hopes that the political climate would be better suited for his *Sexpol* work and that he would be able to get out of the stifling political climate in Vienna and the hostile circle of the Vienna Psychoanalytic Society. Also, the Communist Party was much stronger in Germany than in Austria, thus providing him, so he thought, with greater prospects for his *Sexpol* work. Shortly after he moved north, his increasingly bitter foe Paul Federn had his name removed from the membership list of the Vienna Psychoanalytic Society. At about the same time, the Social Democratic Party removed him from its membership rolls for what they saw as his pro-Communist leanings. Again we see how the conservative, bourgeois, and red-fascist forces utterly failed to understand what Reich was trying to do with his very subtle weaving of social psychology, an emerging energetics, and depth psychology. While Reich was never a great diplomat when under pressure, he was rarely given credit for the fecundity of his categorial system, and his enemies were almost always locked into simplistic dyads that he had long since transfigured, such as the material/ideological, or the pregenital/genital, or eros/death drives, or unpleasure/pleasure, or sublimation/chaos, or character/symptom, or dreams/body work.

In each of these cases he knew both sides of the dyad well but had, like Peirce or Hegel, grounded these sides in a more encompassing *third* category that allowed each member of the dyad its specific role to play within the unfolding dialectic. But he never let the dyad lock itself into a simplistic either/or. In a sense, he had taken the Marxist dialectic seriously (with its movement of position and antiposition, the inner logic of dialectical materialism) but had gone back to its more profound Hegelian roots, albeit perhaps not consciously, with its far more complex momentum of negation, identification, and transfiguration. This loosened up the dialectic so that it could correspond more accurately to the internal rhythms of the psyche. For most thinkers, regardless of their field, this level of thinking is not within their grasp, as it requires simultaneously maintaining several seemingly incompatible conceptual horizons in one expanding categorial and phenomenological space, while also making continual reconstructions and reconfigurations that correspond to an expanding phenomenal data field.

Before we examine his great dialectical synthesis in *The Mass Psychology of Fascism*, we need to take a brief look at an important transitional text, written in 1931, that brings together the Marx-Engels tradition and the anthropology of Bronislaw Malinowski (1884–1942) with Reich's own *Sexpol* work and with his energetic reconstruction of Freud. The text, originally published in Berlin, was *The Invasion of Compulsory Sex-Morality*.[2] The Malinowski text that set him on fire, as it seemed to confirm all of his views on social sexual suppression, was *The Sexual Life of Savages*, published in 1930. To complete the circle, Reich sent Malinowski a copy of what he referred to as *The Invasion*, which brought forth an equally strong affirmative response, leading to a ten-year friendship between them that ended only with Malinowski's death.[3]

Malinowski was a Polish field anthropologist (later moving to England) who made his mark on history by studying the Trobriand tribe (among others), who lived in the northeastern corner of New Guinea. He came to the conclusion that the tribe lived on the cusp between an earlier matriarchal social structure and an emerging patriarchal formation. Reich found strong resemblances between this analysis and Engels's understanding of the ancient form of primitive Communism from which the patriarchal structures of capitalism emerged, where the correlation between women and property in the marriage exchange was the central player. Reich took the best pieces of the Marx-Engels (especially the Engels) theory of primitive Communistic society (which Reich called "work-democracy" in his 1951 revision of the text) and grafted them onto his notions of how sexual suppression must somehow be tied to the emergence of property rights, which could occur only when women were degraded (primarily through marriage) in the transition into patriarchy.

The key point in the transition (in a primitive Communist society) from matriarchy, which exhibits healthy forms of genital potency, to patriarchy, which starts to manifest all of the various sexual dysfunctions, is in the role that marriage comes to play in the social economy between the genders. In the matriarchal form of sex-economic relations, all adolescents of the Trobriand tribe were allowed to live out their healthy genital needs in special huts set aside for them. There were sexual rules of decorum, and certain "perversions" (such as anal intercourse) were strongly abjected by their society, but otherwise sexual pleasure and exploration were encouraged. Reich argued that this free sexuality undercut the need for an Oedipal conflict in Trobriand life because there was no pressure to confine subjective sexual fantasy to a tightly bound nuclear family; that is, the mother or father did not have to be the sole object of sexual desire or cathexis because there was so much free libidinal expression outside the family triad. By the same token, there was no need to develop castration anxiety, as neither the mother nor the father was envisioned as a threat to the penis or vagina, precisely because they were not guilt-invoking cathected objects that must avenge themselves for the transgression of the child. And further, no characterological or muscular armoring emerged, as there were no conflictual unconscious situations to generate the *need* for armor.

At the other extreme, one clear mark of the triumph of patriarchy is somatically/semiotically manifest in the genital zone with male and female circumcision, introduced violently and against the will of the victim and in especially horrific forms for young women. The patriarchal idea is always that if you sexually mutilate a potentially libidinal woman, then you take away her genital pleasure so she has no motive other than an *economic* one to enter into a relationship with a male. Yet in this New Guinea Eden, at least in its precorrupt form, Reich had almost found his symptom-free individual after all, and he extrapolated the data he needed for his larger program of social reform.

When an adolescent Trobriand couple (in the precorrupt era or subgroup) felt that it was time to make a more permanent bond, then they would do so, but at this matriarchal stage they experienced no deep economic repercussions in moving from the sexual free-play of adolescence to a one-partner marriage. The communal bonds were strengthened, but no vertical power structures were erected; nor was genital potency suppressed.

In the transition to patriarchy, the marriage act became formalized and the wife's family was forced to pay a tribute to the family of the husband (which would be ongoing). For the Trobrianders, this tribute usually took the form of vegetable produce. The family group of the male would prosper at the expense of the family group of the female, thus invariably linking the male gender with increasing wealth. Further, male subclans would join together, working toward a larger clan grouping, perhaps under royal protection, thus further concentrating their hold on the commodities of the overall group. Malinowski and Engels ended up with the same understanding of this transition toward the control of social and personal commodities, but Malinowski added at least the rudiments of the sex-economic perspective, which Reich now had to complete. Before going into more precise detail of these arguments, it is appropriate to simply quote Reich's brief definition of the meaning of a sex-economic analysis: "We should call *the way in which society regulates, promotes, or hinders gratification of the sexual needs 'sex economy'*."[4] He paralleled this model or framework with that of a food economy, which also is regulated, either according to primitive communistic (work-democratic) principles or according to capitalistic/patriarchal ones. Just as I can deprive someone of bread (say, in a company store connected with a coal mine), so too can I hinder sexual gratification by internalizing guilt over nonmonogamous fantasies and impulses.

In a matriarchy there is free access to both food and sex on a horizontal (class-free) level without suppression. In a patriarchy sex is suppressed because it is tied to the sexual desire that links women to property rights—that is, for Reich, *"property is transferred by means of sexual interest."*[5] If I, as a female, have a sexual desire for a male, then my sexual interest will be the foundation for a whole host of subsequent unhealthy property relations, such as rights of inheritance (which until a few years ago in Korea, for example, were still father-to-son only, never to widows), or rights of ownership, or rights of education for male offspring against female offspring, and so on. Obviously, if sexuality were allowed to flow along its natural channels, then enforced monogamy, with its material value to the male clans (corporations) would be threatened. For Reich, lifelong monogamy was simply impossible, and the only way it could be enforced, to ensure the economic well-being of the few, was through implanting internalized sexual guilt about nonmonogamous (pre- or extramarital) relationships.

Put simply, to allow men and women to form less permanent sexual unions based on the pleasure principle would undermine the smooth operations of an economy that must bind one woman to one man so that the nuclear family patriarch, working in consort with other clans, can control her assets and basically denude her of economic power. To deepen the irony, in Trobriand society, the patriarchal form of marriage required abstinence even during the early part of marriage (the honeymoon period). Of course, for those who oppose birth control, this patriarchal strategy works out another avenue of social and personal control as sexuality gets confined to the act of procreation and hence gets sharply reduced in frequency and in the number of possible partners. It is only in parts of North America and western Europe that this pattern has been broken (for how long and how deeply, in a consumerist economy?), while for the vast majority of women, this brutalizing sex-economic structure is still an absolute given.

Reich listed four specific steps through which the transition from genitally healthy matriarchy was corrupted into sexually frustrated patriarchy. The linchpin for the entire process was the marriage bond, which was a *bond* precisely because of its economic implications:

1. The transition of power from woman to man. Thereby the power of displacement grows vertically, according to rank. The chief, in contrast to the citizen, has the most power; his wives have the least.
2. The transition from natural genital love life to the compulsory marriage bond.
3. The transition from sex-affirmation to sex-negation, from the affirmation of premarital genital activity to a demand for premarital asceticism. And finally the most important thing:
4. The growing division of society into oppressing upper groups and oppressed lower groups.[6]

So we see how the power relations shifted from primitive work-democratic structures, where women may have had a slight edge in some respects, to a vertical society in which males controlled sexual desire by linking it to property rights. Women became forms of commodity, thus leading eventually to the logical outcome of prostitution, while sexual repression began now with even infant sexuality. Reich took a very bold leap beyond the conservative Christian Socialist position of his erstwhile Viennese colleagues by showing, I think quite convincingly, the links among (1) the devaluation of women, (2) the transformation of sexual desire into property, (3) the need to suppress healthy genital sexuality to maintain the link between one woman and her commodity value, (4) the inevitable result of sexual dysfunction in all forms of patriarchy, (5) the conflict between guilt and desire in the newly constructed patriarchal Oedipal character structure, (6) the rise of characterological and muscular armoring in patriarchy, and most dangerous of all, (7) the link between the emergent post-Oedipal guilt and the hunger for an authoritarian personality to resolve the guilt by transforming genital desire into a desire to work for the State.

In unbridled capitalism there is no question but that sexual potency cannot be fulfilled, and this very fact is a necessary condition for the success of continuing capital accumulation within the hands of fewer and fewer people. Keep people sexually starved, and they will become acquisitive—that is, they will seek substitute gratifications in the sphere of power and external signs of their narcissistic woundedness (as Alice Miller suggests). The almost manic correlation between sexuality and advertising, for example, is a given in cultural studies, and it is especially interesting that the sexuality is merely promised, never really delivered, thus creating an endless chain of deferral in which one desire must drive on to another. It is like trying to masturbate endlessly without a climax. In a wonderfully crisp argument, Reich correlates sexual frustration with the needs of a patriarchal economy:

Apart from the fact that the individual's interests were mainly genital and were *satisfied*, the material needs were slight. Interest in property and avarice increased in proportion to the extent to which genital interests had to be suppressed. During one phase of human history, living conditions (first the union of primeval hordes, later the excessive pressure of the marriage gift) gave rise to sexual restriction and sexual repression. This freed psychic interests for a specific type of economic evolution, i.e., *private economy*. These interests were avarice and the desire to accumulate, and they sprang up at the expense of genital interests.[7]

Totemic or fetish objects function as the new object cathexes in patriarchal capitalism, precisely because they correspond to unfulfilled pregenital drives. Since it is impossible to have a healthy sexual life, either because the power of internal and external repression is too strong or because promiscuity and acting out empty the psyche of meaningful genital potency, it becomes necessary to invest the resultant surplus sexual energy value into highly prized cultural artifacts. If you are unfilled sexually, then you must buy the most expensive automobile in the neighborhood, which in turn keeps your nose to the grindstone, ties you economically to your partner, and further fuels the real or alleged growth of the economy. But if you are sexually fulfilled, then part of your incentive for reinforcing patriarchal capitalism simply goes away; this threat to the system has to be met head-on by state-sanctioned repression.

Reich was able to bring together two seemingly incompatible systems in this smaller text: namely, Engels's analysis of the matriarchal basis of primitive communism and Freud's analyses, from his 1913 *Totem and Taboo*,[8] of how the primal horde of rebellious sons overcame the patriarchal father and set up public totems and taboos as means to eternalize their resultant guilt. Further, Freud argued that incest was prevented by the taboo of exogamy (prohibition of sex with one's clan members). So Reich felt that Engels was right about the priority of matriarchal organization, and its value as a normative social tool, but he also felt that Freud better understood the unconscious mechanisms about how patriarchy actually emerged from guilt structures that became internalized around a dead (but now heavenly) father. This displacement and internalization set the tone for patriarchal *culture*, but the current form of culture was not natural and hence was neither eternal nor necessary: "we repudiate the idea that sexual suppression is a *necessary* component of the development of human society, because we recognize in it a mechanistic view."[9] In sounding the trumpet against mechanism, Reich was signaling his evolution toward his later view of orgonomic functionalism. The latter view stresses the importance of the total and integral organism in contrast to a linear view, which focuses only on strict causal chains that occur in a small part of the organism as a whole. Freud remained trapped within a mechanistic ontology, in spite of his own struggles against it in his early years (especially in Paris). Further, Freud always conflated culture with biology and never grasped the distinction between the secondary (culture-dependent) drives and those rooted in the biological core of the character structure.

Freud's overall argument in *Totem and Taboo* was designed to show the parallel between contemporary ontogenetic neurotic symptoms and their phylogenetic basis in what he called an "atavistic vestige" (perhaps the most Jungian moment in his writings). For example, there is a parallel between the liturgical practices of the individual (ontogenetic structure) in the contemporary church or temple and the primal act of murder and guilt by the primal horde of the patriarch (phylogenetic structure). The liturgy of the church actually serves a neurotic function by both invoking and assuaging the guilt of the individual through an unconscious reenactment of the species-deed in the dim past.

The subtitle of Freud's book was *Some Points of Agreement between the Mental Lives of Savages and Neurotics*. That is, whenever we are overcome by a neurotic compulsion, either to act out or to avoid something, and we have no explanation for the origin of this compulsion, then we may be reaching into primal taboo structures that come from our ancient past. Many of these taboos, as noted by the contemporary Freudian Julia Kristeva, center on the abjection of women (which will dovetail into the framework of the Engels/Reich economic argument). Primitive taboos were often projected onto outward objects that were held to have magical and demonic powers, such that mere physical contact with them could bring harm (which is paralleled by the fear of touch manifest in contemporary neurotic phobias). Freud well understood the ambivalence that emerges in the dialectic between the desire one could have for a taboo object (such as the sexual hunger of a man for a woman during menstruation, or toward the wife of a tribal member—an exogamy taboo).

This desire instantly triggers the guilt of taboo violation, which is reinforced by the power of the public totem object, which represents the power of the clan, the ruler, and the deity—namely, the projected murdered father who had controlled access to all of the desired sexual objects. (Freud is, of course, writing all of this from the standpoint of the primal male.) There are three totemic object clusters in the group: first, the clanwide totem; second, two gender-specific ones that can never be transferred between genders; and third, personal ones that die with their owners. Marking all members of the clan with the sign of the totem reinforces exogamy; therefore to sleep with any one of one's fellow clan members is to almost literally sleep with one's own blood. The clan totem is often an animal or a plant that is tied to the murdered father. The concept of sacrifice emerged at this stage of primitive development, as the guilt-ridden tribe would consume the totem animal to ingest the deity and form an incarnational connection. Religions emerged as public ways of remembering the guilt of the primal murder of the father, via the totemic meal. Freud's understanding of religion and its symbolic systems concerning death, atonement, resurrection, transfiguration, woundedness, exile, healing, community, spirit, and incarnationality was, to be gentle, far from sophisticated. At the end of *Totem and Taboo* he makes an ex cathedra statement, that his inquiry shows that "the beginnings of religion, morals, society and art converge in the Oedipus complex."[10]

Reich's arguments on the relationships between anthropology (the study of "savages") and the rise of neurotic symptoms in a sex-economic analysis of patriarchy are far more complex, multilayered, and empirical than those presented by Freud in *Totem and Taboo*. Freud was about fifty-seven years old when he wrote his anthropological/psychoanalytic text, while Reich was thirty-four; but regardless of the age difference, Reich's work shows much greater conceptual power and willingness to go into the darker places within the economic and social sphere. Again, while Freud could at best work out of one or two categorial horizons simultaneously, Reich, like a chess grand master, could hold a number of horizons in his mind while reshaping each one under the creative pressure of the others, in this case producing a rich skein from the game strategies of (1) transformed psychoanalysis, (2) cultural anthropology, (3) economics, (4) bioenergetics, (5) psychopathology, (6) sociology, and (7) ethics.

One of the most striking moves in Reich's social analysis occurs in *The Invasion of Compulsory Sex-Morality*, where he states that an authoritarian society uses sexual repression to control its citizens and to reshape character structure along the lines of severe armoring and obedience:

1. It powerfully backs every reactionary institution, which by means of sexual fear and sexual guilt feelings deeply roots itself in the exploited masses.
2. It backs the compulsory family and marriage, which require the atrophy of sexuality for their existence.
3. It makes children subservient to their parents and thus, as adults, subservient to the state, by creating fear of authority in the mass individual.
4. It paralyzes the intellectual critical powers and the initiative of the mass individual, for sexual repression uses up much bioenergy that otherwise would manifest itself intellectually and emotionally in a rational manner.
5. It impairs bioenergetic agility in many people, makes them inhibited, and paralyzes their power to rebel against social evil.

All this, taken together, means the *ideological anchoring of the existing authoritarian system in the character structure of the mass individual*, thus serving the suppression of life.[11]

Comparing this summary with his earlier papers and writings, we can see how Reich has now come to recognize that the fundamental basis of the character structure and its armoring is derived from the social inscription of the authoritarian patriarchal state that uses the nuclear family as its means of infiltrating the pregenital lives of children. In the 1920s he was still somewhat reliant, as noted, on certain Teutonic myths of self-creating and defiant individuality. By the early 1930s he had come to the conclusion, which was never to leave him, that individual neurotic symptoms were the result of patriarchal and authoritarian pressures that bent and damaged the character structure, putting in place of healthy genitality a warped and armored individual who could only lash out either in a sadistic/masochistic release of tension (which always failed to produce genital fulfillment) or in uncontrolled acquisitiveness through substitute object cathexes. The authoritarian state, which had its primitive beginnings way back in the first marriage gift and subsequent economic contract, could use sadism and masochism (*both* being manifestations of rage against the *object*, contra Freud) to control undesirable elements within society— they simply became demonized as objects worthy of sadistic cathexis. He was now ready to take the step from *The Invasion of Compulsory Sex-Morality* to the deconstruction of the *Führer* principle, and in taking it Reich produced one of the most important works in the history of the psychoanalytic movement.

Again we are faced with the scholar's problem that the book available to us in English is based upon the 1946 revised third edition rather than the 1933 original. The reasons behind Reich's revisions, however, are not such that the foundation of the original is buried in mist, and the 1946 edition provides a deeper historical perspective on the Nazi era than obviously would have been possible in 1933. Reich's original German typescript of the 1946 version is available and will be referred to herein when and if appropriate. It should be noted that the Gestapo banned the book in 1935.

The 1945 preface to the 1946 edition, written in Maine, gives one of Reich's clearest overall assessments of where his work had taken him by the time of his exile in America. In less technical language than he often used, Reich described how he came to understand the threefold nature of the character structure and how his research had also established that the phenomenon of fascism was not confined to given political movements but was a manifestation of the "little man" in each of us. The triadic model of the psyche asserted that the outer layer, like the shell of an egg, was composed of the social persona (to use Jung's term), which was fundamentally unstable and gave only the mere appearance of rationality. He argued that liberals were stuck on this outer layer of the psyche and that they could not understand the irrational eruptions that emerged from the depths of the unconscious.[12] To plan one's social reconstruction based on a "rational" reconfiguration of the outer social layer was a profound mistake that played right into the hands of the stronger fascist forces; mere liberal autonomy could not withstand fascist heteronomy.

The second layer of the psyche was that of the secondary drives, the domain that Freud thought was actually the core of the self. For Reich, on the contrary, the secondary drives were products of frustrations surrounding the full expression of the third layer of the psyche, the biological core. The image is like that of an egg, with the shell, as noted, being the "rational" social persona, the egg white being the secondary drives, and the healthy life-generating yolk at the center quietly remaining as the bioenergetic core. For Freud the so-called primal aggressive drives were at the root of social conflict, and only sublimation and cultural control could contain them. Thus, the nonfoundational secondary drives emerged whenever there was no genital potency and the natural routes of sexual object cathexis were blocked. This generated frustration, which in turn produced sadism and masochism toward aspects of the object world, which were seen to represent the denial of pleasure.

Of course, we have heard this part of Reich's tale before, but not yet in the context of a brilliant social deconstruction of how such a towering and demonic movement as fascism could take hold of so much of the world. The overall argument to come, more like a symphonic poem than a single argument sequence, carefully entwined an analysis of the triadic self with theories of race consciousness, mysticism, religion, perversions, the authoritarian personality, the rise of socially inscripted Oedipal structures, fear of sexuality (for example, in the form of birth control), and a radically updated Marxism (now called work-democracy).

Specifically, the book works through a reconstructed Marxist analysis of the power of ideology in social formation, thereby paving the way for the microscopic analysis of the German family and its patriarchal center, where this ideology has its effect in generating and sustaining the fascist state. The Nazi racial theory, tied to sexual fears and projection (especially incest fear vis-à-vis the "predatory" Jews), is analyzed, particularly in the ways in which it becomes entwined with the internally contradictory class thinking of the ruling elite of the party. At the heart of *The Mass Psychology of Fascism* is a contrast between a healthy form of sex-economy and the deviant forms of social and sexual interaction found in fascism. Reich concludes this work with a programmatic statement pointing to the intrinsic power of work-democracy as a practice that can open out sexuality while also enabling the members of the workforce to become politically self-governing.

Reich took issue with the idea that fascism was antireligious and argued that it generated its own type of religion, parasitic on the secondary drives that were a distortion of the free-flowing and life-giving bioenergetic core of the character. In the 1942 preface he presented his case:

> Fascism is supposed to be a reversion to paganism and an archenemy of religion. Far from it—fascism is the supreme expression of religious mysticism. As such, it comes into being in a peculiar social form. Fascism countenances that religiosity that stems from sexual perversion, and it transforms the masochistic character of the old patriarchal religion of suffering into a sadistic religion. In short, it transposes religion from the "other-worldliness" of the philosophy of suffering to the "this worldliness" of sadistic murder.[13]

In the 1930s, German Protestantism quickly became very friendly to German fascism, and it was common practice to place two books on the church altar, namely, the Bible and Hitler's autobiography, *Mein Kampf* (*My Fight* or *My Struggle*). Martin Luther's theology of the two kingdoms, one being on earth, where we must show obedience to earthly rulers, and the other being in heaven, which has its own laws, made it easy for pastors to let Caesar be Caesar and rule with an iron first, while maintaining the belief that the kingdom of heaven still awaited the faithful.

The Roman Catholic Church presents a more complex picture be-

cause some courageous bishops stood up to Hitler, for example, on the issue of gassing the mentally disabled or mentally ill, while other church
leaders collaborated with the state in helping suppress disorder or anti-
authoritarian behavior. Even after the war was lost, some priests in the
Roman Church helped Nazi officials (many in the notorious Waffen SS
who had been *directly* involved in the "final solution") flee Germany by
underground routes.[14] But the more international position of the Roman
Church helped it to remain slightly less compromised than the German
Protestant churches. Needless to say, the Italian situation was far more
entangled for the Roman Church than for the German, and the full scope
of the church's co-implication in the Holocaust in both countries has yet
to be fully assessed.

The Nazi revival of paganism, as argued by Reich, did not supersede
other religions but wove it into the sexual perversions that came from the
Nazi intensification of the secondary drives. Nazi religion was a new religion, a curious blend of Christianity (which had strong pagan roots any-
way) and a Norse pagan mythology of blood and soil. There was nothing
new in this part of Reich's argument, but his sudden move to link religious typology to the perversions was striking and bold. The "old patriarchal religion" was rooted in the kind of sexual frustration that generated
masochism. The psyche would suffer because of an implied rage against
the withholding divine Other, taking on the suffering, not as a form of
perverse pleasure, but as an inverted way of dealing with the feeling of
bursting against a repressing external taboo. But masochism was at
least passive on the surface; it did not always manifest the rage of frustrated libido, which goes against other persons. The new Nazi religion, on
the contrary, converted masochism into sadism, in which, via the state,
cathected perverse secondary drives could be turned against other selves
all the way to the extreme of mass murder. Luther's masochistic other-
worldliness (his theology of the cross versus the theology of glory) could
now become the Nazi religion's this-worldly sadistic murder. But in both
cases, Reich was convinced, what was missing, and what caused all of the
subsequent violence, was the absence of full genital potency in the "little
man," Hitler's most ardent disciple.

Reich never rejected Marxism in toto but located it within the much
longer history of patriarchy, as it emerged out of matriarchy four to six

thousand years ago. But Marxist social analysis, according to Reich, lacked several fundamental ingredients: (1) an understanding of the economic structures of twentieth-century capitalism; (2) a grasp of the *subjective* factors that can shape history (Reich's argument was that Marx wrote decades before psychoanalysis and social psychology were created and thus could not have understood the power of internal motives); (3) an understanding of how persons often act *against* their material interests; and (4) a failure to grasp the power of "mysticism" to corrupt character structure. On the other side, he took the Freudian tradition to task for different reasons:

Psychoanalytic sociology tried to analyze society as it would analyze an individual, set up an absolute antithesis between the process of civilization and sexual gratification, conceived of destructive instincts as primary biological facts governing human destiny immutably, denied the existence of a matriarchal primeval period, and ended in a crippling skepticism, because it recoiled from the consequences of its own discoveries.[15]

If the Marxists limped along with a wooden antisubjective materialism combined with a rigid and overly optimistic dialectic, the psychoanalysts still tried to project an unmodified personal psychology onto social structures and fell into the trap of conflating destructive aggression with the true bioenergetic core of the self. Marx's dialectical optimism, which can be traced to both Jewish and Christian millennial traditions, simply could not understand the psychic contradictions that occurred within the worker, namely, that her or his desire for rebellion was in an eternal struggle with an even stronger need to overcome castration anxiety by appeasing the patriarch and repressing all rebellious impulses. This primal contradiction made a mockery of any optimistic dialectic that assumed that a change in material conditions would bring about a change in the consciousness of the so-called proletarian class.

Reich was highly critical of "economism" insofar as it posited a onedirectional and causal dialectic going from the ruling class that shapes material economic conditions to social and personal ideology and hence character reconstruction. Economism asserts that the lower classes think about the world in the way that they do because of their economic situation, and the ruling class helps create an ideology as a mask to cover the tragic exploitation in the situation. Reich wanted to probe into the real to-and-fro of the dialectic, namely, to ask about how ideology functions, not as a mere social superstructure but as a powerful nonmaterial subjective field-in-itself that could rework economic conditions.

There is a fourfold structure to this process. Iconically, for Marx, a ruling class (R) shapes an economy (E), while it in turn creates an ideology (I) to mold a character structure (S) so that S will be compliant with its own exploitation. Hence, for the Marxist (in a rough and simplified form): $R \rightarrow E \rightarrow I \rightarrow S$. Thus the ruling class shapes both the economy and the ideology that changes character structure (all *right*-pointing arrows). For Reich, the dialectic was much more complex: $S \longleftrightarrow I \longleftrightarrow R \longleftrightarrow E$, but also $I \rightarrow S \rightarrow E$. Here we see that the ruling class shapes ideology but is also shaped in turn and that character structure is deeply shaped by ideology but can also exert pressure backward toward the economy. Reich's implied icon of left-pointing arrows shows this more clearly. The question Reich raised here was about how ideology could change character structure regardless of one's social class.

What was the sexual link not seen by the Marxists, and what was the mechanism that internalized the patriarchal state (ideology) in the individual? With these two questions Reich opened up the problematic in a way that is still, I think, valid and fundamental. In providing his detailed answer, he not only found the depth structure of the Nazi mythos but also isolated the character structure in all persons (albeit manifest differently in the two genders) that makes fascism a perennial human prospect. The key to his argument was that the nuclear family was a microcosmic reconfiguration of the macrocosmic state and that it did the state's controlling work for it by internalizing its imperatives in young children during their vulnerable Oedipal years (and actually helping to create the Oedipal structure in the first place). Remember that he had extrapolated from Malinowski that in a matriarchal organization there would be no Oedipal structures or manifestations of castration anxiety. Both of these pathologies were manifestations of a historically conditioned and finite framework, namely patriarchy. It followed that neither was eternal and that they could be transformed under the right social conditions.

The link between micro- and macrocosm was combined with the psychoanalysis of childhood sexuality and further layered with a deconstruction of the church as an agent of the state (this third piece being right out of Marx). Given what we have said above about how the German churches generally caved in to Hitler and even enthusiastically endorsed the policies of National Socialism, it is clear that the Marx/Reich analysis is largely correct, although it ignores the prophetic role that the church *can* play in social reconstruction, such as in the American or South African civil rights movements. Reich stated:

> The psychoanalysis of men and women of all ages, all countries, and every social class shows that: *The interlacing of the socio-economic structure with the sexual structure of society and the structural reproduction of society takes place in the first four or five years and in the authoritarian family.* The church only continues this function later. Thus, the authoritarian state gains an enormous interest in the authoritarian family. *It becomes the factory in which the state's structure and ideology are molded.*[16]

The process starts with the suppression of childhood sexuality, usually around masturbation issues, and then continues until it creates an Oedipal triangle, precisely because there will be no sexual experimentation outside of the family until postadolescence or later. In turn, of course, castration anxiety emerges, and "every vital life-impulse is now burdened with severe fear."[17] The power of sexual repression soon thwarts rebellious impulses, but the libidinal psyche still seeks out substitute gratifications. Our natural aggression converts to "brutal sadism," the unhealthy aggression of our secondary drives. The pattern is soon locked in place for the fascist control over character structure.

The child learns obedience as a way of outflanking castration anxiety but has no way to find healthy sexual outlets. The contradiction between rebellion and fear becomes so powerful that the grown individual will ignore self-interest or material welfare in order to lower the anxiety threshold, and obedience to the patriarch is the path to an anxiety-free utopia. In his psychoanalytic study of Hitler, based in part on a careful reading of *Mein Kampf*, Reich saw this conflict in the adolescent Hitler as he violated his father's wishes and struggled to become an artist, while also idealizing the maternal:

Yet alongside this rebellion against the father, a respect for an acceptance of his authority continued to exist. This ambivalent attitude toward authority—*rebellion against it coupled with acceptance and submission*—is a basic feature of every middle-class structure from the age of puberty to full adulthood and is especially pronounced in individuals stemming from materially restricted circumstances.

Hitler speaks of his mother with great sentimentality. He assures us that he cried only once in his life, when his mother died. His rejection of sex and his neurotic idolization of motherhood are clearly evident in his theory on race and syphilis.[18]

Reich insisted that the lower middle class was the most likely breeding ground for fascism as it resented its status most acutely. Psychologically, Hitler divined, it became easy to link maternal sentimentalism with a fear of sexual pollution. For Hitler, the connection of other races with sexual disease came naturally, as it represented a tragic but logical projection of his own miscathected sexuality with a fear of violating his mother in an Oedipal embrace. The Jews, blacks, Slavs, Bolsheviks, and others *wanted* to violate the pure Aryan mother and forever contaminate her blood. (Hence the "need" for the Nuremberg Laws of 1935 to determine race— that is, blood—credentials.) And the sexually repressed and economically depressed Germans understood this "logic."

As in the transitions from matriarchy to patriarchy that Malinowski found, correctly or incorrectly, in the Trobriand Islanders, the Third Reich used the structure of the suppression of women in enforced monogamy to secure the state's (clan's) interest. The father and the son in their own way reinforced this process, and the son in particular was unconsciously driven to oscillate between identification with the *Führer* principle and the painful suppression of sexual desire:

What this position of the father actually necessitates is the strictest sexual suppression of women and the children. While women develop a resigned attitude under lower middle-class influence—an attitude reinforced by repressed sexual rebellion— the sons, apart from a subservient attitude toward authority, develop a strong identification with the father, which forms the basis of the emotional identification with every kind of authority.[19]

Yet this process was, of course, far more complex and presented another and deeper contradiction at its heart. The abjection of sexuality by the son, so as to avoid castration by the state and its psychological enforcers, got inverted into a longing for the maternal principle as it got disguised in the nationalistic language of "blood and soil." Suddenly a diabolical solution to the unconscious and unresolved Oedipal situation showed itself—namely, that the son could love his mother in the guise of the "German Mother," as the ground for the regeneration and protection of the *Volk*.

Again, Reich reminded the reader that the Oedipal complex was not something rooted in our primal nature but was in fact a product of the patriarchal confinement of childhood sexuality within the harrowing constraints of the authoritarian family. In the reactionary Nazi state it was impossible to even *recognize* an Oedipal longing for the mother; therefore it was much easier to project it onto the demonized Other, and then to link that demonization to race and sexual disease. The repressed Oedipal object cathexis in the male is displaced onto Mother *Deutschland*, who will nurture, protect, inspire, and purify through her blood. The interweaving of Christian and pagan themes became another means of activating the unconscious through the new Nazi religion that displaced all sexual anxiety into a great embracing, but sexually pure, maternal ground.

The contradiction within Nazi religion was the war between an abjected religion of the soil (with its connotations of sensuality) and a utopian longing for a transfigured heaven (with its connotations of purity). The contradiction was manifest in the fact that the Nazi mythic system could not function without a strong sense of the dark abysmal elements in the ground (*der Abgrund*) from which arose the blood, the soil, and the maternal. This Norse and pagan element was desexualized as much as possible, but the original mythical material simply would not remain bound by such conscious attempts to control its chthonic (erotic and earthly) power. Further, the so-called "pure" Christian side of the new religious hybrid rejected any Christology that stressed suffering or the centrality of the drama of the crucifixion. More literally, the crucifix was to be replaced by the image of fire, which better connoted the masculine virtues of honor and bravery. Fire lifted upward and had an eschatological heart (the thousand-year *Reich*), while the pagan gods, in spite of Nazi remythologizing efforts, pulled downward into the abyss.

The subtle interpretive point, very clearly grasped by Reich, was that the pagan gods and goddesses (Norse and Greek in particular) were originally part of a matriarchal mythic structure and thus fully chthonic. The Nazi reconstruction of Greek history read the stories of the classical gods and goddesses through the lens of patriarchy and privileged the high Athenian period (fourth century B.C.E.) as the norm of Greek self-consciousness. By the time Athens had reached its cultural fullness around 400 B.C.E. (Socrates was executed in 399 B.C.E.), the social system and its supporting gods and goddesses were already under patriarchal control. In mythical terms, Zeus had conquered his wife, Hera, by taking sexual control over all desired mortal and immortal women, thus privileging the phallus and the power of light consciousness over the chaotic and uncontrollable "feminine" power of the soil. Put differently, the power of linear solar consciousness had displaced, often by violence, the cyclic power of maternal lunar unconsciousness.

The life of Plato's Athens was not a life of matriarchal natural law and healthy genital sexuality. On the contrary, the Greek norm (championed by countless German and British scholars in the nineteenth and twentieth centuries) was in fact brutally patriarchal and unjust. In a sense, the Nazis were canny in sensing an affinity for classical Greece, but they utterly ignored the preclassical and archaic matriarchal period and its chthonic mythological structures. Reich laid out the truth of Greek life in the era of Plato in an uncompromising way and made it clear that he considered the Nazi glorification of only one isolated moment of Greek civilization to be the result of a deep pathology:

> Among the ancient Greeks, whose written history does not begin until patriarchy had reached a state of full development, we find the following sexual organization: male supremacy, hetaerae for the upper classes and prostitution for the middle and lower classes; along with this the wives leading an enslaved and wretched existence and figuring solely as birth machines. The male supremacy of the Platonic era is entirely homosexual.[20]

For the most part, this was an accurate reading of the Athenian city-state during Plato's lifetime. The upper-class hetaerae were women who demanded some independence for their own sexuality and their own self-education, but they still served married men and attended to their needs. Married women were desexualized and often literally confined to the household grounds. The one less valid claim is that "the Platonic era is entirely homosexual." Plato, for example, was extremely critical of homosexuality, seeing it as a crime against nature (see especially his later *Letters*), and his mentor, Socrates, made it clear, especially at the end of the dialogue *The Symposium*, that he would never succumb to homosexual solicitation even by someone as handsome as the notorious Alcibiades. It is more accurate to assert that the Athenians were conflicted about homosexual practice and that a number of moralists strongly condemned it. Also, it was much more the practice among the economic elite than among the working classes.

Thus, by eulogizing a cleaned-up patriarchal paganism, the Nazis were able to graft it onto a "masculine" nationalistic Christianity that abjected the cross and all that it implied. Reich asked the crucial question: given this contradictory mixture of suppression and desire, paganism and sadistic Christianity, the cross and the flame, the Teutonic mother and *der Führer*, what kind of symbol would best pull all of this together and hold the contradictions around one visual icon? Clearly the image/symbol could not be the cross; nor could it be an obvious phallic power. It had to activate the unconscious, as all great symbols do (whether demonic or healing) and contain unconscious meanings that were sexual in nature. In essence, it had to be sexual without being too obvious about it, and it had to connote male power and a strong sense of fusion with the State.

Hitler experimented with a number of variations of this ancient symbol, finally coming up with his *Hakenkreuz*, or hooked cross—the swastika. This symbol, with the arms turning either clockwise or counterclockwise, had roots in ancient civilizations, such as the Indian, Native American, and even Middle Eastern. It always conveyed a sense of sexual and religious power (for example, the power of *prana* or *kundalini* in the Hindu tradition) and activated unconscious libidinal forces. Hitler's perhaps unwitting choice of the clockwise-turning swastika was a masterstroke insofar as it maintained both sides of the various contradictions of the fascist personality. It was at once sexual and antisexual, semi-

Christian and patriarchal/pagan, and maternal and authoritarian. The black swastika at the heart of the red and white flag was, certainly for Hitler, according to Reich[21] a direct symbol of anti-Semitism, evoking the "dark" Jew with his twisted sexuality. Hitler was aware that the ancient swastika had some Semitic roots. Hence its inversion into an Aryan symbol could play with and against those roots. This internal contradiction again manifested his twisted attitude toward Otherness, sexuality, and sexual disease.

The swastika functioned unconsciously to reshape the sexual conflicts that patriarchy inevitably generated. Each "little Hitler" could gaze upon this symbol, ensconced in a white circle surrounded with a red rectangle, and find a locus for harmonizing conflictual rebellious and guilt-discharging feelings. More precisely:

Thus we can assume that this symbol depicting two interlocked figures acts as a powerful stimulus on deep layers of the organism, a stimulus that proves to be much more powerful, the more dissatisfied, the more burning with sexual desire, a person is. If, in addition, the symbol is presented as the emblem of honorableness and faithfulness, it can be accepted more readily. In this way allowances are made for the defensive strivings of the moralistic ego.[22]

The twisting and energized arms of the swastika represented two lovers in the act of coitus but under the guise of "honorableness and faithfulness," thus invoking sexuality while simultaneously keeping sexual taboos in place. The symbol worked so well because of its long track record in human phylogenetic evolution as an unconscious reconciliation of the contradictions of patriarchy. Sexual contradictions multiplied without let-up in the Nazi state, leading to the ultimate moral corruption of Aryan breeding farms to service the Third Reich's future needs for cannon fodder.

A true symbol, especially in its demonic/patriarchal form, activates the unconscious and reshapes the character structure by generating new characterological armoring against that very activation. But of course, the sexual dilemma is not overcome, and the repressed but very powerful energy of the psyche must find an out. Because this energy is linked to the morally inferior secondary drives, it can manifest itself only through

sadism and brutalism. The psyche "reasons" that its lost virility and genital impotence can be redeemed by destroying the "evil" virility of the
Other. If one could remove the Jews or Bolsheviks, then a sexual utopia
might come—all of this thinking taking place on the unconscious level.

The ideology of German fascism stressed racial pollution as the greatest fear of the *Volk*, and the state therefore needed to take strong measures
to keep this pollution out of the national bloodstream. But what was *this*
fear based on? Was there something even more primal than racial fear
that might be *its* foundation? Reich used his reconstructed Marxism in a
fascinating and evocative way when he linked the fear of other races to a
more original *class* consciousness, namely, a fear that mixing outside of
one's economic and social class was itself a form of pollution. Consequently, the people lower down on the social scale were the original Jews,
blacks, and Bolsheviks:

> If, in the final analysis, it is the idea of the interbreeding of members
> of the ruling class with members of the ruled class that lies at the
> root of the idea of racial inbreeding, then we obviously have here
> the key to the question as to the role played by sexual suppression
> in class society . . . Since sexual suppression has its origin in the
> economic interests of marriage and the law of inheritance, it be-
> gins within the ruling class itself. At first the morality of chastity
> applies most rigidly to the female members of the ruling class.
> This is intended to safeguard those possessions that were acquired
> through the exploitation of the lower classes.[23]

Clearly, to have sexual relations with a member of the ruled classes was
to expose oneself to those social elements that did not have proper sexual
control or "chastity." The tight link between commodity acquisition and
the sexual control of ruling-class women was reinforced by the abjection
of those from whom surplus value is appropriated. The poor and victimized
were the original Jews, blacks, and Bolsheviks. Yet this primary rejected
ground must itself be displaced onto so-called "external" others so that
the more basic class war is fully disguised. The reactionary Nazi social
system had a genius for convincing the middle class to turn against the
lower classes rather than against the rich, who were their true exploiters.
The Nazi Party lived out this reactionary logic in a variety of ways, some-

times deliberately privileging the industrial capitalists, and at other times praising the "revolutionary" powers of the workers. All forms of fascism must work both sides of the contradiction (whether sexual or economic) and play them off of each other as shifting conditions dictate.

In practice the ruling class allowed itself all kinds of sexual "perversions." Nazi officers certainly did not confine themselves to an idealized Mother *Deutschland* any more than they restricted themselves to monogamy. The contrast between party theory and actual practice created another contradiction at the heart of the ruling class, the same class that shut down public forums for sexual release such as the wilder cabarets. They acted out both sides of the contradiction between desire and suppression with no effort to integrate them; that is, they were as sexually impotent as Don Juan. But if the lower classes dared to act this way, the results could be swift and deadly. Reich recounted how a young woman was paraded through the streets of Nuremberg on August 13, 1933. Her head was shaven, and she had to carry a placard that stated, "I have offered myself to a Jew." The SA (Hitler's storm troopers, Sturmabteilung, who were later liquidated by the Gestapo during the "Night of the Long Knives") escorted her through the town, making sure that she was presented before all of the prominent international hotels. Had a wealthy capitalist "experimented" with a Jewish maid (in a pre–Nuremberg Law era), no fuss would have been made. Transgression was first defined in class terms, then became a racial/blood issue for the ruled class. Of course, the ruling class must at least pretend to uphold the patriarchal code, but it also had the secret privilege of violating it.

The primary drives of the biological core manifest a deep sexuality and a cosmic matriarchal religiosity, which is grounded in the "osmotic plasmatic sensation" of the organism. Any hint of this sensation, however distorted through the secondary drives, works by producing a longing for a very dimly sensed deeper source of genuine orgastic potency. Pathology works because it opens up yet abjures the healthy core. By abjecting what it secretly evokes, orgastic potency is tragically cathected through sadism:

> The cohesion of sadistic brutality and mystical sentiments is usu-
> ally to be met with wherever the normal capacity to experience or-

gasm is disturbed. And this is as true of a mass murderer of our time as it was of the inquisitors of the Middle Ages or the brutality and mysticism of Philip II of Spain. If a hysteria does not stifle unresolved excitation in nervous impotence, or a compulsive neurosis does not stifle the same excitation in futile and grotesque compulsive symptoms, the patriarchal-authoritarian compulsive order offers sufficient opportunity for sadistic-mystical discharges. The social rationalization of such behavior effaces its pathological character.[24]

Thus if personal pathology (such as hysteria or compulsive neurosis) does not do its perverse job of transforming the psyche into a fully armored and neurotic character structure, then the state has the means to do so. Therefore both the primal father figure and the displaced Oedipal object have already captured any neurotic patient who could have potentially become a healthy individual. Once the state does its uncanny work, through its microcosmic agent the patriarchal family, then individual therapy will have only limited effect. The transition from personal psychoanalysis to the *Sexpol* agenda is necessitated by the loss of individual autonomy (and any personal hero myth) within the fascist structure, itself grounded in the veiled class war. In this social/psychological analysis, a neurosis is a product of antecedent social/patriarchal forces, and its embeddedness within the total character structure places it beyond the curative reach of the Vienna model of psychoanalysis.

Mysticism, which Reich defined as sadistically tinged amorphous longing for what has been taken away—the orgasm—was the perfect religion for the fascist personality type. It could pick and choose from among earlier religious symbols and orchestrate them so as to hold the contradiction between sexuality and repression in place, while hiding the contradiction in the unconscious. The dialectic between what was hidden and what was unhidden, maintained by constant patriarchal vigilance, had implications for the one human enterprise that stresses the centrality and moral force of unhiddenness. Reich contrasted the drive of science with the demonic drives of mysticism. While the fascist mystic conceals as much as possible of the mechanisms of social control, the scientist, especially the *Sexpol* researcher, must bring to light as much consciousness as *is* possible, always bringing unconscious contradictions into the sphere of social awareness and critique. Insofar as the fascist leadership understands this difference between its mysticism and genuine science, it must repress scientific inquiry in favor of using pseudoscience to reinforce its own ideology. In Nazi Germany the biological sciences were bludgeoned into "recognizing" the truth of the race theories of the Third Reich. True biological inquiry had to go underground. But physics—except so-called "Jewish" physics—could continue its work provided that it generated useful weapons for the war machine. Obviously a physicist could not hope to make an atomic bomb, for example, without a full reliance on "Jewish" science, but *this* embarrassing contradiction was overlooked.

With an eye on the larger international picture, Reich pointed out that all patriarchal nations use and misuse science by a variety of means. The biological sciences have a special emotional charge because they have implications for our understanding of the human character structure. Hence fascist ideology must go after Darwinian models in particular (even as they misuse Darwin by isolating several of his concepts out of context, such as the idea of the survival of the fittest) because they compel us to root ourselves back in the natural orders from which we have evolved. Not only is this a blow to our narcissism, but it is also a blow to the patriarchal religion that can maintain its psychological policing only by the fantasy of a male god who directly models the human being in his own narcissistic image. To accept the full, if open-ended, implications of the neo-Darwinian synthesis would be to loosen the grips of the patriarchal state, which would uproot the sovereign self from the indifferent ground of nature. Reich also pointed a warning finger at America:

> The methodical withholding of scientific findings from the masses of the population, and "monkey trials" such as we find in the United States, encourage humility, lack of discrimination, voluntary renunciation and hope for happiness in the Beyond, belief in authority, recognition of the sacredness of asceticism, and the unimpeachableness of the authoritarian family.[25]

Since something analogous to the Scopes monkey trial, conducted in Dayton, Tennessee, in the summer of 1925,[26] has recently resurfaced in American political life (the 1999–2000 conflict within the Kansas School

Board concerning the suppression of genuine evolutionary science in favor of creationism), it is imperative to bring the contradiction between (1)
science, healthy sexuality, and work-democracy on the one side, and (2)
mysticism, fascism, and sexual pathology on the other side, into the full
light of day. The links between antiscience, anti-Darwinism, and the authoritarian family, where the patriarch uses a negative male-centered "religion" to sexually constrain his family, are very much of a piece with the
emergence of Nazi ideology in the 1930s. Science, at least in Reich's understanding of the term, is by definition antifascist and antipatriarchal
(even if it often gets captured by the state). Put simply, to be against the
neo-Darwinian synthesis is to be against democracy, precisely because
science continues to affirm that synthesis through overwhelming empirical evidence, conceptual fecundity, and sheer logical coherence. The
choice for Reich is that between democratic scientific inquiry and fascist
mystical authoritarianism, which is really a masked *theocracy*. Reich
would have perfectly understood the contemporary American antievolu-
tionism campaigns and their emergence from a sexually repressed and
sadistic patriarchal family power structure.

But what is to be done when a specific, overwhelming fascist movement arises from out of the "little Hitler" in the mass psychology of
the individual person? If the Vienna model of slow and careful *symptom*
analysis with the individual is impotent against Hitler and his analogues,
then the *Sexpol* worker must work differently by challenging the total
class structure: "Thus, it is not a question of helping, but of *making suppression conscious, of dragging the fight between sexuality and mysticism
into the light of consciousness, of bringing it to a head under the pressure
of a mass ideology and translating it into social action.*"[27] Faced with the
rise of fascism, the scientific sex researcher must combine reconstructed
psychoanalysis with work-democracy in order to show the contradiction in
action. As the ever-precise taxonomist, Reich was able to find the political
bacillus in its hiding place and to see its spoliative motility in action. The
political disease body had its own life trajectory, just like any bacterium
or virus, and a social psychoanalyst (or a vegetotherapist) must be trained
to see it within the context of healthy antibodies and the surrounding
organism. As an astute historian, Reich saw that such social infection
was usually the statistical norm in patriarchal societies and that only a
medical-style intervention could have any chance of saving the organism.

Reich went a step further by arguing that there is a causal correlation between social/political pathology and physical disease. If the fascist personality structure is already a disease body and entails that the organism live under the constant pressure of the physical contradiction between the desire for orgasm and the external (but internalized) control mechanisms for thwarting that healthy desire, then it follows that diseased biophysical bodies, like cancers, will emerge from this biological warfare. We saw how Reich applied a version of this argument to Freud when he asserted that Freud's jaw and palate cancer were caused not so much by his intense abuse of tobacco as by his rigid character and muscular armor, coming from his form of patriarchal Judaism, that forced him to "swallow" his natural aggression and sexuality. This swallowing caused his cancer and manifested it precisely in the part of the body that had symbolic connection with the emotional suppression itself. Hence in an intensified form of conversion hysteria, the subject unconsciously converts emotional armoring into a physical disease, one quite real, as a manifestation of the contradiction within. This political disease–to–biopathological disease argument marked the beginning of Reich's turn to more direct investigation of cancer and the role of diseased bions ("T bions," from the German word for death, *Tod*).

This fascinating conceptual leap represents one of those Hegelian-style syntheses that we have seen so often before in Reich. Two antipodes (Peirce's seconds), namely, the political sphere and the domain of "private" physical health, are now seen to be linked via a third category, that of the "biopathic" illness. It is one illness (a unified third) with two manifestations, fascism and cancer (or some other physical pathology). Reich argued:

An additional objective factor, which is closely related to [anti-birth-control movements], is the rapid increase of neurotic and biopathic illnesses as an expression of disturbed sexual economy, and the intensification of the contradiction between real sexual demands on the one hand and old moralistic inhibitions and child education on the other hand. The increase of biopathologies means that one is more prepared to acknowledge the sexual cause of so many sicknesses.[28]

Given what Reich had argued in *The Invasion of Compulsory Sex-Morality* in 1931 as the Hitler phenomenon was emerging, it seems to follow that fewer physical biopathologies would emerge in a matriarchy than in a patriarchy. If a lowering of the general sexual potency of the individual causes something like cancer, and if that lowering is a *direct* result of patriarchy, there must be a patriarchy-to-cancer link that is statistically significant. Nazis must be sicker than Trobriand Islanders, at least those who still live under some lingering forms of matriarchy. At the deepest physical level, physical pathologies are caused by sexual conflict, which in turn make the organism more vulnerable to internal and external bacteria and viruses. The immune system is stronger in those who are genitally potent and weaker in those who cannot withstand the corroding forces of their own "little Hitler" within.

Returning to direct political analysis, Reich argued that the German and Soviet states had betrayed the socialist principles from which they derived their rhetoric and had in fact created an odd amalgam, which he called "nationalistic internationalism," as a way of holding onto the contradictions inherent in their projected Oedipal and patriarchal structure. The Soviet Union had a more complex evolution in this direction because of the genuine struggle for internationalism in the Lenin era, which was brutally shattered by Stalin and his desire for an absolute state based on its own principles of "blood and soil." Lenin promised the workers a true internationalism, something Reich also championed, while Stalin on some level recognized that he could maintain power only if he appealed to the Oedipal struggle between desire and repression in the mass individual. The so-called dictatorship of the proletariat was replaced by the dictatorship of the party. Reich was among the first to recognize the demons in Stalin's program and made it clear that by 1934 the true Russian Revolution of 1917 was over and that the era of red fascism had begun. This was especially evident in the sudden about-face in the Soviet Union on sexual issues. A growing form of repressive puritanism replaced a liberated *Sexpol* approach. As noted, Reich's own *Sexpol* writings lost the imprimatur of Moscow, and he was forced to publish them without their support. He was not removed from the rolls of the German Communist Party because that party was dissolved by the Nazi state before it could take any such action against him. It was in fact the Danish Communist Party that canceled Reich's membership on November 21, 1933.

Soviet-style fascism had its own mythological structure, which tied the longing of the repressed masses to the soil of Mother Russia, the womb of all creation, and the eschatological promise of deliverance from the hands of the numerous enemies who surrounded the sacred soil of the people. In the official newspaper of the Communist Party of the Soviet Union, *Pravda*, an article on March 19, 1935, presented the Oedipal mythic universe of the "new" Russia. Reich quoted extensively from it. A typical passage is:

The ideas of Soviet patriotism breed and rear heroes, knights and millions of brave soldiers who, like an all-engulfing avalanche, are ready to hurl themselves upon the enemies of the country and obliterate them from the face of the earth. With the milk from their mothers, our youth are imbued with love for their country. It is our obligation to educate new generations of Soviet patriots, for whom the interests of their country will mean more than anything else, even more than life itself.[29]

With only a few words changed, this text could easily be mistaken for a Nazi propaganda broadside. Maternal milk, the sacred knights, the surrounding horde of less-than-human people, and the great pseudogenital "avalanche" all work the reader into a sexual state that is more than willing to hand its cathexis over to the party. If you cannot sleep with the woman who gave you her milk, you can certainly love the country that is rooted in the sacred soil. And why not add Stalin to the patriarchal mix? In the *Leningrad Red Times* of February 4, 1935, the following appeared: "All our love, our faithfulness, our strength, our hearts, our heroism, our life—everything for you, take it, O great Stalin, everything is yours, O leader of our great homeland . . . When my beloved wife bears me a child, the first word I will teach it will be 'Stalin.'"[30] The Stalin-era Soviet Union, Reich believed, had developed a red fascism that was a mirror image of the black fascism of Nazi Germany, because of its creation of a dialectic between a miscathected maternal ground and a strong identification with the *Führer* principle. Healthy sexuality could no longer be a desideratum in this hidden contradiction, and any attempts to do genuine *Sexpol* work were suppressed.

After his diagnosis of black and red fascism (he paid less attention to Italian fascism but took due note of its imperialistic expansion into North Africa), Reich worked out his positive proposals for a truly international work-democratic society. The correlation between repressed sexuality and alienated labor was an obvious one for him to make. Insofar as a worker is genitally impotent, she or he will also fail to derive pleasure from work. Three conditions had to be in place before a democratic work structure could function: (1) healthy work conditions, such as a well-lighted and ventilated workplace with nonrepetitive work; (2) free expression of sexual energy in the overall life of the worker outside of the workplace; and (3) the pleasure principle experienced through the work itself. If the second condition was not met, then workers would rebel against the lack of pleasure in the work. The true origin of strikers' rage must be located in their deep genital frustration, even if their grievances were also objectively warranted. Reich was interested in the *rage* that both strikers and strike-busters manifested during labor disputes and carefully traced this rage to the patriarchal tyranny that enslaved both sides, albeit in very different respects.

The third or bridging position that Reich sought—the underlying connecting reality between sexuality and work—was the biological energy that propelled the organism outward. At the heart of the international workers' movement and its seemingly innate sexual stasis was the thwarting of the basic biological core by the state and its agent, the authoritarian family. The cure for this social disorder would be to make material work libidinal:

When a man takes pleasure in his work, we call his relationship to it "libidinous." Since *work* and *sexuality* (in both the strict and broad senses of the word) are intimately interwoven, man's relationship to work is also a question of the sex-economy of masses of people. The hygiene of the work process is dependent upon the way masses of people use and gratify their biologic energy. *Work and sexuality derive from the same biologic energy.*[31]

Thus a total reconstruction of the biological core of the character structure would be necessary in order to bring Lenin's vision to fruition, even if Lenin lacked one of the key ingredients for understanding the failure of all previous revolutionary attempts: understanding the sexual dynamics in patriarchy. There could be no reconstruction of systems of power without a more primal reconfiguration of the dynamics of eros.

Once the basic biological energy of the psyche (whether personal or collective) was manifest in both genital satisfaction and work pleasure, Reich argued, then a personal or social revolution would already have taken place, but without violent means. Whenever a "revolution" expresses itself through overwhelming violence, it is clear that the perverse secondary drives are in play, not the nonviolent core drives. An international matriarchal work-democratic society would, by definition, be nonviolent, as violence has no biologic value other than in the very limited sphere of healthy self-preservation. Even sexual competition would be less intense in a work-democratic world. The elimination of the class war would take away the need for class inbreeding and the selection of certain class-desirable sexual traits in one's partner.

Work-democracy would function very differently from Stalin's horrific five-year plans, which used strong military rhetoric to compel workers into nonlibidinal work for the state. While Stalin's approach took many lives, the movement of work-democracy would preserve the life principle and protect each individual worker from exhaustive patriarchal exploitation. Reich defined his new normative political model:

> Work-democracy is the natural process of love, work, and knowledge, that governed, governs, and will continue to govern economy and man's social and cultural life as long as there has been, is, and will be a society. Work-democracy is the sum total of all functions of life governed by the rational interpersonal relations that have come into being, grown, and developed in a natural and organic way.[32]

Reich conflated the descriptive and honorific here (as he did elsewhere); that is, he argued that work-democracy *was* (descriptive) what governed social life, and also that it *ought* (normative) to emerge whenever the rational overcomes the irrational. This slight conflation aside, Reich clearly had a very rich understanding of the "rational" and a very subtle understanding of the "irrational." He never reduced reason to analytic deduction or mechanistic one-dimensional induction but (like Hegel before him) saw reason as being a primal part of the depth structure of nature itself—not a mere human tool to be used by only one organism in the currently known universe but a trait that pulsated from the heart of nature and was thus manifested in all living things insofar as secondary and irrational forces did not thwart them. Hegel put it thus: "The real is the rational and the rational is the real." This made reason (*Vernunft*) an ontological term rather than an epistemological one.

The irrational was that within the human that raged against the depth structure of reason, namely, our true biological core. In the German Romantic tradition of the nineteenth century, Schelling struggled to find a place for the irrational (*der Abgrund*, the abyss, or *das Regellose*, the unruly ground) within nature, while Hegel abjected the irrational and worked with overwhelming energy to gather it up into the rational (through his concept of *Geist*).[33] Insofar as Reich was at least unconsciously an inheritor of this fecund and brilliant philosophical tradition, he sided with the Hegelians against the followers of Schelling. At this point it is appropriate to once again ask the speculative question: was Reich fleeing the unruly ground of his own and nature's unconscious in order to survive his own internal travail? And further: can Reich's enlarged conception of the rational be capacious enough to give proper space to the irrational, or must the irrational be conceptually driven out of nature altogether? But what of the irrational pulsations that lie within the depths of prehuman nature or of the human unconscious? Do these movements exist, and if so, how must we relate to them?

We will conclude with Reich's concise eleven-point summation of his discoveries about personal and social life as it emerged from the matriarchal to the patriarchal period. Here as elsewhere Reich summarized his own categorial and empirical framework better than his interlocutors had done, and he zeroed in on essentials in a way that reinforces my claim that he was a master conceptual taxonomist:

1. Mankind is biologically sick.
2. Politics is the irrational social expression of this sickness.
3. Whatever takes place in social life is actively or passively, voluntarily or involuntarily, determined by the structure of masses of people.

4. This character structure is formed by socioeconomic processes, and it anchors and perpetuates these processes. Man's biopathic character structure is, as it were, the fossilization of the authoritarian process of history. It is the biophysical reproduction of mass suppression.

5. The human structure is animated by the contradiction between an intense longing for and fear of freedom.

6. The fear of freedom of masses of people is expressed in the biophysical rigidity of the organism and the inflexibility of the character.

7. Every form of social leadership is merely the social expression of the one or the other side of this structure of masses of people.

8. It is not a question of the Versailles Peace Treaty, the oil wells of Baku, or two to three hundred years of capitalism, but a question of four to six thousand years of authoritarian mechanistic civilization, which has ruined man's biological functioning.

9. Interest in money and power is a substitute for unfulfilled happiness in love, supported by the biological rigidity of masses of people.

10. The suppression of the natural sexuality of children and adolescents serves to mold the human structure in such a way that masses of people become willing upholders and reproducers of mechanistic authoritarian civilization.

11. Thousands of years of human suppression are in the process of being eliminated.[34]

I need add very little to this summary. I shall point out only, once again, the logical consistency within Reich's framework (regardless of what one thinks of some of his presuppositions, such as those about matriarchy). He connected his anthropological data with his earlier psychoanalytical research, while he simultaneously brought in his social case study of Nazi-style fascism. Each strand within the logical structure reinforces the others, not just in the linear structure of an "if A then B" model but in the larger conceptual design.

During this creative period in his life, while he was in Berlin

(1930–33), Reich wrote two fundamental texts that together should ce-
ment his reputation in the history of thought. His enthusiastic discovery
of Malinowski opened him to the idea that there was a fundamental divide
between healthy matriarchal culture and the unhealthy patriarchal culture of the past millennia. He took this idea and made cogent extrapolations from it, which he then applied to the self and to the social order. His
deconstruction of the Nazi mythos that was unfolding around him relied
on all of his previous insights into neurosis, character structure, the Oedipus complex, biological pathology, class war, the oppressive nuclear family, and even impulsivity. He also worked out a fundamental analysis of
the human character, producing what is certainly his most famous text,
Character Analysis. Although it was written slightly before *The Mass Psychology of Fascism*, it represented a different side of the very same coin.
It helped to create a whole new approach to therapy and showed, to those
friendly to the Reichian framework, that the Vienna model simply could
not do all that it was said to do in healing the biopathically broken individual. The next chapter will be devoted to a careful examination of *Character Analysis* and its implications for the bioenergetic work that followed
from it.

We will also see Reich's first marriage finally collapse, partly due
to his growing relationship with Elsa Lindenberg, and he will flee the
untenable situation in Berlin for a Vienna that was itself growing unsafe
for him and his *Sexpol* program. From Vienna he quickly emigrated to
Copenhagen, where the first truly virulent anti-Reich campaign began.
Yet he also struggled on with his work and created his own publishing house, as noted, because there was no other publishing venue open
to him. From out of this internal and external chaos, *Character Analysis*
emerged as the fullest statement of his postpsychoanalytic perspective on
the self and its armoring.

5

Character Analysis

While he was still in Berlin, Reich wrote *Character Analysis*, the text that is considered by many to be his masterpiece. Pulling together his research and clinical experience from 1925 to 1933, he laid out his program for moving psychoanalysis away from symptom analysis and toward a total reconfiguration of the neurotic character structure by working through resistance to the muscular armoring that was the source of the individual's nongenital forms of sexuality. He made the struggle against the latent negative transference in the analysand the central point of attack in the initial stages of the therapeutic drama. He also had a good deal to say about sexual stasis, different character types (such as the narcissist and the compulsive), armoring, and the techniques of therapy. In the third enlarged edition of 1949, he added material pertaining to the emotional plague, schizophrenia, and orgone therapy. In this sweeping work of over five hundred pages, he in essence created a whole new way of regrounding psychoanalysis in the biosphere (the entire energy field in and around the self) and in the movements of the libido as they deny any possible death drive in the self.[1]

We will pick up the biographical thread in the next chapter, as I want the elucidation of *Character Analysis* to take center stage here. The clinical and theoretical material of this book developed naturally out of his work on psychopathology in the 1920s and was a perfect complement to his work on the fascist personality (*The Mass Psychology of Fascism*) in the same period. Each book should always be read in conjunction with the other, as they together serve to deepen the categorial structures that

Reich unfolded to probe into the complex interweave of the social and personal dimensions of the psyche.

Right at the start Reich made it clear that the character structure of the individual derived from the social process, and he used an illuminating metaphor to express this correlation—the character structure was the *congealed* social process. As we saw in the previous chapter, the social process worked out its patriarchal and antisexual designs through its concentration in the nuclear family. The child, like the parent before him or her, became the locus for a congealing of these hidden fascist traits, and no amount of purely individual therapy could hope to enter into the depth dynamic of the self-in-process. Yet Reich also felt that some of the basic core dimensions of the individual self could be illuminated on their own terms and thereby provide a link from the isolated narcissistic and defensive individual to properly reconstructed social forces.

Reich argued against Freud's belief that the expression of a repressed memory would entail the release of its corollary neurosis. He asked the simple question: how do you explain those many cases where the return of the repressed memory brings no relief from the neurotic symptom? After all, the foundational truth of psychoanalysis was that the process of making something conscious was virtually the same as that of removing the neurotic cathexis. But Reich's extensive clinical experience had taught him otherwise. The question was transformed into a positive insight: is there not some kind of correlation between the *way* an experience is remembered and the extent of relief that is obtained? A patient could remember a whole host of Oedipal conflicts and castration anxieties and yet be unmoved by them.

This was especially the case with those analysands who used ironic detachment as a defense against the castration anxiety produced by the analysis itself. The ironic patient could entertain any number of "truths" about her or his condition but never let them become affectively charged. Further, the patient could be using irony in a sadistic defense/offense against her or his negative transference to the analyst. That is, the analysand might not trust the analyst because the analyst, for example, activated a father complex with a castration component. Rather than get too close to the analyst/father, the analysand would cover over the unconscious negative transference by using the distancing tool of irony. Thus the patient seemed to be saying, "I will not let you get inside of me and castrate me further, so I will put up this powerful wall against you and go along with the analytic game and use its vocabulary, and I will even allow myself to remember lost childhood experiences, but one thing I will never do is *feel* them intimately."

Remembering became the easy part, and the resistances that blocked childhood memories might not be so deep after all. The analyst could certainly stay in the dimension of interpretation and look at individual symptoms and dream material, but something else was needed to really break open the heart of the resistance. What Reich wanted to know was the source of resistance per se, not its more immediate and observable manifestations. Why was there resistance at all, and what made it so powerful in the individual psyche? Could there be a *somatic* core that was even more important in the economy of the psyche than the sphere of meanings that emerged into consciousness? In fact, could the interpretive approach itself be one way of avoiding the issue of resistance? Reich discovered in his own practice that it was far easier to discuss the meanings of neurotic symptoms, or even the neurotic character structure, than to look at why meanings were so easily had and how they tended to blind the analyst and the analysand to the more urgent work of probing into the transference and how it activated resistance. The issue was thus shifted away from paying attention to remembered material in the order in which it presented itself to the tactic of looking directly for signs of a latent negative transference that would be the locus for resistance to analysis. For Reich it wasn't until the analysand started to hate the analyst that the true work of analysis could begin.

But how did the analyst discover the status of the unconscious negative transference? Were there any clues in the behavior of the analysand that would point (semiotically) to the emerging hatred toward the father/ mother/analyst? Reich argued that these clues could easily be found in the overlooked areas of body language and behavior. Consequently one could try to find evidence of the negative transference not just in dreams and symptoms but in such things as (sadistic) silence, failure to pay one's bill in full or on time, an absurd desire to please the analyst, ironic distance, lateness for appointments, body rigidity in the analytic sessions, a monotone speech pattern, or an attitude of suspicion and distrust of the analyst. Each of these behaviors or bodily attitudes was a sign pointing to an underlying object—the emerging negative transference. The transference was negative because it was a symptom of the analysand's profound fear of the analytic work as it in turn reawakened parallel childhood material, especially the Oedipal (patriarchal) complex and its necessary corollary castration anxiety. The analyst was cast in the role of the castrating father or the hated mother, but this entire process was, of course, unconscious to the analysand. Hence getting the patient to remember childhood traumas was one thing, but getting the analysand to face into the transference situation (always negative at first) was something else entirely. Reich sensed that other analysts did not do the latter kind of work because it was, quite simply, a nasty business.

The situation could be described as follows: the analysand developed a transference vis-à-vis the analyst that on the surface looked positive. When probed more fully, however, the "positive" transference showed its harsher face, namely, that it was a latent *negative* transference masking the initial stages of the hatred the analysand had toward either the mother or father, which got projected onto the analyst because of the power of the unconscious transference. Most analysts, because of their own narcissism, refused to look into the true depth dimension of the transference structure, preferring to live in the more controllable world of memories and interpretations:

> It can be said generally that *resistances cannot be taken up soon enough in the analysis, and that, apart from the resistances, the interpretation of the unconscious cannot be held back enough.* Usually, the procedure is the reverse of this: the analyst is in the habit, on the one hand, of showing much too much courage in the interpretation of meaning and, on the other hand, of cringing as soon as a resistance turns up.[2]

Given that the process of analysis would bring up Oedipal struggles and their attendant castration anxieties before anything else, it followed that the transference, in which the analyst became mother/father, would have to embody the fear and hatred suddenly stirred up by the reactivation of the childhood material. It was certainly understandable that the analyst would prefer to stay away from this boiling morass of hatred and flee to the slightly more daylight world of meanings and interpretations.

But analysis required that both analyst and analysand had the courage to evoke and intensify the negative transference so that the affects connected with the childhood material *really* got activated—that is, the analysand had to truly hate the analyst and to cathect a lot of rage onto the new transference object. If the analyst had the courage to ignite this firestorm, then the analysand was well served, and eventually the distrustful attitude of the analysand could evolve into one of openness and trust toward the analyst. But without acting out the negative transference first and uprooting it from its innumerable hiding places, there would be no positive transference (which was an absolute necessity for the later stages of therapy). Reich argued that it was often necessary to confront the patient directly with the evidence of hidden negative projections, but he also cautioned that it had to be done with care and precision so that the confrontation was one that the analysand could integrate at that time, thereby avoiding the problem that even stronger resistances could be generated as a defense reaction against wounded narcissism—that is, a positive self-image that could not tolerate the idea that rage against the father/mother existed. Only a powerfully intuitive analyst could know when the timing for confrontation was right.

In his fourth chapter, entitled "On the Technique of Character Analysis," originally given as a paper at the Tenth International Psychoanalytic Congress in Innsbruck, Austria, in September 1927, Reich presented in much more detail how the analytic process actually worked, both in terms of the economy of the psyche and in terms of the analyst/analysand relationship. The "basic rule" of psychoanalysis insisted that the patient open him- or herself fully to the analyst and therefore not hold back any unconscious material. But Reich noted that very few patients were even capable of following the basic rule and that this was because their unconscious resistances were far too strong to permit a trusting and non-defensive relationship. Patients had a double layer of resistance. The deeper layer was the resistance itself, one that held back any recognition of the covered-over Oedipal struggles and their castration anxieties. The second layer, perhaps less deep but even more complex, was the resistance to dealing with the very *awareness* of resistance. That is, the analysand would be incredulous when the analyst pointed to an unwillingness to recognize that resistances existed. This was itself a painful truth that had to be resisted, and both layers of resistance were, of course, unconscious, hence difficult to deal with in the opening stages of therapy.

So Reich envisioned therapy as a struggle between the analyst who saw the resistances and the analysand who was driven to not see them in order to protect a wounded ego ideal. The analytic process was also unconsciously seen as another form of castration—that is, of the threat to the penis or clitoris now enacted by the all-powerful analyst who took on the mantle of the father. For the patient, it was far easier to present "material" in a steady and predictable flow than to let even the hint of a negative transference emerge, because any anger expressed toward the analyst would immediately evoke castration and humiliation, as it had done in childhood. Thus while Reich fully honored dreams and symptoms, he used them to probe into the resistances first and then, if appropriate, would interpret them in more traditional, Freudian terms. A key issue was that of finding out what the analysand was resisting *today* and how that in turn tied in with any childhood material. The archaeological work of digging down through the symptom to its animating childhood experience was deprivileged so that the more powerful work of looking at contemporary resistances could be linked to the latent negative transference and therapy could really begin to open up the psyche.

Hence castration anxiety and a need to protect an ego ideal thwarted resistance analysis, compelling the analyst to be especially alert to signs of the latent negative transference. As noted, Reich thought that the best analytic strategy was to wait before directly invoking childhood or infantile material. Current material, since it was obviously deeply related to the earlier struggles, would be a better starting place:

In the beginning of the treatment, it is merely necessary for the analyst to discern the *contemporary* meaning of the character resistance, for which purpose the infantile material is not always required. This material we need for the *dissolution* of the resistance. If, at the beginning, the analyst contents himself with putting the resistance before the patient and interpreting its contemporary meaning, it is not long before the infantile material emerges and, with its help, the resistance can be eliminated.[3]

The obvious starting point for resistance analysis was to look into the transference that the analysand unconsciously projected onto the analyst.

First it would be necessary to show the patient that the transference existed and that it was a necessary and healthy part of therapy (under proper conditions). Second it would be necessary to link the transference to any contemporary event that might have Oedipal or castration anxiety components, such as a current work relationship involving an authoritarian personality. Later other strategies would be used to release the awareness of the latent negative transference that was actually lurking within a misidentified positive transference.

A dialectic soon emerged as the patient began to sense where analysis was going. The ego became identified with the analyst, and the ego/analyst was used as a defense against the intensified libido. In a sense, the analyst became the authoritarian father who was ultimately a mirror of the state. In microcosm one saw the entrance of the fascist mindset whenever the threat of the libido became too great. This was the moment when therapy had to push past the resistance to open up the libido in a healthy way:

The ego projects onto the analyst its defense against the striving of the id. Thus, the analyst becomes an enemy and is dangerous because, by his imposition of the irksome basic rule, he has provoked id strivings and has disturbed the neurotic balance. In its defense, the ego makes use of very old forms of defensive attitudes. In a pinch it calls upon hate impulses from the id for help in its defense, even when it is warding off a love striving.[4]

Were there no analytic intervention, the old balance between ego and id could proceed with all of its compromises and cunning intact. But as soon as the analyst loosened up the ego structures by undermining some of their forms of resistance, the id became freer to unleash its own built-up energetics. The economy of the psyche shifted from strong ego control to an anxious state in which the id was reawakened. And one of the first manifestations of the loss of a resistance was the increase in the amount of anxiety in the psychic system. From his phenomenological observations Reich was able to develop a law that stated that there was always an increase in anxiety whenever there was a lack of genital potency combined with an initial loosening of the character armor (somatic resistance) in the self. Needless to say, most individuals would initially prefer to dampen anxiety than to proceed with the intense demands of the analytic work. Anxiety could be lowered by simply putting the ego back in its place as controller of the id.

Every successful analysis required that the analysand experience powerful emotions that turned toward a hatred of the analyst. The unfolding of the latent negative transference into one that was no longer latent but manifest was a clue that the therapeutic relationship was moving in the right direction:

> Finally, the patient rebels against the threat of the analysis, rebels against the threat to his protective psychic armor, of being put at the mercy of his drives, particularly his aggressive drives. By rebelling against this "nonsense," however, his aggressiveness is aroused and it is not long before the first emotional outbreak ensues (i.e., a negative transference) in the form of a paroxysm of hate. If the analyst succeeds in getting this far, the contest has been won. When the aggressive impulses have been brought into the open, the emotional block has been penetrated and the patient is capable of analysis. From this point on, the analysis runs its usual course. The difficulty consists in drawing out the aggressiveness.[5]

In a sense, what was meant by analysis proper could begin only after the "paroxysm of hate" had loosened the emotional block that was embedded in the character armor. This would increase the amount of anxiety in the system in the short run but would lead to its replacement by sexual satisfaction in the long run. Genital potency could not emerge without the initial penetration of the emotional armor of the individual, an armor that formed what the world saw as that individual's character structure. And it wasn't until the negative emotional outburst of the patient occurred that she or he could even know that there was a character armor blocking the natural flow of biological energy in the psyche/soma.

Imagine the terror in the psyche of the analysand when she or he was suddenly confronted with insights that shattered the neurotic compromise between the ego ideal and repressed sexuality. For Jung this would be equivalent to the discovery of the *shadow*, namely, that part of the unconscious that manifested the feared and denied part of the *persona* (the positive ego and its external social ideal). Patients were more likely to flee therapy during this time, when they experienced the sudden demoralizing effects of confronting the shadow, than at any other time. Here Reich's insights ran on tracks parallel to Jung's as he, like Jung, saw the "shadow" as being composed of deeply abjected ego-ideal-shattering drives and conflicts that generated intense resistances, which in turn compelled the less strong analysand to leave therapy. To prevent the analysand from acting on the flight response, the analyst had to know how much true ego strength was available in each case and also properly gauge the recovery powers of the repressed libido. This analytic process required the utmost from the analyst, as a more passive or listening approach would fail to enter into the resistances that the analyst should have helped excite in the first place. For Reich the method of free association no longer held any prospects for a cure on the *character* level. Only a more direct and probing method would work—a method that looked for the negative transference first and then heated its intensity until it became an incandescent presence in consciousness.

As always, the transference was fundamental to Reich (as it was for Freud and Otto Rank), especially insofar as it was the road by which the patient could travel back to infantile conflicts. But in the initial stage of therapy all forms of transference were both negative (even if masked by a so-called positive transference) and the locus of resistance. This occurred because it placed the analyst in the role of the castrating father or the Oedipal mother (for a male analysand) or of the castrating mother and Oedipal father (for a female analysand). In either event, the analyst was the castrator *and* the object of sexual desire, neither prospect being congenial to the analysand's ego ideal, therefore causing the patient's psyche to resist any awareness of its current and infantile situations. Reich insisted that only an inexperienced analyst would believe that a positive transference was possible at the beginning of therapy:

It is correct that all neuroses result from a neurotic character and, moreover, that the neurotic character is characterized precisely by its narcissistic armoring, then the question arises whether our patients are at all capable of a *genuine* positive transference, in the beginning. By "genuine," we mean a strong, nonambivalent, and erotic object striving, capable of providing a basis for an intense relationship to the analyst and of weathering the storms entailed by the analysis. Reviewing our cases, we have to answer this question in the negative: there is no genuine positive transference at the beginning of the analysis, nor can there be, because of the sexual repression, the fragmentation of the object-libidinal strivings, and the restrictions of the character.[6]

Object-libido strivings were fragmented because they were still tied to pregenital fixations that could not weave themselves into a whole genital cathexis. Insofar as the negative transference could evolve into a positive one, it would follow that the object-libido strivings could begin to cathect onto *one* object, namely, the analyst. Put simply, when the patient fell in love with the analyst and knew that she or he was doing so, the libido could be worked with in a conscious way. The transition was from castration anxiety and Oedipal struggle toward a state of healthy and guilt-free object cathexis. The role of the analyst was to be the midway point from castration anxiety to a healthy extra-analytic relationship. Only through a positive transference could the analysand evolve into a genitally healthy person. By loving the analyst, the analysand could work past fear of the father/mother castration and overcome incest desires.

Pregenital strivings (oral, anal, phallic/clitoral) must become genital in the full sense. Seeing that they did was a key part of the analyst's job. If the analyst were loved only orally or in an anal/sadistic way, then the analysand's psyche would remain in a state of sexual stasis. Analytic skill would gather up the pregenital fixations into the genital and allow the analysand to see the analyst in terms of "sexual realism":

> From the economic point of view, the task of handling the transference might best be formulated as follows: the analyst must strive to bring about a *concentration of all object libido in a purely genital transference*. To achieve this, the sadistic and narcissistic energies, which are bound in the character armor, must be freed, and the pregenital fixations must be loosened. When the transference is correctly handled, the libido, built up as a result of the liberation of those strivings from the structure of the character, becomes concentrated in the pregenital positions. This concentration of libido induces a temporary positive transference of a pre-

genital, i.e., more infantile, nature. This transference, in turn, is conducive to the breakthrough of pregenital fantasies and incest drives and thus helps to unbind the pregenital fixations. However, all the libido which analysis helps to free from its pregenital fixations becomes concentrated in the genital stage and intensifies the genital Oedipal situation, as in the case of hysteria; or reawakens it, as in the case of compulsion neurosis (depression, etc.).[7]

Again the analytic dialectic is manifest, this time in terms of the transformation of the pregenital into the genital, but only through a temporary regression that, in true Hegelian style, must initially negate the very goal that is sought. When therapy evokes the pregenital through a positive transference, there is a step backward into fantasies and incest longings that divert the libido away from its goal of full genitality. But this regression in the dialectic is actually a necessary stage in that it brings the rejected pregenital material into consciousness, thereby allowing it to transcend itself and take the next step of gathering its fragments into a unified genital drive that is directed toward the analyst. This last turn in the dialectic requires, of course, an unleashing of genuine affect and a loosening of the character armor.

It is one thing for the analyst to work with the transference fields of the analysand, but it is another entirely to be aware of her or his own countertransference tendencies. For Reich, two elements within the countertransference were essential. The analyst had to be fully aware of any sadistic or aggressive drives within him- or herself as well as his or her own level of genital potency. An aggressive countertransference would result in a power struggle between the analyst and patient, as the analyst would interpret any sign of a negative transference as a threat to his or her power and authority. The issue of sexual potency was especially important to Reich insofar as most of the earlier forms of analysis had failed in his view because the analysts were themselves unfulfilled genitally. A sexually impotent analyst would resent any healthy flowering of genitality that would point to an object cathexis outside of the analytic context. In effect, the prospective lover in the outside world would be a threat to the possessiveness of the analyst. Or the impotent analyst could misuse the analytic work to fulfill pregenital fixations, such as the act of masturbating female patients under the guise of therapy.

If the analyst had overcome aggression/sadism and had found a healthy genital life, then the countertransference would be far less dangerous and would be less likely to contaminate the analytic relationship. But if the analyst were still unconscious of her or his own thwarted sexuality, the analysand would catch on fairly quickly:

> The analyst, to be sure, has the right to live according to his own light. But the fact remains that if, *unconsciously*, he adheres to rigid moral principles, which the patient always senses, if, *without knowing* it, he has repressed polygamous tendencies or certain kinds of love play, he will be able to deal with very few patients and will be inclined to hold up some natural mode of behavior as "infantile."[8]

What about another key piece of the countertransference in which the analyst falls in love with the patient? Did it follow that only a genitally impotent analyst became vulnerable to the enticing effects of the transference? Remember that in his autobiography Reich had identified the transference *with* love, and he made no distinction between transference (which was unconscious) and *genuine* love and mutuality (which were largely *autonomous* and free from unconscious bonds). Clearly he was right when he asserted that the analyst must not be a rigid moralist, but had he looked more fully into the dangers of the countertransference? My sense is that Reich had his own fears about this most dangerous dimension of the countertransference, precisely because he, like Jung, was especially susceptible to the erotic dance between analyst and analysand.

In addition to dynamic issues, Reich was interested in the categorization of neurotic *types* and in contrasting the basic neurotic type per se with the genitally healthy individual. He led into the former issue by first laying out the fundamental distinction between the total neurotic character (vis-à-vis armoring) and the flexibly armored potent type. In neither type is armoring absent, but in the neurotic character armoring becomes rigid and holds back true emotion, infantile memories, and libidinal expression (except in the twisted forms of phobias or reaction formations, the latter being a species of countercathexis). In the neurotic type the ego builds up a strong reactive defense against the id, precisely because the id has not been allowed to develop naturally under the conditions of patriarchy. Any cathexis outward that threatens to reawaken castration anxiety would be met with a countercathexis from the ego in which libidinal energy is blocked and pushed backward into the unconscious. The place where the countercathexis confronts the initial outward-bound cathexis becomes the locus for the character armor. The armor can be seen as a solidified sphere of the deposits of the militant countercathexes that protects both the ego and the ego ideal from fissure. Of course, this is a neurotic compromise formation, and analytic intervention threatens to fragment the hard-won ego defenses; hence the resistances and the latent negative transference to the analyst as another form of countercathexis.

In a sense, character itself is a "narcissistic defense mechanism." Again Reich asks a more basic question than his colleagues: why do humans have character structures in the first place? Is character biological, or is it a secondary social inscription? If it is the latter (which Reich assumed), then how is it formed, and is this process inevitable? His conclusion is that all character is to some degree an embodiment and expression of defense and resistance, rooted in the patriarchal Oedipal drama and castration anxiety. And since patriarchy is only a relatively recent social construct, it follows, for Reich, that a return to matriarchy would make defensive structures far less necessary, as they would be based on the reality principle rather than on fantasies of castration.

The ego was forced to do two jobs simultaneously. It had to defend the psyche against the "stimuli of the outer world" while also defending the psyche from the internal pressures of the id. In order to be successful in both tasks, it was forced to develop prohibitions and align itself with the superego, but neurotic defects were the necessary consequence of this process. The pleasure principle was met with the hypermoralism of the ego ideal, as that ideal was infused with the codes of the superego. But what happened to the erotic component per se in the neurotic versus the healthy individual?

Genital orgastic gratification of the libido and sublimation prove to be prototypes of *adequate means*; all kinds of *pregenital gratification and reaction formations* prove to be *inadequate*. This qualitative difference is also expressed quantitatively: the neurotic character suffers a continually increased stasis of the libido precisely because his means of gratification are not adequate to the needs of the instinctual apparatus; whereas the genital character is governed by a steady alternation between libido tension and adequate libido gratification. In short, the genital character is in possession of a *regulated libido economy*.[9]

The neurotic character had the following traits: (1) a pregenital fixation, which when isolated into oral, anal, or phallic/clitoral would manifest the distinctions among the hysterical, compulsive, and phallic-narcissistic subtypes; (2) libido stasis, because of the blockage of a realistic object cathexis; (3) reaction formations that represented the dynamics of the ego's countercathexes; (4) strong superego structures; (5) castration anxiety; (6) unresolved Oedipal tensions; and (7) a rigid armor to suppress anxiety. The genital character, on the other hand, manifested (1) full genital gratification; (2) sublimation in creative outlets such as work-democracy rather than in phobias; (3) a lack of sexual stasis—that is, an *outward-moving* sexual economy; (4) relative freedom from castration anxiety and Oedipal tensions; (5) very flexible armoring that could adjust to the shifting reality demands; and (6) limited superego prescriptions against sexual expression.

It must be noted that Reich's use of the concept of sublimation here was quite different from Freud's post-1920s use of the concept vis-à-vis cultural ideas. Sublimation was not a substitute for genital gratification, as it was for the Freud of *Civilization and its Discontents*, but a way for sexuality to positively and creatively express itself through nonsexual objects. Reich argued, for example, that no artist could be successful as an *artist* without using sexuality in his or her work. Thus for Reich sublimation actually become a way of sexualizing the world rather than of fleeing from the drives of the libido. With his 1939 conceptualization of orgone energy, this sexualization took on more cosmic forms.

Sublimation, now in the honorific class of concepts, differed sharply from neurotic reaction formations. Reich was quite clear that the ego structure was at stake and that the reality principle could never break into the open if reaction formations stood in the way:

What strikes us about these phenomena is that the reaction formation is spasmodic and compulsive, whereas the sublimation flows freely. In the latter case, the id, in harmony with the ego and ego ideal, seems to have a direct contact with reality; in the former case, all achievements seem to be imposed upon a rebelling id by a strict superego.[10]

The energy of the id could flow freely only when no rigid forms of character armor stood between its need for outward cathexis and the reality principle. What Reich denoted as "sexual realism" was a component of the contact between the libido and the proper genital object. By contrast, what could be called "sexual idealization" would be manifest when the libido or id met with a superego that put back pressure on its outward-bound drive. The pressure of the countercathexis would be manifest in the forms of spasmodic muscular contraction (especially in the pelvic floor) and a restriction of the blood flow to the skin surfaces. Thus reaction formations (unconscious reactions against id impulses) were particular and chaotic, whereas sublimation was unified and rational.

More specifically, what of the differences between a weak ego and a strong ego vis-à-vis unity and armoring? How would a weak ego manifest itself? How would a strong ego present itself?

Whereas the emergence of a phobia is an indication that the ego was too weak to master certain libidinal impulses, the emergence of a character trait or typical attitude in place of a phobia constitutes a strengthening of the ego formation in the form of a character armoring against the id and the outer world. A phobia corresponds to a cleavage of the personality; the formation of a character trait, on the other hand, corresponds to a consolidation of the personality. The latter is the synthesizing reaction of the ego to a conflict in the personality which can no longer be endured.[11]

From Reich's perspective, a phobia—say, an irrational fear of the dark or of spiders—emerged because the ego did not fully integrate the rush of the libido. The phobia represented a fragmented psyche that could deal with sexual anxiety only by creating a specific fear that becomes the focus of the anxiety. Sexual stasis and its corollary, generalized anxiety, were masked by reducing anxiety to a finite and located fear, but this simultaneously kept the ego from being integrated both with itself and with the libido. Fear of spiders, for example, was an unconscious transformation of a more generalized fear of the devouring mother, which in turn was a localized fear of the power of sexuality.

A character trait, on the other hand, like an assertive posture in the world, manifested a more integrated psyche. While phobias were uncontrollable and were connected with spasmodic irruptions of the character armor, character traits emerged rationally out of an integrated ego that was also able to negotiate the twin pressures of outer stimuli and internal sexual drives. Put differently, the appearance of a phobia was a sign of a broken psychic economy. The character trait was a sign (Peirce's *symbolic* sign manifesting thirdness or concrete rationality) of the wholeness of the psyche and its ongoing bond to the reality principle. A phobia was an irruption in the psyche awaiting meaning, while a character trait already had meaning.

Working further with Peirce's semiotic and metaphysical categories, we could reconstruct the basic Reichian model in a philosophically richer way. In the initial stage of therapy the analyst was usually concerned with finding meanings—that is, thirdness as reason in action. The analysand would be more than ready to accommodate the conscious and unconscious expectations of the analyst by letting signs (symbolic) with meanings emerge into the analytic space between analyst and analysand. In this "betweenness" zone thirds, or units of conscious meaning, would be available for public scrutiny and could in turn be woven into a narrative that both analyst and analysand would affirm as warranted. This process would also allow for the irrational and unpredictable irruption of seconds, in this case, meaningless surds (undefined and unshaped units of reality) that break into consciousness through symptoms and/or dream material. But the analyst would not allow their secondness to be secondness. He or she would immediately struggle to convert each irruption of a second into a portent of meaning/thirdness. Hence analysts had a tendency to fear raw secondness and would want to impress thirdness upon it.

Reich had the courage to stay in the realm of secondness for as long as it took to find out what made a particular irruption a form of secondness—that is, a resistance. In this application of Peirce to Reich, it is appropriate to equate secondness with resistance. On one level resistance is without meaning in the usual psychoanalytic sense. We could say that a resistance is an irruption that has no immediate thirdness. Yet here we have to make some subtle distinctions. A dream has a symbolic semiotic structure—that is, it has symbols that already have a sphere of meaning, usually related to infantile material (for Freud and Reich) as it illuminates contemporary material. To talk of the thirdness in a dream is perfectly appropriate. What the analyst contributes is interpretants—that is, further signs that draw out the meaning already presented, albeit cryptically, in the symbols of the dream. In this sense we could say that the analyst deepens the amount of thirdness within the dream by unfolding its bursting contents.

But the sudden emergence of a resistance is not the presentation of an already-attained third awaiting further ramification by interpretants (new signs). Rather, the resistance is a true second that can only become a third by a very different *kind* of analytic work than the work of interpretation. The interpretive approach moves from thirdness to thirdness while resistance analysis moves from secondness to thirdness. And most analysts, as noted, are not comfortable with wrestling with secondness, as it frustrates the almost imperial demands of semiotic elucidation. Put differently, the patient's unconscious will continue to throw curve balls at the analyst through those seconds that frustrate meaning analysis. This increases the anxiety in the countertransference.

When the analysand presents a resistance, the analyst is directly confronted with a brute causal relation producing a sign with almost no direct meaning. The resistance is more of an unconscious *act* than a meaning-filled structure that can be rotated through analytic circumspection. And what does the resistance produce in the countertransference? It generates its own brute causal second that the trained analyst has to identify as such. Resistance analysis binds the analyst to the analysand on an even deeper level than does interpretive analysis because secondness lies further down in nature and the psyche than does thirdness. For Peirce, thirdness is an evolutionary emergent from secondness and not the other way around (except in the case of entropy). Interestingly, the concept of entropy can be well applied to the psyche insofar as attained thirds can unravel and decompose into chaotic seconds that are not rewoven into meaningful patterns. In this sense of the term, a psychosis, while having much meaning for the analyst, is a clear form of entropy for the analysand.

The *forms* that character took were thus forms of thirdness as they could be seen to have emerged out of the taciturn and dark ground of secondness. Each character type was an expression of how emotional and muscular armoring evolved to produce a relatively stable contour for the relevant self-in-process. Thus a type was a constellation of seconds and thirds in a unique configuration. Reich used his categorization framework differently in changing contexts, thus producing a complex schema that we can now elucidate more precisely. His initial triad of character forms was (1) the hysterical character, (2) the compulsive character, and (3) the phallic-narcissistic character. He also added the masochistic character, and we have seen his basic dyad between the genital and neurotic characters. Or one could develop a Reichian categorial scheme through an analysis of specific pregenital fixations, thus producing oral, anal, and phallic/clitorial character types. Or again one could use Reich to create a typology based on the use and misuse of the reality principle, or yet again in terms of the openness to transference currents. These differentia are all ways of rotating the psyche through different interpretive lenses, but they all in the end point to a reliable typology (given Reich's presuppositions) that can be found through a variety of routes. We have discussed the genital and neurotic types and the problems of phobias and reaction formations in the structure of the emotional armor. To round out Reich's typology, we must discuss the four remaining types as presented in *Character Analysis.*

All four of the following types (hysterical, compulsive, phallic-narcissistic, and masochistic) are species of the neurotic character type. The genital type does not present species in the same way, as it has already transcended the genera or species of psychopathology. So we can say that there are two primal psychic types, the genital and the neurotic, with only the latter having species. In Aristotelian terms (also used by Saint Thomas Aquinas) we would thus say: there are two psychic genera (classes) in opposition to each other. Genus A is the nonpathological class of those who have attained full genital satisfaction. Genus B is the pathological class of everyone excluded by A. Genus B is the larger class, as it has more members, that is, more scope or instantiation. Genus B has several species (subtypes), but they can be configured in different ways depending on the therapeutic or pedagogical context. But these different species in genus B have a consistent contour of traits regardless of which trait may be privileged at a specific time. For example, to talk of the *anal type* is roughly commensurate with talking of the *compulsive type.* Philosophically we thus distinguish between the *genera* (largest classes of the area of investigation) and the *species* under one or more genera. Psychoanalytically we use the parallel language of *types* and *subtypes*. Either pair of terms is appropriate. All four terms refer to the scope of thirdness, with the genus and the type obviously "having" more thirdness than the species or subtypes.

Again, each type, from genera A and B to the species of B, are manifestations of thirdness as it has emerged from the swirling darkness of secondness. But for Reich, the therapist has real access to these types only through the use of resistance analysis rather than interpretive or hermeneutic analysis. Hence to accept his typology, it is also necessary to accept his method for unfolding the types and subtypes. It is always the case, in whatever discipline, that typology and theory of method go together, even if they are not fully clarified in advance (which may not be possible). The method shapes the way the material appears, while the material shapes the way the method is formulated and rendered public. This is a reasonable dialectic from which it is impossible to escape. For many philosophers the only lasting criteria in forming issues of validation out of this dialectic are pragmatic ones. That is, method and typology Z have some validity only insofar as they generate desired pragmatic and measurable results, such as symptom relief. Given this pragmatic model, which I accept, Reich's resistance model has obvious positive pragmatic consequences, while his typology may require some refinement if it is to do service and have good pragmatic consequences in the future configurations of gender, race, and class. Let us then look at the species under genus B.

The first species of the neurotic character type was that of the hysterical character (remembering that the term *hysterical* can be partially redeemed if it is understood in terms of volatility and extraversion). Of all the pathological character types, the hysteric was the most transparent to analysis. She or he presented with a dialectic of coquetry (psychosexual flirtation) with a transition to passivity. This type was prone to quick and easily excited fixations on other persons, which actually were without true emotional depth or any sense of long-term commitment. The hysteric would use the lure of his or her sexual powers to create a circle of genitally frustrated admirers. But the hysteric was frozen in the phallic/clitoral stage and had a deep Oedipal attachment that blocked any adult forms of sexual relationality. Anxiety was very high for the hysteric and could be controlled only by the repression of healthy genital impulses.

Was the hysteric honest about her or his use of intense sexual energy to shape and control both the object world (of external sensations) and the inner pulsations of libido? Could the hysteric take ownership of the chaotic mixed signals that were sent out over and over again to hapless victims of the dance of eros denied? Reich quite rightly pointed to a deep dishonesty in the hysteric type, a dishonesty that had painful and disruptive consequences for other people:

> Thus, the sexual displays in the hysterical character are an attempt to find out whether dangers are present and where they might be coming from. This is also clearly demonstrated in the transference reaction in the analysis. The hysterical character never recognizes the meaning of his sexual behavior; he violently refuses to take cognizance of it and is shocked by such "insinuations." In short, one soon sees that what stands out here, as sexual striving is basically sexuality in the service of defense.[12]

Pseudosexuality thus replaced full genital sexuality, as the latter would be too dangerous to the fragile compromise between the ego and the id. Whenever the hysteric sent out a sexual probe, via coquetry, she or he was in fact testing the dangers that lurked in the object sphere. If anyone acted on these signals, he or she would be immediately charged with inventing them or with being a demonic sexual aggressor. Hence the hysteric type was using sexuality in a dishonest way, projecting this power onto the Other, who in fact had been compelled to misread the signs because her or his sender was unaware of his or her complicity in sending genuinely sexual invitations.

Thus the hysterical type presented with hypersexuality, a need for immediate gratification, excitability, shallow relationality, a fixation on the phallic/clitoral stage where immediate gratification was the norm, a somewhat looser character armor than the other pathological types, and a high degree of somatic and psychic anxiety. The intense vacillations between sexual evocativeness and sharp denial when these invitations were accepted marked a personality that had a fragile ego structure with an unstable armoring that was far less solidified than in the compulsive type. Whenever someone sent the signal of yes to the hysteric's implied invitation, she or he would be met with the reaction of no coming from the sudden increase of anxiety released by the hysteric's newly activated libido, which was barely recognized for what it was in the first place. For the non-hysteric in the situation, it was a no-win scenario.

In a sense, the hysterical subtype was similar to the impulsive character type that Reich had analyzed several years earlier, especially insofar as they both manifested chaotic and uncontrollable forms of hypersexuality that were not seen as such. Impulse control was the one major weakness of the hysteric, combined with anxiety recoil when the impulses were met with an objective response. Sublimation was weak for both types, making it difficult for them to put long-term energy into lasting cultural or social artifacts. We would not be violating Reich's categorial schema to say that the hysterical character type (subtype) acted out the traits of the impulsive or borderline personality.

While the hysteric was somewhat narcissistically tied to phallic/clitoral displays of outward pseudosexuality, the compulsive type was tied to anal and sadistic impulses and fixations. This type has entered the consciousness of the public imagination in a much clearer way than the other types, perhaps because its traits are so obviously distasteful. The compulsive had a pedantic sense of order in which the world of outer sensations had to be controlled, as well, of course, as the world of the libido. The compulsive was methodical in his or her behavior, cheap in financial dealings, often collected things that could be tightly controlled, such as stamps or coins, and was driven by an anal eroticism that had a sadistic component.

How did the compulsive type evolve out of its infantile and childhood experiences to become a fully compulsive character? What conflicts were at the center of the psychosexual drama that made full genitality impossible? Reich again showed his genius at taxonomy as he described the compulsive type both historically and structurally:

Historically, we have a central fixation on the anal-sadistic stage, i.e., in the second or third year of life. Toilet training, because of the mother's own particular character traits, is carried out too soon. This leads to powerful reaction formations, e.g., extreme self-control, even at an early age. With the rigid toilet training, a powerful anal obstinacy develops and mobilizes the sadistic impulses to strengthen itself. In the typical compulsion neurosis, the development continues to the phallic phase, i.e., genitality is activated. However, partially because of the person's previously developed inhibitions and partially because of the parents' antisexual attitude, it is soon relinquished . . . Hence, in the compulsion neurosis the repression of the genitality is typically followed by a withdrawal into the immediately preceding stage of feces interest and the aggression of this stage. From now on, i.e., during the so-called latency period—which is especially pronounced in the compulsive character—the anal and sadistic reaction formations usually grow more intense and mold the character into a definite form.[13]

Reich added a footnote to the above passage in which he insisted that the latency period (from ages five to twelve) was shaped by cultural forms of sexual suppression and was not a biological imperative in any sense. The compulsive type thus became fixated during the end of the Oedipal stage, in which anal aggression was the norm for interacting with external stimuli. Whatever phallic/clitoral experiences became manifest were soon repressed by the maternal or paternal superego, so that the anal stage became the highest rung on the ladder of fixations.

The compulsive, often acting like someone who had obsessive compulsive disorder, manifest, for example, in activities such as constant hand-washing to ward off germs (libido), used ritual and repetition to control the internal and external worlds. Affect and thought were divorced from each other, and the realm of thought was used as a means to escape the power of the repressed affects. Reich pointed out that scientists were often compulsive types because of their attention to controllable detail and their need for a more totalizing control of the environment. The greatest fear was loss of self-possession through something unpredictable (an irrational second). Thus the compulsive used thirdness in a deliberate way as a means to escape from secondness. By contrast, the hysterical type was more comfortable moving into and out of the realm where secondness can give birth to thirdness. The hysteric could honor secondness especially insofar as he or she thrived on a kind of impulsive chaos to cathect the phallic/clitoral excitations and fixations. This was a realm of experience utterly alien to the compulsive type, for whom any hint of change would induce a rapid increase in anxiety.

Externally, compulsives had a rigid musculature (hypertonia), in which the body presented itself as being awkward and uncomfortable with its surrounding world. As a child, the compulsive learned to hold in his or her feces by intense muscular control at the behest of the mother. This holding in became the norm for subsequent development through the latency and adolescent periods into adulthood. The entire body had to hold in the anal aggression of the libido, letting it out only through reaction formations such as repetitive ritualized behavior. (Reich here refers to a patient who used to "pass his hand over the fly of his pants three times before each session," while also reciting a particular verse.) Rituals controlled the potential uprush of the libido. Freud had linked the compulsive neurosis with religious ritual to show the connection between the need to control sexual power and competition, on the one hand, and the equally compelling need to shore up the ego through reenactment and return to a threat now controlled by the suppression of the affects, on the other.

The third subtype in this list of psychopathologies, the phallic-narcissistic, was quite different from the first two. Unlike the compulsive type, the phallic-narcissistic character would not generate a reaction formation (a protective countercathexis) against aggression. This type would let aggression out and would usually attack first rather than wait for an attack, real or imagined. Reich gave a clear capsule summary of the three types:

> The phallic-narcissistic character differs even in external appearance from the compulsive and the hysterical character. The compulsive is predominantly inhibited, reserved, depressive; the hysteric is nervous, agile, fear-ridden, erratic. The typical phallic-narcissistic character, on the other hand, is self-assured, sometimes arrogant, elastic, energetic, often impressive in his bearing.[14]

The phallic-narcissistic character would not have a complex inner world of introspection but would more likely be a person of decisive action without regard for real consequences. Reich listed Napoleon and Mussolini as two exemplars of this type. Addicts also tended to be phallic-narcissistic, and this was the type behind most forms of homosexuality.

The phallic-narcissistic type did not generate countercathexes against aggressive drives, as did the compulsive, but rather gave those drives free rein as a form of defense against external stimuli. Nor did the phallic-narcissist try to control the environment through ritual. Rather, a direct assault was more effective in bending the world to his or her will. Phallic aggression warded off those impulses that were defended against by character armoring. Further, phallic and sadistic violence was compensatory for childhood genital deprivations. Like the other types, the phallic-narcissistic was genitally impotent even with the unrelenting display of pseudogenital potency. The hysteric lacked the sadistic piece that was central to the phallic-narcissist, even if he or she shared a tendency toward exhibitionism. The compulsive was far too rigid and self-protective to act out in full pseudogenital splendor.

We can consider these three types (actually subtypes) of the neurotic type as forms in which the emotional and muscular armoring became shaped. The hysteric and the phallic-narcissist had more flexible forms of armoring than did the compulsive. But unlike the genitally healthy type, the neurotic subtypes used (or were used by) armoring as a means of protection against the twin threats of external stimuli and internal libido. Any threat to the armoring generated resistance and produced an increase in anxiety. The hysteric controlled anxiety by sending out pseudosexual probes of the object world to gauge any real threat. The compulsive controlled anxiety by sadism toward the object world and by a ritualistic struggle to manage the irrational. The phallic-hysteric controlled anxiety by a roosterlike display of bravado or some kind of addiction that blunted the effects of anxiety. But none of these types could find the right correlation of ego and libido that would assure full genital potency while allowing for a healthier form of armoring that was reality driven and fully flexible.

The masochistic character was the fourth subtype dealt with in *Character Analysis*. Like the preceding types, the masochist was also caught in the dialectic of libido and ego using armoring as a defense against the inner and outer demands of reality. Reich again attacked Freud's view of masochism, which he read as rooting the drive for punishment in a biological urge toward self-destruction—namely, the death drive. For Reich there simply was no biological evidence for a death drive, and further, the cultural aspects of what appeared to be a secondary-level death drive were also misconstrued. Even on the level of cultural inscription, the phenomenological evidence—that is, the evidence derived from a very close study of the way death anxiety was *actually* experienced by the attending psyche—pointed to a sexual tension within a continuum, not a separate counterdrive that worked against the libido. Was the masochist really concerned with self-punishment, a kind of inverted self-sadism, or was another mechanism operating?

Reich remained a staunch believer in the pleasure principle (*Lust*) and still insisted, as he had in the 1920s, that unpleasure (*Unlust*) was itself a part of the pleasure spectrum rather than its opposite. So the psyche could not go "beyond the pleasure principle" in Freud's sense, but rather it would experience tension as a kind of constricted sensation within the pleasure continuum. This sense of "constriction" was a central piece of Reich's view of masochism, tied to his phenomenological awareness of the bursting sensation that came from the back pressure of emotional armoring on the libido. Thus "the masochist, far from striving after *unpleasure*, demonstrates a *strong intolerance of psychic tensions* and suffers from a quantitative *overproduction of unpleasure*, not to be found in any other neurosis."[15] The masochist was caught in an overload of anxiety and sexual tension that produced a sensation of unpleasure, but the masochist was *not*, contra Freud, desperate to punish him- or herself in order to assuage a guilt-consciousness (although that might be a *piece* of the tension).

Punishment was not directly sought, but substitute punishments would emerge that would actually take away some of the anxiety of feared punishments. Thus the masochist would imagine possible punishments and then work out an internal scenario in which they could be dealt with. This ongoing internal dialogue deflected anxiety away from the reality principle toward a domain of internal and somewhat manageable false punishment narratives. Interestingly, the masochist, unlike the phallic-narcissistic type, would run from sexual rivals because of a fear of the castrating father. This cut off any possibility of sexual fulfillment because the genital ideal was always translated into anal passivity in the face of a perceived threat from the phallic type:

His true nature, his *ego,* is rooted in passivity because of the anal
fixation. As a result of the inhibition of exhibitionism, moreover, his
ego has developed an intense inclination toward self-deprecation.
This structure of the ego stands in opposition to and prevents the
realization of an active phallic ego-ideal. The result of this is again
an intolerable tension, which serves as a further source of the feeling of suffering and thus nourishes the masochistic process.[16]

Praise from another person was perceived as a threat to the stability of the
ego and libido compromise formation, as it would heighten the possible
phallic tendency of the ego ideal, thus threatening a sudden rush of sexual release in the direction of the object. Hence masochists tended to
downplay their own accomplishments so as not to "tempt the gods" with
hubris. For the phallic-narcissistic type, on the other hand, the gods were
on his or her side, and there was no issue of hubris from which one had to
be protected.

How did the masochist operate in the dance of eros? While the hysteric was wrapped up in anxiety, and the compulsive hated and denied the
love object, and the phallic-narcissist approached the object directly, the
masochist used the tactic of self-abasement, a "show of misery" that was
designed to elicit a love response from the Other. The masochist was saying, "Love me because I suffer for you, and if you love me, I will escape
from this torment."

But what was the masochist *really* afraid of? What caused such a defensive attitude that cut off outgoing phallic/clitoral power? The answer
was clear—namely, that the masochist was actually afraid of an increase
in pleasure out of the sea of unpleasure. That is, the masochist had a fear
of bursting or exploding out and through the emotional and muscular armoring that had held anxiety at bay. This could also be a fear of a "melting feeling" in which the self would disappear in the orgasm. As a
reaction formation against this disappearance, the pelvic floor would contract spasmodically and thwart the release of orgastic energy, that is,
there is an inhibition at the height of excitation. Any possibility of "surrender" was blocked at this point where the sensation of bursting and
melting was at its most intense and frightening. Further, for the male
masochist there was the fear that the penis would dissolve in the vagina

and cease to exist. For Reich this was a three-step process: "(1) I am striving for pleasure, (2) I am 'melting'—this is the fear of punishment, (3) I have to suppress this sensation to save my penis."[17]

But how did the masochist become free from this dialectic in which a sense of dissolution evoked the fear of punishment? Was there a way past the anal passivity that blocked genital health? For Reich two things had to be done in therapy to liberate the masochist type from the fear of bursting or melting—namely, to move the libido from the anal to the genital domain and to eliminate genital anxiety (the fear of losing the penis for the male). On the bioenergetic level, the masochist also had to be liberated from the spasms that constricted the pelvic floor (which made real intercourse impossible). With these strategies, the analyst, working first through the resistance, could bring the masochist out into a healthy relationship with the object world.

Underneath all of the four neurotic subtypes was the problem of anxiety. Each type experienced anxiety in a different way and had different defenses for dealing with it, as noted. But within the phenomenon of anxiety itself, there were two species, two subtypes that were related to each other in their own dialectic. Reich distinguished between what he called "real" anxiety and "stasis" anxiety, with the latter being the more encompassing category. Real anxiety emerged in a more finite way as a means for coping with specific threats, whereas stasis anxiety was the foundational sensation for the entire psyche in all of its neurotic modes:

Thus, anxiety is and always must be the first manifestation of an inner tension, whether this is brought about by an external frustration of the advance toward motility or the frustration of the gratification of a need, or whether it is brought about by a flight of the energy cathexes into the center of the organism. In the first case, we are dealing with stasis or actual anxiety; in the second case, with real anxiety. In the latter, however, a condition of stasis results of necessity and consequently there is also anxiety. Hence both forms of anxiety (stasis anxiety and real anxiety) can be traced back to *one* basic phenomenon, i.e., the central stasis of the energy cathexes. Whereas, however, the stasis anxiety is the direct manifestation of anxiety, real anxiety is initially merely an antici-

pation of danger; it becomes affective anxiety secondarily when
the flight of cathexes toward the center creates a stasis in the central vegetative apparatus.[18]

Actual or stasis anxiety was the primal form that anxiety per se took when
the neurotic character could not manifest proper sexual cathexes through
genital potency. It was all pervasive and varied in intensity as armoring
was created to mute it. Like existential analysts (such as Ludwig Bin-
swanger), Reich insisted that anxiety was fundamental to the human condition. But he further added that it could be radically reduced through a
total remaking of the character structure (a point *not* shared by the exis-
tentialists, for whom anxiety was tied to the realization of being-toward-
death and hence not reducible except through deception or "bad faith," to
use the language of Sartre). On the other hand, real anxiety was *real* precisely because it was tied to a specific, if changeable, object in the world.
Yet it had *its* ground in stasis anxiety and would emerge out of and return
to its ground.

Freud had not fully understood the distinction between real and stasis
anxiety and hence had not probed more successfully into how stasis anxiety related to armoring, resistance, and the defense mechanisms. Reich's
advance was to show the intense dialectic between finite and specific *real*
anxieties on the one side and global totalizing stasis anxiety on the other,
as *this* dialectic was in turn correlated to the dialectic between anxiety
per se and libido. Only the genital character type would lower the anxiety
level to the point where it was not the determining factor in life.

We move now into the third part of *Character Analysis*, where Reich
presented his more sophisticated bioenergetic concepts pertinent to character as he had come to formulate them by 1949. He actually began this
division of the text with a 1935 essay based upon one that he had read before the Thirteenth International Psychoanalytic Congress in Lucerne,
Switzerland, in August 1934. The focus of the essay, which proved to be
controversial, was on the relationship between psyche and soma around
the issue of "orgastic contact anxiety and its overcoming." This paper analyzed the concept of contactlessness in the libido and world correlation
where the psyche was cut off from a genital relationship to the object pole.
The lack of genital contact between self and Other was seen as a basic
trait of various forms of neurosis.

One distinction needs to be made here. In many contexts Reich seemed to use the concepts of libido (*die Libido*) and id (*das Es*) interchangeably; but there was a refinement in *Character Analysis* in which the id was equated with the pleasure ego rather than the more, for him, global libido. In the spirit of this distinction, the id was somehow used by the libido as its point person in the ego structure. It is not clear if this distinction was absolutely fundamental for Reich, and it may have had only practical or tactical implications in certain orders of analysis. Yet it was an intriguing distinction nonetheless. For Freud the concept of the id basically covered the unconscious per se (c. 1923), while his earlier use of the concept of the libido (c. 1905) referred to the sexual drives *within* the unconscious.[19] Thus Freud seemed to see the id as being more encompassing than the libido (even touching on the ego),[20] while Reich, because of his privileging of biosexuality, made the libido the more generic term. This reversal of genus and species showed the gulf between these two thinkers toward the middle and end of the 1920s.

Before his psychoanalytic colleagues in Lucerne, Reich presented his bold model for character analysis and its specific tactics for overcoming the total neurotic character structure. His summation of the six stages of therapy was one of his most concise and compelling to date (1935):

Character analysis that has been correctly carried out, notwithstanding the endless diversity in content, conflicts, and structures, exhibits the following typical phases:

1. Character-analytic loosening of the armor.
2. Breaking down of the character armor, or, put another way, specific destruction of the neurotic equilibrium.
3. Breakthrough of the deepest layers of strongly affect-charged material; reactivation of the infantile hysteria.
4. Resistance-free working through of the unearthed material; extraction of the libido from the pregenital fixations.
5. Reactivation of the infantile genital anxiety (stasis neurosis) and of genitality.
6. Appearance of orgasm anxiety and the establishment of orgastic potency—upon which depends the establishment of the almost full capacity for functioning.[21]

To work on the psyche of the analysand, the resistances had to be isolated, named, and brought to the surface within the context of the transference. Once this was done, enough trust could be established within the
analytic hour to move into a carefully timed loosening of the muscular
and emotional armor. The neurotic compromise between the ego and the
libido, which appeared in one of the four neurotic character types (hysteric, compulsive, phallic-narcissistic, or masochistic), had to be shaken
free so that a new ego/libido correlation could occur. Put in Peirce's terms,
the neurotic blockages of secondness had to be transfigured into future-
directed forms of thirdness that were reality oriented and rational. Once
the armoring had become loosened, childhood material would flow automatically, sometimes through contemporary material, and the analysand
would truly undergo the intense affects that had been covered over by the
countercathexis of the armoring. This entailed going from unconscious
pregenital fixations to conscious genital primacy, but not without reenact-
ing infantile trauma. In the end, the analysand would achieve full orgastic potency and a profound lowering of anxiety.

By 1935 Reich had moved from psychoanalysis in the classical sense,
however modified by him, into his bioenergetic and vegetative model. He
wanted to reduce "all psychic activity to the primal vegetative function."
The vegetative function was one that could be studied bioelectrically (as
he set out to prove empirically) and could be brought under some kind of
therapeutic control through a measurement of the flow of libido throughout the musculature. What was this deep energy in the biological system?
As if to frustrate our carefully drawn distinction between libido and id
above, Reich in 1945 appended a footnote that equated id with orgone:

> What the psychoanalytic theory calls the "id" is, in reality, the
> physical orgone function within the biosystem. In a metaphysical
> way, the term "id" implies that there is "something" in the biosys-
> tem whose functions are determined beyond the individual. *This
> something called "id" is a physical reality, i.e., it is cosmic orgone
> energy.* The living "orgonotic system," the bioapparatus, merely rep-
> resents a particular embodiment of concentrated orgone energy.[22]

I have been arguing that Reich was rather negative about the term *metaphysics* but that he certainly had one, as all language users do. Here we

see him use the term in a positive way, denoting a sensibility to the larger cosmic setting in which his research was taking place. He was in essence saying that his modified psychoanalysis was driven by its inner logic to affirm the depth energy of the world by empirical means. The biosystem of medical psychoanalysis was fully embedded in an energetics that governed it and that had its own knowable laws and principles. Again, psychoanalysis was the antechamber to the house of orgonomics or orgone analysis proper.

Yet the concept of orgone, while sharing family resemblances with such concepts as id, entelechy (Aristotle), and élan vital (Bergson), is distinctive in that it can be measured, according to Reich. Orgone has empirical manifestations that can be traced by known means of electromagnetic measurement, such as temperature variation and galvanic response, although on a conceptual level orgone functions as an almost pre-empirical unifying principle. One way of understanding Reich is to say that he remains a monist but translates his scientific materialism (a form of monism) into a concept of what we could call spiritualized matter. He is not exactly a panpsychist for whom matter is "effete mind" (in the words of Peirce) or for whom matter is constituted by "drops of experience" (in the language of Whitehead and Hartshorne), but a thinker who affirms that matter is really a manifestation of a deeper organic pulsation that is the underlying dynamics of an evolutionary nature. Put in more theological terms, Reich is not asserting that orgone is a conscious or even personal divine being but that it is a dynamic energy that is a form of nature creating nature out of itself alone. Insofar as we are in healthy contact with orgone, especially in the sexual sphere, we are also in contact with the ground of the world. Hence direct contact with orgone (or vegetative currents) is crucial, and lack of contact with it is a pathology that cuts off the organism/psyche from its own powers of renewal.

The ego instincts were seen as being the condensation of all of the defensive reactions of the organism to outside stimuli and the inner power of the libido. Would character analysis entail an extinction of the ego structure insofar as it was the locus of resistance and negative transference? Was Reich becoming a crypto-Buddhist with this move to place the ego in a negative light? For the Buddhist philosopher, the ego is the source of desire while desire was in turn the source of suffering. To eliminate suffering, it was necessary to destroy its source—namely, the desiring ego. Is there a difference here? Reich saw the ego not as the source of desire but as its gatekeeper. The source of desire was the bioenergetic libido that could never be extinguished by internal introspective means. Unlike the Buddhist, Reich wanted natural genital desires to become manifest in an outward way. If they did not do so, as in the more ascetic forms of Buddhism, then the entire organism was already in a state of decline (an argument used by Nietzsche against both Christianity and Buddhism). Reich did not so much want to extinguish the ego (as in Buddhist nirvana or Hindu samadhi) as to open up the ego's armoring so that it could still perform its reality functions while letting healthy genitality pulsate through it. His strong monistic (perhaps even mystical) tendencies, which didn't become fully expressed until his period in America, were modulated by a deep Western sense of ego autonomy and separateness.

When the flow of the vegetative current was blocked, the psyche experienced an "inner isolation," or an "inner deadness." In extreme cases this condition degenerated into a schizoid depersonalization in which the affects were totally cut off from the intellect. The best term for denoting these states was *contactlessness*, which entailed that the blocks against the libido were rigidly in place and had sunk beyond the reach of consciousness or even (perhaps) therapeutic intervention. The armoring that was the concrescence of the countercathexes could take on any variety of forms. Reich used an iconic representation of armoring that likened it more to a branching tree with no single trunk than to a single linear counterthrust against the outward-bound libido. Fear of an outward and inward orgasm was actually a fear of *"direct psychic contact with persons and with the processes of reality."* For the neurotic character, contactlessness lowered the anxiety threshold by quashing the libido, but this, sadly, entailed the loss of the dialectic with a human community and with reality in general.

Julia Kristeva's term *abjection* is appropriate here, with its combination of a sense of desire and fear. For Reich the ego structure denies the desired object that it is mortally afraid of. But this object is also the stimulus to the blocked libido and the goad that compels the libido to bang against the armoring of the ego. Or one can invoke Freud's key concept of ambivalence, which entails the same kind of love/hate relationship with the object. Resistance emerges out of the fiery trial of abjection and am-

bivalence, causing the ego to ossify and take on the shape of the surrounding authoritarian culture as it is microcosmically reenacted in the
nuclear family. There is clearly a logical and empirical connection between the authoritarian personality and the abjection of sexuality.

Thus far I would argue that Reich remained logically consistent in his
categorial scheme and also used his native phenomenological gifts to full
capacity. He had ferreted out the latent negative transference by actually
looking at the analytic data as they presented themselves to him. This entailed moving past semblance into the phenomenon itself as it showed itself in its own terms. For the phenomenologist, the phenomenon had a
kind of energy in and through which it would emerge past and through its
theoretical encrustations (or ideological superstructures) into the light of
more circumspective sight. Put technically, the true phenomenon showed
itself from out of itself by itself and not through another phenomenon. For
Reich the so-called positive transference (in the initial stages of therapy)
was a mere semblance of the deeper negative transference that showed itself as itself through resistance, which was its *how* or *way* of self-showing.
That is, the negative transference was the primal phenomenon that showed
itself, but it emerged into awareness through its secondary resistances.
The resistances did not create the negative transference; rather, the
negative transference created and intensified the resistances. Reich's
phenomenological intuitions were in attunement with the phenomena
themselves, thus forcing him to move past the conceptual projections of
his less intuitive colleagues. It should be noted that the term *intuition* as
used here does not connote something like a "hunch" or a "prophecy" but
refers specifically to the act of direct seeing into the essence of something.

Moving into the 1949 material in *Character Analysis*, which we will
deal with in an adumbrated way in the next chapter, we can see how
Reich's energetic model slowly took over the terrain of psychoanalysis
and replaced it with a biophysics that talked primarily of energy flows,
and how a working model, which he now called "orgonomic functionalism," became an extension of the 1933 model of character analysis. Put
differently, the new shift in focus was away from a study of character to an
analysis of the body, its musculature, and its relationship to the flow of orgone. The study of orgone, the great cosmic energy that played *through*
the psyche, was fully functional rather than topographical or historical—

that is, it was directed toward a transformation of actual currents within the body regardless of where their historical configurations came from.

Specifically, how does orgone energy flow through the body, and how does body armoring function in relation to orgone? Since bioelectricity is in some sense orgone, it follows that orgone will flow along the axis of the central nervous system. The main current of orgone is thus up and down the spine, but orgone also follows other paths as well, and in the genitally healthy person this flow will be unimpeded (insofar as allowed by the reality principle). But in the neurotic individual there will be a counter-tendency for the body to form circular armor rings that are perpendicular to the spinal column. These armor rings are in effect segmented cross-sections that encircle the central nervous system. Reich asked the reader to think of a segmented worm as an analogue to the orgone/armoring structure. Lengthwise along the worm we would have the flow of libido or orgone, while in the horizontal axes we have the segments that were perpendicular to the longitudinal main axis of the worm's body.

The segmented armor rings became manifest through their effects on the observable musculature of the body so that a trained analyst could quickly gauge where an armored segment was located. The most obvious and important of these perpendicular segments were (1) the ocular area, (2) the oral area, (3) the neck area, (4) the chest segment, (5) the diaphragm segment, (6) the abdomen segment, and finally, (7) the pelvic armor. Each of these needed to be dissolved in turn before the therapist could proceed onto the next one.

The basic energetic model was quite straightforward: "the liberated body energy spontaneously attempts to flow *lengthwise*. It runs into the still unresolved crosswise contractions and gives the patient the unmistakable sensation of a 'block,' a sensation which was only very weak or altogether absent as long as there were no free plasmatic currents whatever."[23] The analyst had to know which specific muscular activities or configurations were signs of an underlying armoring. Each muscle could function as a symbolic sign of a meaningful third or piece of armor.

Thus the analyst would look for such symbolic signs as a rigid chin, an immobile pelvis, expressionless eyes, a masklike expression, stiff-neckedness, a knot in the throat, rigid breathing, or a tensed back. These would all be signs referring to an object (the armor) in a certain respect. Here Reich implicitly combined phenomenology with a kind of pragmatic semiotics. That is, his phenomenological probes into the phenomenon of the armoring were reinforced by a sign theory that went from the secondary phenomenon (what Peirce would call the "immediate object") to the deeper primary phenomenon (what Peirce would call the "dynamic object"). The immediate object of analytic intuition was the muscular spasm or contraction, while the dynamic dimension of the same phenomenon was the underlying neurotic armor that represented a defense against the twin powers of the outer and inner worlds. The therapeutic answer to this rigid horizontal segmentation was to dissolve the blockages in each of the seven major rings and to let the libido flow along the vertical axis so that it could move from a contactless state toward one that established full genital contact as routed through the pelvis.

The armoring model is fully consistent with most of what Reich had written about before 1945, but what about the underlying dynamic object—namely, the libido or orgone energy (which was cosmic)? Here I need to introduce the last of Peirce's ontological categories to provide a philosophical underpinning for Reich's orgonomic funtionalism. We have seen the pertinence of Peirce's categories of *secondness* (brute meaningless causality) and *thirdness* (concrete reasonableness manifest in symbols and conscious meanings). But we have not probed into his most difficult and controversial category, that of *firstness*. This category is the foundation for and generative of the other two categories (or principles of reality). It is a category that is almost impossible to describe, as description already entails at least a minimal degree of thirdness or of secondness becoming thirdness. How does one describe that which is referred to as a kind of oceanic sea of possibilities or as pure immediacy without any differentiating qualities? Perhaps one can only point (as Wittgenstein argued about the domain of the mystical).

Firstness is manifest in Reich's concept of orgone insofar as orgone is the deepest phenomenon that underlies anything that we can talk about, assimilate, or manipulate. It is pre-semiotic (a feature of firstness) insofar as it is not a body of signs in itself but the place where signs fall away into darkness. It is the ultimate dynamic object that is known through its immediate objects and ramified through interpretants (new signs), but it is never a second or a third. But did Reich see it this way? My sense is that in his initial encounters with orgone, he was compelled to see it as a kind of mysterious ground that had no direct properties that could be pointed to—that is, as firstness. But as he probed into some of what he thought were its more pertinent manifestations, such as the bions that emerged out of organic or inorganic decay, he came to apply his own notions of secondness and thirdness to orgone, leaving behind its inexplicable origins in and as firstness. One could say that Reich violated the inner logic of firstness by saying too much about it. Insofar as he did so, I suspect that there are roots in his theory of the unconscious.

Is the unconscious conscious, and if so, in what respect? Earlier I noted that Jung had asserted that the unconscious had a special *kind* of consciousness that enabled it to function in a teleological and compensatory way vis-à-vis the ego. That is, for Jung the unconscious, both personal and collective, seemed to know what the ego needed if it was to help it reach a more integrated state with its unconscious. Reich seemed more reticent to assign the predicate of consciousness to the unconscious, seeing it as more like a blind surging id or energy flow. But is there another way to frame the issue that moves us past this major contradiction within the psychoanalytic tradition? Is there a type of consciousness that is unique to the unconscious, and can we find a language to exhibit this uniqueness? The answers come from rethinking Peirce's three categories as they apply to the transactions between consciousness and its unconscious ground.

Clearly, consciousness entails thirdness, namely, a meaningful rational (in the largest sense) structure of intelligibility. Without thirdness there is no meaning. But does the issue end here? Is there a way of expanding the concept of consciousness beyond the traditional Western sense of a centered awareness tied to an individual self (that is, a form of *self*-consciousness)? Do we not conflate the notions of consciousness and self-consciousness? If that is the case, perhaps it makes sense to work out a view of consciousness that deprivileges any sense of a reflexive turn backward into self-consciousness. In Reichian terms we can ask: does orgone have any thirdness (as Reich came to believe), or is it merely a manifestation of firstness (pre-intelligible oceanic being)?

When philosophers are caught in a conundrum, they often make a distinction. Here the distinction I would like to make is between what we can call *sheer thirdness* and *manifest thirdness*. The latter category refers to the intelligible structures that take shape within the ego and its self-aware constructions. This is the type of thirdness that we are all aware of—that is, it is the fully circumspect and semiotically available con-sciousness that the analyst can access via symptoms and neuroses. The former category, which is newly introduced here, denotes a dimension of thirdness that does not show itself directly but that has a minimal kind of prethematic awareness/consciousness nonetheless. This sheer thirdness is not yet the kind of thirdness envisioned by Jung for the unconscious, but something deeper down that has another kind of awareness. For Jung the unconscious is very much alive as a kind of scanning system that knows both the outer world and the world of the psyche. It can know in its own way when the ego is one-sided in its relationship to the world, and it can provide what is needed to compensate for that one-sidedness. But the orgone/id of Reich does not have this more manifest and exalted type of knowledge. Still, the orgone does know in its own muted way what the ar-mor is doing to thwart its healthy momentum. It is aware in a *sheer* way, rather than in a public semiotic way, of its psychic environs. The longitu-dinal energy of the psyche knows where the horizontal rings are that rep-resent its countercathexes.

Hence for Reich, were he to have used this language, the orgone is aware of its locations even if not in a fully semiotic and reflexive sense. This awareness is somewhere between the "awareness" a falling rock has of its gravitational pull and the awareness that a self-conscious psyche has of, for example, a dream interpretation. Thus we can conclude that even for Reich the unconscious has thirdness and that it is a full partici-pant in the drama of self-transformation. The firstness of the orgone is it-self a unique kind of firstness. Again, were we to make a distinction, we could say that orgone is a form of *developmental firstness* rather than *bare firstness*. For firstness to be developmental it must be pulsating outward toward the stream of consciousness. Insofar as firstness is bare firstness, it is self-encapsulated and fully mute. As Peirce put it, pure (bare) first-ness would be like the unnamed world on the day it was discovered by Adam. Developmental firstness (a concept not used by Peirce) would re-sist self-enclosure and, like the id, move toward the light of awareness without, however, itself being a center *of* awareness.

Hence I am willing to argue (or speculate) that orgone is an absolutely unique combination of developmental firstness and sheer thirdness. No other ontological form or energy in the world shares this dual categoriza-tion. Yet at the same time orgone also participates in the domain of *sec-*

ondness insofar as it has causal effects and interacts with bodily material. When we look at some of Reich's American writings in the next chapter, we will see that there is a profound tension between a lingering scientism vis-à-vis orgone and an emerging ontopoetics that wants to see orgone in almost religious terms. My sense is that this tension is perfectly appropriate, given the unique status orgone seems to have in terms of the categories of being.

Returning to *Character Analysis*, we must explore two final themes that Reich included in his third edition of the text. They were the analysis of schizophrenia, written in English in 1948, and the study of the emotional plague, which was written in German in 1943. His rethinking of schizophrenia represented his mature reflection on how orgonomic functionalism applied to the problem of a major psychosis, a theme that had occupied his mind as early as the mid-1920s when he still lacked the categories (in his mind) to understand the true dynamics of intrapsychic catastrophe. In working through this essay we will see how orgonomic functionalism looked backward toward the psychopathological material that had been the launching pad for Reich's career.

Reich's primary concern in this essay was with paranoid forms of schizophrenia rather than with catatonic or hebephrenic forms; the former are characterized by an extreme withdrawal from the world, and the latter are characterized by a slow deterioration of the biosystem. In contrast to these less active and expressive forms of schizophrenia, the paranoid form was "characterized by bizarre ideas, mystical experiences, ideas of persecution and hallucinations, loss of the power of rational association, loss of the factual meaning of words, and, basically, a slow distintegration of organismal, i.e., unitary, functioning."[24] Paranoid schizophrenia manifested itself in a split psyche in which the prospects for reintegration were blocked by a powerful dialectic of natural libido and armoring. But unlike the neurotic character, the paranoid schizophrenic was fully aware of the orgonotic streamings within the body and could not stop them from breaking through the armoring, thus producing the profound psychic split that the neurotic avoided. In this sense, for Reich the paranoid schizophrenic was more honest about the id or libido than the neurotic was.

Insofar as the consciousness became split into two primary parts, it was compelled to project aspects of the split onto the outside world. The feared and desired organic streamings were converted into external agents that threatened to engulf the self with demonic threats. The concept of the devil, an increasing concern for Reich's mature philosophy of religion, emerged from the split psyche as the most intense manifestation of the id as it rushed past the armor and terrified the individual. The hallucinations and paranoid delusions of the schizophrenic were aspects of the split self read backward from an external source, such as the walls of the room in which the patient sat. There were no filters left in the reality ego, which was smashed by the uprush of bodily orgone, through which the analysand could find and stabilize a reality principle. Only the external world of delusions remained, and these voices and visions had their own absolute and unmediated validity. It was like going from a world of testable thirdness to one of entropy and chaos in which bizarre thirds swirled about without a knowable contour. For Jung there was profound meaning in this process, and each third could be traced back to specific archetypal structures, while for Reich the process revealed less about disclosable meanings than about biophysical conflicts.

In one of his clearest passages he marked the transition from psychoanalysis to biophysics by comparing their respective triadic schemas. But not everything from psychoanalysis survived in its evolution to orgonomic functionalism:

> The psychoanalytic arrangement of mental functions according to the three great realms of the ego, the superego, and the id has to be sharply distinguished from the *biophysical* arrangement of the functions of the total organism according to the functional realms of *bio-energetic core* (plasma system), *periphery* (skin surface), and *orgone energy field* beyond the body surface. These two theoretical structures describe different realms of nature in a different manner. Neither is applicable to the other realm of organismic functioning. There is only *one* meeting point of the two theoretical schemata, i.e., the *"id"* of psychoanalytic theory, where the realm of psychology ends and that of biophysics *beyond* psychology begins.[25]

Reich seemed to be saying that each language was appropriate in its domain but that the earlier language of psychoanalysis would prove to be unhelpful in the more fundamental and curative domain of biophysics in which the orgone energy of the system was dealt with directly. One could still talk of ego and superego, as both structures remained real in their own way. But their form of reality was actually parasitic on the more primal forms of orgone as it worked in and through the armoring segments of the body and psyche. The older dualism of body and mind (one that Reich never felt fully comfortable with) was replaced with a pragmatic functionalism in which the distinction of body/mind was not ontological—that is, denoting two substances—but pragmatic. Hence in one context it might make more sense to use the earlier language of mind, while in another analytic context it might make more sense to use the language of biophysics. Where the two languages converged was in the equation of id and orgone.

How could the analyst proceed to heal the schizoid character that saw all "forces" as being external and alien? The neurotic character could at least learn that his or her projected traits were in fact internal, but the paranoid schizophrenic was bereft of such insight. The forces were "out there" and represented a command system that would compel the schizoid character to act destructively. Reich presented a case study of a female patient who had an overwhelming impulse to push someone onto the train tracks because of a command hallucination that told her to do so. She did not act on the impulse. How did the external become the internal again?

The answer emerged slowly for Reich in the 1930s as his conception of biophysics began to encompass, but not negate, his character-analytic theories. What was the paranoid schizophrenic in fact dealing with? The answer: the schizoid character was intensely aware of the organic life forces (more so than the neurotic) and felt them as being manifest in the world as the psyche split into two segments precisely because of the unbridled power of the id/orgone. Two therapeutic guidelines emerged from this insight: (1) the analysand had to be brought *slowly* to the point where he or she could tolerate the streamings in a less catastrophic way, and (2) the analysand had to *slowly* learn that the source of the devils in the outside world was actually the healthy "melting" sensations within the body that often became mixed with the "fear of bursting" associated with sexual stasis on the verge of overcoming itself. The sensation of melting and the fear of bursting were two sides of the same coin, although the ultimate

Wilhelm Reich, age three, 1900

Wilhelm Reich (indicated by arrow) in the Austrian army, 1916

Reich with
his first wife,
Annie Pink

Reich with his
second wife,
Elsa Lindenberg

Reich's third wife, Ilse
Ollendorff, with their
son, Peter, at Orgonon

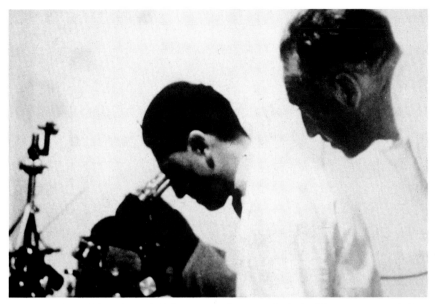

Reich (right) in the Oslo laboratory with Roger du Teil of the University of Nice

The orgone energy accumulator

Reich in the students' lab at Orgonon, 1946

Reich with the Cloudbuster at Orgonon, mid-1950s

Reich in his study at the observatory, 1955

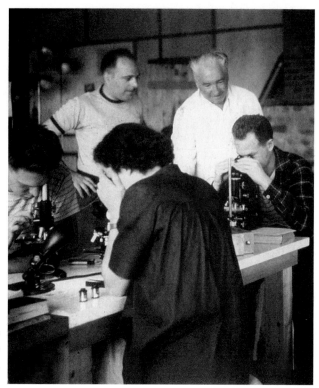

Reich with students
in the students' lab
at Orgonon

Reich on his way to prison, March 1957

goal of therapy was to link the self to the true melting sensation (orgonotic streamings) once it had experienced the "burst" and no longer feared it. These streamings were especially powerful in the pelvic floor area but quickly spread throughout the entire body after and with the orgasm.

Even more precisely Reich stated, "The more and better contact she made with her plasmatic bioenergetic streaming sensations, the less the fear of the forces would be. This would also prove my contention that the *'forces' in schizophrenia are distorted perceptions of the basic orgonotic organ sensations.*"[26] The centrifugal power of these sensations drove outward with such force that they took on a gestalt of their own in the three-dimensional world of external reality. They then turned backward centripetally and reentered the expelling psyche to haunt the barely existent ego. In this framework the expelling psyche manifested a form of secondness that simply drove orgone outward. The world into which the cathexis had been thrown was a manifestation of secondness insofar as it had no rational structures of its own. The countercathexis of the now free-floating orgone was yet another manifestation of secondness that had no conscious logic or meaning on its own. As always, therapy consisted in the drive to weave secondness into thirdness, but always at the right pace.

Thirdness emerged whenever the schizophrenic learned to accept his or her orgonotic streamings as being from within and as being true expressions of the life force. Insofar as this took place, the split within consciousness could be healed and a unified psyche would emerge, in turn making genital health possible. Raising an age-old question, Reich argued that the difference between the genius and the schizophrenic was that the genius could accept and work with (sublimate) her or his orgonotic streamings whereas the schizophrenic would only suppress them. This distinction makes it clear that schizophrenia and genius are incompatible categories, even if genius and manic-depression are almost always coimplicated.

In the schizophrenic, then, perception is split off from the orgonotic sensations within the psyche/soma. In the genitally healthy individual, perception coincides with the id and its outward expressions. That is, a streaming is seen for what it is, and it does not become displaced into some image of the devil or other malevolent force that produces commands that go against the fragmented ego for the schizophrenic. All dev-

ils are thus socially embedded constructs that arise from the split person-
alities that frequently emerge in society. A paranoid schizophrenic's devil
can easily become a neurotic character's Satan and thus enter into an entire theological tapestry.

Reich rounded out his analysis of schizophrenia by arguing that this
extreme psychosis could also be correlated to a more or less permanent
brain lesion that was itself produced in the natal period from an orgoni-
cally sick mother. Like many contemporary psychiatrists and neuroscien-
tists, he was convinced that some micro- and even macroscopic changes
took place in the very young brain of the vulnerable individual, making
the later fragmentation of the personality likely. From this he inferred that
care for the orgonotic well-being of the mother was as important as care
for the newborn. In the womb the seeds were laid for psychopathology, precisely insofar as the carrying mother was not in tune with her own healthy
genitality.

Schizophrenia, in its catatonic, hebephrenic, and paranoid forms, was
clearly an individual psychosis with *some* social antecedents and *some*
social implications. But Reich was persuaded that there is another form
of psychosis that was *primarily* social in its expression, transmission, and
genesis. He referred to this newly discovered but age-old psychosis as the
"emotional plague." We probed into aspects of this disease in Chapter 4,
when we analyzed *The Mass Psychology of Fascism*, but it was in his final
essay of *Character Analysis* that Reich's earlier social and political theories became more sharply focused on the issues of medical analysis and
medical prophylaxis. His questions became (1) what *is* the emotional
plague? (2) how do we *detect* it in ourselves and in others? and (3) how do
we *protect* society against it if the normal agents of our self-protection may
be the plague's chief agents?

In answering the first question, Reich argued that the emotional
plague was an epidemic or a contagious disease just like bubonic plague
or cholera. Instead of eruptions on the skin or lesions on the body, the
emotional plague was manifest in "violent breakthroughs of sadism and
criminality." Was it transmitted like a virus through blood or the air, or
did it have a different kind of transmission? This question was never fully
addressed, but it is clear in this context that the emotional plague was
transmitted through social suppression of the genital impulse. Yet in another sense, one could "catch" the plague from another person or a group,

and this transmission could be sudden and catastrophic. Why did Reich call this plague "emotional"? Precisely because it presented with a strong affect tone that blocked out rationality and measured self-assessment. It was a "biopathy of the organism" that distorted the entire character structure, much like schizophrenia. When in the grip of the emotional plague, the individual had no means for even seeing the plague *as* a plague, let alone finding a way past its delusional projections.

In Reich's implied philosophy of history, all of the crimes of the patriarchal period of humankind (c. 4000 B.C.E. to the present) stemmed from the emotional plagues that had coursed through the communal psychic systems that shaped individual lives. Having lived through the human emotional plagues that spawned the two world wars, Reich saw that none of the major events of wartime could be blamed on the will of selected individuals acting rationally. Rather, those travails were products of leaders and followers who *could not* act rationally because they were trapped in an overwhelming disorder that had its roots in the unconscious and its shaping by the antisexual forces of patriarchy. By the same logic, such plague responses as racism, sexism, and xenophobia were all rooted in ancient patriarchal structures that abjected otherness in the same way that they denied the unconscious, even while being in its grip.

Hence we can say that the emotional plague was a viruslike organism that spread throughout a community through social means of genital suppression but that could also have a person-to-person transmission even after puberty. After all, the Oedipal and castration complexes were in place, and a contemporary plague structure had only to activate what was there. Further, Reich argued, the plague masked the fact that it existed and hence it was hard to detect. But how did the trained medical person come to recognize that the emotional plague had descended upon a community? In answering this second question, we see Reich once again use his phenomenological gifts to pry loose a phenomenon from its self-concealment.

The first trait that became manifest in the phenomenon of the emotional plague was the split between an individual's or group's action and the motives that the individual or group assigned to the action. In one of Reich's examples, he noted the behavior of typical parents during a divorce proceeding. Both parents wanted only the "best" for their children and for themselves and saw their actions and their motives as coinciding.

But upon analysis it soon became clear that the motives did not agree with the actions. In fact, each parent wanted to inflict pain on the other by arguing for what was "best" for the children, which always happened to coincide with the interests of the accusing parent. Hence the parent was *really* saying, "You betrayed me by sleeping with X; therefore I want to punish you by taking away the children." Of course, the children are reduced to mere means. By the same logic, a social group could want to convert a "backward" people to its own religion for their own good. Yet in the cunning of the emotional plague, this social group was actually manifesting a sadistic need for authoritarian control over a group that would be susceptible to such manipulations.

Secondly, the plague drove people to restrict the life force or natural genitality of others. The logic was quite simple: if I am not sexually fulfilled, you cannot be either. A moralizing attitude emerged that equated sex with chaos or disease or even social anarchy. Yet behind it was an armored individual who could not tolerate nonarmored (actually flexibly armored) persons. In all forms of the plague, the energy for the negating drives was derived from genital frustration and was thus a secondary drive rather than a healthy one. The secondary drives ruled the social world and had to be transformed back into primary drives if there was to be any hope for work-democracy and a full genital life for everyone.

Another schema that well presents the traits of the emotional plague lists four aspects that are always present in predictable ways:

1. Motive given for an action never coincides with the real motive, which is hidden. Nor does the ostensible goal tally with the real goal.
2. There is a total belief in the ostensible goal.
3. Conclusions are not the result of thinking but are predetermined. Thinking serves to confirm and rationalize the predetermined conclusion.
4. Use of defamation (generally sexual, moralistic).[27]

Hence the medical psychiatric practitioner can recognize the presence of the duality of motive and action, the totalizing belief in the goal, the determinism in thinking, and the tactic of defamation toward anyone who manifests healthy genitality. Clearly the plague person will use sexual defamation above all other tactics. Gossip is a very interesting phenomenon because it can have strongly relevant effects on an individual even when she or he is not aware of them. Certain employment possibilities, for example, can disappear for no known reason because the shadow of "deviant" or "unprofessional" sexuality has been placed over the genitally healthy person by an impotent plague person. Sexual gossip may well be the strongest glue in any plague society, precisely because it emerges from the very heart of the neurotic blocking of sexual energy.

How, then, could the medical practitioner hope to provide a cure for this dangerous social psychosis? Reich's answer, which was adumbrated only in this 1943 essay, was that all of our prophylactic attention had to be turned toward the issue of rescuing healthy childhood and adolescent sexuality from the educational establishment, which was in the hands of the plague people. Most forms of education imposed an authoritarian order on children as a way of controlling their native and robust sexuality. A new pedagogy must allow for proper outlets for sexuality so that the natural genital energy in the psyche could be untrammeled and thus freed for learning and growth without neuroses. Ultimately Reich concluded that *"it is solely the reestablishment of the natural love-life of children, adolescents, and adults which can rid the world of character neuroses and, with the character neuroses, the emotional plague in its various forms."*[28]

What was to come next for Reich? By 1933 he had written two of his greatest works, *The Mass Psychology of Fascism* and *Character Analysis.* In his additions to these works during the period of his American "exile," he wove in material from his orgonomic functionalism and concept of work-democracy to inform the reader of his understanding of the transition from psychoanalysis to biophysics. Between 1933 and the time of his revisions in the early to mid-1940s, he passed through an intense period of biological and electrical research into the organic foundations of the psyche and the body itself. He "discovered" bions, those extremely small organic forms on the cusp between the living and the dead, and he thought he had developed an understanding of how cancer cells come into being from degenerated bions (the T bions). During this period of the late 1930s, he also experimented with the direct electrical impulses that were manifest during orgasm and worked toward a quantifiable structure for the orgone theory. But most important was the orgone theory itself as it emerged toward the end of his European period. In the next chapter we will focus on the orgone theory rather than on the highly controversial bion and cancer theories, and conclude with his religious metaphysics and his own mythological identification with Christ. The tale will end with a brief analysis, based on newly published material, of his battle against the Food and Drug Administration.

6

Displacement, Orgone,

Cosmic Religion, and Christ

Between 1933 and 1939 Reich was forced into deeper forms of exile, first from Berlin, then from Copenhagen and Malmö, Sweden, and finally from his home in Oslo. But this six-year period was also especially rich for him, both in terms of his evolving research into bioelectric energy, the bions, cancer, and sexual-electric energy, and in terms of his personal life, which involved a new marriage (never legally contracted), a series of displacements from his several public organizations, and an estranged relationship with his two children, Eva and Lore. Reich and Annie finally divorced in 1934, after several years of intense estrangement and two years after he met the woman who may well have been the love of his life, Elsa Lindenberg, his only "Aryan" wife (to use his language). Like his first marriage, his second was fraught with sexual tension, although Elsa was closer to him on the matter of political activity and *Sexpol* work than Annie was. It is significant that Reich placed a photograph of Elsa in his study at Orgonon long after the marriage was over. Elsa was an absolutely stunning beauty who at that time (the 1930s) made her living as a dancer in serious theater. Reich met her on May Day in Berlin in 1932. They became intimate while Reich was still married to Annie.

In the American period, from August 19, 1939, until his death in 1957, Reich probed into such phenomena as weather formations, flying saucers, a new kind of naturalistic mysticism, and issues in cosmology and atomic physics. It is a frightening fact that soon after his arrival here, he was arrested and imprisoned on Ellis Island on the grounds that he might be a German spy and might harbor un-American sentiments. He was freed after some high-level pressure from well-placed friends, but the experience deeply colored his subsequent feelings about the government and American life. He also had an important encounter with Albert Einstein in the winter of 1941 that has left more questions open as to the nature of orgone than, I would argue, Einstein cared to pursue. In his letter to Einstein of February 20, 1941, Reich clarified his position and defended his experimental results concerning the unique thermal properties of the orgone accumulator. Einstein did not reply to this letter, which can be interpreted in any of several ways: (1) he was too busy; (2) he was genuinely vexed by its implications; or (3) his personal secretary didn't pass it on to him. On May 1 and 17 Reich wrote follow-up letters to Einstein that also went unanswered. This rejection by Einstein, while bitter, did not deter Reich from positing a thermodynamic anomaly of the accumulator in his subsequent writings. The primary counterfactual phenomenon that he tried to point out to Einstein was that the temperature inside the accumulator remained higher than the ambient temperature, which classical thermodynamics ruled out.

The political situation in 1933 Berlin soon became untenable for Reich. In the words of Mary Boyd Higgins, Reich found himself in an extremely precarious position because of his public notoriety vis-à-vis the *Sexpol* movement, which advocated birth control, legalized abortion, and civil rights for homosexuals:

> On 28 February 1933, he returned to Berlin from a trip to Copenhagen, where he had lectured on race and fascism to a Danish student organization. That night the Reichstag was burned. He only escaped immediate arrest because he had not held an official position. But soon afterward, a newspaper article on his youth book [*The Sexual Struggle of Youth*, 1932] appeared and he had to leave Germany. He returned to Vienna, where he found little understanding of the German disaster and increasing personal hostility from his psychoanalytic colleagues.[1]

Vienna held no further prospects for him either, so he was forced in a few months to move to Copenhagen (at the invitation from some analytic friends and admirers), where he established himself as a teacher of analysts rather than as a therapist working with patients. As noted previously, he came into direct conflict with the Danish authorities, who suspected the sexual aspects of his work, and with the Danish Communist Party, to which he never officially belonged, for his renegade Marxism. Because of these twin pressures, especially the government's cancellation of his visa, he moved with his new wife, Elsa, in September 1933 to Malmö, Sweden, where he continued his research and continued to function as a training analyst. Yet once again the gossip mill got stirred up, and he was tarred by some Swedish analysts and spied upon by the Swedish government. One rumor had it that he and Elsa, allegedly not his legal wife, were running a brothel in town and that Reich was engaged in strange sex experiments with his students. In June 1934 the Swedish government canceled Reich's residency and work permit, and he was forced to return to Denmark under an assumed name.

At the end of the 1934 summer season, Reich and Elsa moved to Oslo, where he had a number of supporters. He was given access to the University of Oslo's research facilities and quickly established his own laboratory where he could study the bioelectrical aspects of sexuality and later pursue his growing interest in bions and cancer cells. He was deeply in love with Elsa; his children were under the protection of their mother, Annie, first in Vienna and then later in Prague. His experimental research marked a new departure for him, although its main outlines had been worked out theoretically in the early 1930s and he was, for the moment, free from the Nazi plague.

But once again the apple in the garden of paradise became riddled with worms, this time in the form of an intense vilification campaign mounted against him in the leading Norwegian newspapers, the editors of which merely revised the old rumors from Denmark and Sweden; former analytic friends now willingly betrayed Reich to the press. Later his third wife gave this account of the period: "The campaign lasted from September 1937 through November 1938, comprising more than a hundred articles in Norway's leading newspapers, and running the gamut from 'the quackery of psychoanalysis' and 'the Jewish pornographer,' to 'God Reich creates life.'"[2] At the same time he was surrounded by a small and loyal band of fellow researchers who were convinced that a unique form of energy (soon to be called orgone) existed and that it was somehow connected with the orgasm. The net effect of the smear campaign, however, was to force Reich into a highly introverted attitude in which he would rarely appear on the streets of Oslo for fear of being spotted and stared at as if he were some kind of bizarre oddity. This fear of public ridicule became so intense that he refused to go to restaurants during his final six weeks in Oslo and preferred to eat beans and franks in the apartment of a friend.

Even some of his friends began to have problems with dimensions of Reich's personality and with his tendency, they argued, to develop an uncritical cultlike following among his fellow researchers. The Norwegian psychiatrist Nic Waal, who worked with Reich both in Vienna and in Oslo, made this assessment of Reich in 1958:

> It seems to me that his published papers often lacked objectivity. They often attacked other schools of thinking and were lacking both scientific proofs and scientific language. The [Oslo] group seemed to become rigid and unwilling to co-operate under pressure of attack. The group thereby missed perceptions of new ideas and directions and could not follow the new developments in other schools of thinking. This made for isolation.[3]

Her comment, in an otherwise appreciative memorial essay, points to the constant stream of criticism that followed Reich from his post-Vienna days. But the worst criticisms came in Norway and the United States, precisely when Reich had begun to show the results of his new functional science of orgone energy.

His letters and journals from this period reflected his growing concern with fascism (the *full* nature of which the Norwegians did not grasp until far too late); the extreme thrill he experienced over the direction of his work; some strong hints of psychic inflation; his conflicted attitude toward Annie and his children, Eva and Lore; his growing infatuation yet ambivalence toward Elsa; and his strong desire to reach out to the academic communities of Europe and America. What is especially important for our psychbiography are the signs of Reich's growing psychic inflation that marked a reaction against the hostility of the world and also something more primal, more disruptive of his psychic structures. My belief is that during the Scandinavian period, in which the hostility of the professional world was at its most intense, Reich could no longer hold back his native tendencies toward inflation. Would he have been so inflated had the external hostility not been there? My sense is that he still would have been inflated but to a lesser extent. My further sense is that the very energies that he was probing in the laboratory were destabilizing per se and that his ego was decentered because of the onrush of bioelectric energy. One reason for my use of the term *displacement* in the title of this chapter is that I wish to steer clear of the more sterile term *exile*, which denotes a mere physical and geographical displacement. The fuller term *displacement* encompasses ideas of psychic decentering, the changing of the ego/id ratio, and the tendency toward psychic inflation, especially during highly energized transition periods.

Specifically, how was Reich's psychic inflation manifest in this period, and how did it relate to the larger issue of displacement? In a letter to Annie written on November 17, 1934, Reich positioned himself as a savior of science who has been misunderstood to be a "psychopath":

I am not a megalomaniac, I just have agonizingly good intuition; I sense most things before I actually comprehend them. And the most important "intuitions" usually turn out to be correct, like the belief I expressed in Seefeld in 1923 that an erection is identical with the reaching out of a pseudopod, that anxiety is a retreat into oneself. Now, eleven years later, a whole new area of physiology revolves around that. You will be reassured to know that this has been confirmed to me by a physiologist.[4]

Reich may have been engaging in a bit of bravado before the woman whom he had rejected, but a number of other letters and journal entries show how strongly psychic inflation had begun to entwine itself with Reich's dramatic attempt to rewrite his relationship to the history not just of psychoanalytic science but of science as a whole. He became increasingly interested in the issue of martyrdom, a trait he had noted in himself at the time of the death of his mother. He was especially fascinated with such victims of the emotional plague as Galileo, Kepler, Bruno, and Jesus, and he began to see himself as belonging to their lineage, with an expected martyr's fate awaiting him.

He was not always aware, I suspect, of the powerful influence he often had on analysands and was not fully in tune with the scope and power of his countertransferences. But he noted how others saw him in this regard,

writing again to Annie on February 26, 1935: "In addition, I now realize
that people are simply afraid of me because I am 'too seductive.'"[5] His
seductive powers enabled him to hold analysands and analysts in the
transference bond long enough for their character armor to become de-
rigidified.

Two dreams from this period—the first a daydream, the second nocturnal—have special pertinence to the theme of psychic inflation and his
need to compensate for his perceived failures in the public scientific and
academic worlds. Reich's friend August Lange recorded the daydream
during their 1936 Easter vacation together in the Norwegian mountains.
Lange later reminisced about the trip:

> When we were in the chalet in the mountains, Willy loved to hear
> Ravel's "Bolero." Once, after the record had been played, he told
> us about a dream he had for the future: He saw himself riding into
> Berlin as a triumphant knight mounted on a white horse, while the
> band played Ravel's "Bolero."—I was astonished that a man like
> Willy could have such a naïve daydream, and at the same time I
> admired that he was not afraid of telling us about it![6]

Obviously we see here a straightforward expression of Jung's hero myth,
with the dream ego playing the role of the social redeemer in the midst of
impending chaos. The hero riding the shining white steed into the corrupt
city brings the light of awareness into the darker places of the emotional
plague. Ravel's "Bolero" conveys the slow but unrelenting emergence of
sexual potency and is a perfect complement to Reich's version of the hero
myth—that is, the hero as the fully genital character who can awaken sexual potency in the prostrated masses. He is a gallant knight, perhaps still
mired in the patriarchal courtly tradition, but fully seen in his shining
forth (clearly a narcissistic-exhibitionist moment, or a manifestation of
the phallic-narcissistic character in Reich). Lange pointed out how simplistic this daydream was, but other things were afoot in Reich's unconscious during his Scandinavian period.

In the second dream, a true nocturnal product of the unconscious,
Reich presented striking symbols that manifested a manic compensation
for his unhappily restricted place in the social world of Oslo. He recorded
the dream in his journal on March 18, 1939:

Had a dream: I was an express train rushing over wide plains night and day. Stars above me, thundering earth beneath me. Occasionally I stopped at stations. Passengers got off, others got on. Some traveled for a long distance, some took only short trips. Again and again the train stopped, people got on, others got off. Many of them were motion-sick because of the terrific speed. I came from far away and rushed headlong into the unknown, through the world, with no certain destination.[7]

Reich gave no interpretation of this striking dream. Needless to say, one can approach it in several ways. Was it an expression of phallic-narcissistic power, namely that the psyche *was* a great, almost unearthly locomotive? Was it a cry of despair over the fact that people forced the locomotive to stop, getting on and off at will, and that many were not up to the ride at "terrific speed"? Was it an anxiety dream focused on the fact of "rushing headlong into the unknown," with no governing framework or map to guide the way? I want to suggest that all of these are pertinent and useful interpretations but that a deeper one is also called forth from the phenomenon of the dream itself.

If Jung is right that all dreams are to some degree proleptic—that is, they predict a possible tendency that the psyche could take in the future—then this dream, I would argue, points toward the threat of manic overcompensation for a stasis anxiety as well as toward a response to the hostility of the external world. In the former prospect, the dream is presenting Reich's conscious ego with the possibility that there is great phallic power still left in his psyche, especially as his analogical identification is with a locomotive that spews forth great clouds of white and black smoke. At the heart of the locomotive is a powerful steam boiler that drives the pistons and the drive shaft, while the power behind the expanding gas in the boiler comes from the fiery red coal that intensifies the molecular momentum of the water. The visceral sensation of *being* a great locomotive must have been remarkable during the dream experience itself (after all, Reich recorded very few of his dreams, and this one made it into his journals).

In the second prospect, the dream is a clear expression of his sense of displacement in the world. While as a train he must go down prelaid tracks, there seems to be no preestablished guide-plan governing the lo-

comotive/track relationship. He must move at terrific speed in his own
measure against the clinging powers of a negating world. If the world rejects him, he rushes on to the next station. But the dreamer/locomotive is
always in control in its own way and will not let the external world arrest
its headlong rush into the unknown.

While privileging one daydream and one nocturnal dream hardly represents a good *inductive* analytic strategy, it at least gives us two brief
glimpses into Reich's internal psychic career in the mid- to late 1930s.
These dreams are certainly not random ejecta from the unconscious.
Their content is fully consistent with all of the rest of the biographical and
autobiographical material that we have probed thus far. They are semiotic
markers, filled with thirdness, of Reich's own struggles with potency and
professional rejection. Clearly, external rejection is internally related to
the sense of potency, and Reich's dream material reflects this psychic
connection. To say that Reich had some stasis anxiety of his own to wrestle with is merely to recognize that part of his brilliant diagnostic and taxonomic gifts came from his unconscious projection of inner conflicts. For
me this is a necessary condition for theoretical work in psychoanalysis
and orgonomic functionalism.

Returning to the more external saga, Annie too felt the growing pressures of fascism while living in Prague with Eva and Lore and her new
husband. She was able to move to the United States with her family, ar-
riving on July 21, 1938. But she also fanned flames of conflict between
Reich and his daughter Eva, having the view that Reich's liberal conceptions of childhood sexuality had hurt Eva's development into adolescence. This was a point over which Annie and Reich had fought bitterly
in earlier years. But once in America, five weeks after their arrival, Eva
reached out to her father by sending him a heartfelt letter. In the words of
Reich's student and biographer Myron Sharaf, "However, Eva was wor-
ried that she had 'lost' Reich because she had been unwilling to visit him
before leaving Europe. She still found it difficult 'for me to be quite honest with you.'"[8] After some awkward attempts on Reich's part to reestab-
lish parental contact, he and Eva became more fully reconciled.

Toward the end of May 1939 Reich expressed both his feelings about
his lowly worldly status and his extreme confidence concerning his lasting scientific discoveries. The journal entry from the twenty-third of the

month represented a very concise self-analysis of what he thought he had achieved to date:

> I am sitting in a completely empty apartment waiting for my American visa. I have misgivings as to how it will go. I have lost faith in pushing things through rapidly.
>
> I am utterly and horribly alone!
>
> It will be quite an undertaking to carry on all the work in America. Essentially I am a great man, a rarity, as it were. I can't quite believe it myself, however, and that is why I struggle against playing the role of a great man. What have I discovered?

> 1. The function of the orgasm
> 2. Character armoring
> 3. The life formula
> 4. The bions
> 5. The electrical function of sexuality
> 6. Orgone radiation
> 7. The processes involved in cancer formation
> 8. The processes involved in rheumatism
> 9. The processes involved in schizophrenia, including the organic causes of neuroses
> 10. The sociology of sexual repression
> 11. The dynamics of fascism
> 12. The spinning-wave theory[9]

I would agree with Reich that he had successfully established at least the pragmatic truth of numbers 1, 2, 5, 9, 10, and 11. Further, there is at least some phenomenological, perhaps even inductive, evidence for numbers 3 and 6. Numbers 4, 7, 8, and 12 require far more justification, although I do not assume that his claims in these four assertions are *necessarily* false. I have noted that some serious and qualified researchers have (in their lights) replicated Reich's bion experiments and have insisted that most of these data are fully replicable by others should they take the trouble.[10] Clearly the cancer theory remains the weakest link in the chain, but *if* the bion theory has any validity, then the cancer theory bears further probing. Finally, I have noted my own tentative sense that something like orgone exists and that the ramification of this concept and its claimed empirical details will probably come from the biological sciences rather than from physics, although physical theory may someday evolve in this direction.

At this point I want to put direct biographical reflections on hold, since they will appear indirectly in the theoretical analyses and will return explicitly at the end of this chapter. For our focus here I have selected the crucial 1941 letter to Einstein, four essays, and four short books. Two of these books, written mostly in English, represent what I have been calling Reich's universalistic ecstatic naturalist religion: *Ether, God and Devil* (1949) and *Cosmic Superimposition* (1951). Finally, in a more psychobiographical vein, I will analyze his 1946 *Listen, Little Man!* (published in 1948) and his 1953 *The Murder of Christ*. These works do not cover all of Reich's astonishing output during the period from the mid-1930s until the mid-1950s, but I am persuaded that they are the most pertinent material and that much of the other material represents an alternative way of saying many of the same things. For example, Reich's 1947 version of *The Function of the Orgasm* contains very little that we have not already examined at some length, although it is well worth reading in its own right. The chapter will conclude with some final biographical analyses, with particular attention to Reich's struggles against the Federal Food and Drug Administration, about which much more is now known.

Reich's encounter with Einstein has been the source of fascination for many scholars, perhaps because of what it *didn't* accomplish. Reich carried one of his orgonoscopes down from his house in Forest Hills, New York (in Queens), to Princeton so that Einstein could see with his own eyes the evidence that Reich claimed he had found for a unique kind of energy—an energy that, once established, Reich held, would overturn all of the then current theories about matter and energy. On a second visit to Princeton two weeks later, Reich took Einstein an orgone accumulator. Evidently Reich did not think that he had explained his conception of orgone energy well enough on that second visit, especially in the light of criticisms from one of Einstein's assistants, who came up with the theory that the real temperature differences came from convection currents in the room. So four days after their meeting he wrote a long letter that detailed his research methods. To validate his claim that the temperature inside the accumulator was higher than the ambient temperature and that a heretofore unknown type of radiation inside the box was responsible for the variation, he explained how he had placed his accumulators in a variety of situations: aboveground, underground, partially underground, wrapped in a blanket, freestanding without a blanket, and so forth, thereby countering the argument that convection currents were involved.

Reich's orgone accumulator consists of a box of almost any workable size (from a shoebox to a medium-size room) that is constructed with alternating layers of such organic and metallic material as fiberglass and steel wool, designed to reflect and deflect orgone energy toward the center of the box. In each case Reich found that the temperature deviation from classical theory was clear and that he had isolated any and all possible external variables that could have contaminated the experiment. The difference in temperature between inner and outer was found to be 0.9 degrees centigrade. Reich's conclusion, as written to Einstein: *"The original arrangement of the apparatus results, under all circumstances, in a temperature difference between the thermometer in the box and the control thermometer, in the absence of any known kind of constant heat source."*[11]

The orgone accumulator intensified *something* that classical physics did not account for. This new form of massless energy not only had thermal properties, or at least thermal manifestations, but also extended outside the accumulator; that is, it was manifest in the world with as much scope as electromagnetic energy, which includes light, heat, magnetism, electricity, and all other forms of radiant energy (such as gamma and X rays). So far as we know, Einstein was satisfied that the thermal variation inside the accumulator could be accounted for by a reexamination of the measuring process itself. He saw flaws in procedure and in the placement of the accumulator in what was most likely a drafty environment. By eliminating any possible draft and by having more refined measurements, one could explain the alleged temperature difference produced by the control (external) versus the internal thermometer. But Reich had a ready answer to these two criticisms and showed in some detail that he was fully aware of any unwanted variables in his derivation of his sensitive data.

Reich pushed further in his letter to Einstein, insisting that orgone was indeed the long-sought life energy itself, responsible for the internal and external dynamics of all growing systems.

> In the *atmosphere*, in the *soil*, and in the *living organism* there exists a type of energy which acts in a specifically biologically way and which I have called "orgone." With the aid of the orgonoscope, this energy is visible as scintillation in the atmosphere and in the soil as well as on bushes (in the summer); it can be measured electroscopically and thermally, and it can be concentrated through a specific arrangement of materials. Several pieces of photographic proof exist, but they have not yet been separated out in unambiguous fashion from the control results. Photographs taken with Kodachrome film show the color *blue* or *blue-gray*, and this is also how the radiation appears subjectively to the viewer.[12]

The orgonoscope visualized orgone energy as visible wave patterns, as measurable as the thermal properties of orgone. The color manifested by orgone in the human visual spectrum could be seen photographically and by the unaided eye. Thus in 1941 Reich argued that orgone, while not strictly part of the electromagnetic spectrum, had properties that could be measured through instruments that normally functioned to quantify electromagnetic traits. Orgone, Reich asserted, could be seen and felt, with and without instrumentation.

In his research during this period (early 1940s), Reich speculated that orgone might even counteract the effects of gravity—that is, make a given organism lighter in weight. Hence orgone in that case not only would be without mass, it would be almost like an antimatter or antigravity force field. In a note of October 7, 1940, Reich asked: "Does orgone charge actually make something lighter—i.e., does it overcome gravity (weight)? I am afraid to think of it, but I must consider all eventualities. If it is not the direct radiation pressure, then it must be an energy which works against gravity."[13] The conceptually and empirically difficult problem is determining which traits of orgone are definitely not electromagnetic, while at the same time demarcating those that are either electromagnetic or are at least causally connected to electromagnetic phenomena. To Einstein he stated: "The relationship of orgone energy to electromagnetic energy is very unclear. According to preliminary observations, it seems to work in the same direction of magnetic force and at a right angle to electrical force."[14] Here Reich posited a causal connection between orgone and both electricity and magnetism, inferring that whatever orgone is, it cannot be of a completely different nature from electromagnetism. And yet it was not a reality that could be brought under the umbrella of known electromagnetic phenomena and their laws.

The Einstein letter, and the psychological currents it stirred in Reich, represented a frustrating attempt to enter into the public academic world of physics. Three years after his letters to Einstein he defended himself in what he called the "Einstein affair" by claiming that Einstein had not followed proper experimental procedure in trying to replicate Reich's original proof of the temperature difference inside and outside the accumulator. He further argued that Einstein was fully aware that he (Reich) was right but that he did not have the courage to accept the full implications of the orgone theory for his own research. In a letter of February 18, 1944, to his friend and early translator Theodore P. Wolfe, Reich stated: "I found the fact that my letter and subsequent reports were not answered so impossible to understand, and the thought that Einstein could act irrationally was so repugnant to me, that I consciously and with considerable effort rejected any possibility of this being the case [that he had misunderstood the orgone theory and evidence]."[15] For Reich, Einstein's refusal to affirm him in public for personal and professional reasons spoke volumes about Einstein's failures as a person and a physicist and, indirectly, about how conformism can affect even high-level science.

His ultimate defense of his research vis-à-vis Einstein's was that he was working out of a new discipline that he called "functional astrophysics," as opposed to the older "mechanical astrophysics." In functional astrophysics it was possible to develop a unified theory that combined the insights of the biological sciences with those of a more radical physics of energy fields. He finally decided that Einstein had protected himself from the new functional universe and was living in a form of denial: "It was understandable that Einstein did not want to contribute to the collapse of his life's work, although this would have been demanded by strict scientific objectivity . . . It is possible that Einstein underestimated the scope of my discovery and its consequences."[16] Thus Einstein understood what was going on with orgone but failed to see its full dimensionality and did not live out the ethical imperative of all scientists: namely, to probe into nature regardless of the impact on a preestablished paradigm. It did occur to Reich that Einstein might have had nontainted reasons for rejecting the orgone theory and its real or alleged existence.

Reich's close collaborator and loyal friend, the Norwegian Ola Raknes, gave his own reasons as to why other scientists found it so difficult to accept that orgone existed, in spite of what could be counted as evidence. While studying with Reich in Oslo on bions and orgone, Raknes was in a position to see the negative responses to this research at first hand:

> Several factors combine to account for the difficulty in discovering the orgone energy and also for the resistance against accepting the discovery once made. The ubiquity of this energy, its presence in every happening, made it difficult to isolate as a separate entity. The impossibility of bringing it under exact measure made it refractory to scientific research, as western science hesitates to recognize as facts what cannot be weighed or measured. And finally emotional factors will make obstacles to the acceptance of the discovery: first of all the reluctance to recognize that one's emotions, thoughts, and actions are in part motivated by unknown forces; second, that the existence of a ubiquitous universal energy, when once discovered, must of necessity raise a number of problems in every field of human knowledge and experience, as this energy—in its primordial form or as other energies derived from it—enters into every happening, be it action or sensation or emotion or thinking or non-human event.[17]

Put in epistemological terms: how can we know something that has no real contrast term or reality? If everything whatsoever in the universe is and/or manifests orgone, then how orgone is isolated and defined experimentally and theoretically becomes a special problem. In this sense, Raknes was correct, but Reich was able to find contrast terms of lesser scope—for example, the tension between orgone and gravity, or between orgone and ambient air temperature. That something is ubiquitous does not strictly require that it be unknowable, although it does entail that all knowledge claims must be made with special attention to a different form of contrast from that between equal and finite polar opposites (like the north and south poles of a magnet). The fact that orgone is *in* everything doesn't mean that *what* it is in has no traits of its own that are nonorgonic.

We move on to examine a series of four brilliant papers entitled "Orgonotic Pulsation," now available in the journal *Orgonomic Functionalism: A Journal Devoted to the Work of Wilhelm Reich*. The papers were written in the period 1939–44 and together constitute a succinct statement both of Reich's bioelectrical researches in Europe and of his orgonomic theories as developed in America. In these four essays Reich used the device of a fictional dialogue between an *electrophysicist*, represented as E, and an *orgone biophysicist*, represented as O. The tone of the dialogue is that of a congenial pairing of two honest researchers, both of whom are sensitive to any counterexamples or disconfirming evidence to the orgone biophysicist's claims about his experimental results and their conceptual implications. Reich started the essays with issues involved in biology and then moved on to a discussion of the inorganic sphere and the nature of electromagnetic energy vis-à-vis orgone energy. By the time he finished the fourth essay/dialogue, he had prepared the groundwork for a cosmic theory of orgone and the prospect of a universal "religion" that would be sustained by a full-blown cosmology encompassing everything from the origins of life to the fundamental structures of astrophysical events. Philosophically his cosmology presented a form of intense, even ecstatic vitalism, functionally based, that opened up a radical naturalism. In the sense I am using here, any naturalistic perspective will assert that nature is all that there is and that there is nothing discontinuous with nature. But a *radical* naturalist will go a step further and also assert that the "one" nature manifests (and is) a deep pulsating energy that spawns new life out of itself—that is, nature is conceptually expressed by Spinoza's notion of *natura naturans* (nature naturing) or nature creating nature out of itself alone. Also, very much like William James in his *A Pluralistic Universe* (1909), Reich expressed his belief in swirling centers of vitality that occur in a variety of forms throughout the physical, biological, and astrophysical orders.[18] This new and radical naturalism was fully continuous with Reich's earlier psychoanalytic work and represented the next stage in the process of developing a therapy for pathology, in the personal, social, and even ecological orders.

In the first essay Reich, functioning as O, stated his primary thesis about the nature of orgonomic science and its grounding belief structures.

It is clear that he had come to these conclusions after many years of research and after walking down many false trails (what Heidegger called
Holzwege, or forest paths ending nowhere):

> First, [orgone biophysics] assumes the existence of fluid transi-
> tions from the realm of nonliving to that of living nature. Second, it
> dispenses, of necessity, with the mechanistic physical conception
> of living processes. It demonstrates a specific biological energy
> which governs all living processes on the basis of simple natural
> laws. This energy, called orgone, governs living as well as purely
> mechanical natural processes. The functions of this energy make
> comprehensible the manner in which living matter develops from
> nonliving matter, that is, the process of biogenesis.[19]

Reich crossed a great deal of conceptual ground in this utterance of O,
combining a cosmology of biogenesis with a functional metaphysics that
refused to become either mechanistic or materialistic. He refined his
metaphysics further by rejecting any kind of monism that would speak of
two modes of reality, mental and physical. Rather, there was an evolutionary continuum that moved fluidly from less mobile orgone to what
Plato might call self-moving orgone, as expressed in the human psyche.
A functional approach, like the monistic, is antidualistic, but *un*like
monism, functionalism does not posit an underlying static substance. Orgone is neither static nor a substance. The one predicate that Reich assigned to it over and over again was that of pulsation (hence the title of
these four dialogues). Instead of saying that orgone radiated or that it
flowed along a conducting substance, Reich argued that it pulsated without regard to an originating physical source. More precisely, orgone was
indeed tied to objects, persons, structures, and events, but it was not dependent upon them for its existence. Electromagnetic energy required
some separate source—say, a dense iron mass for magnetism, or a propa-
gating force field for electricity or radio waves. Orgone, as we shall see,
was actually the *ground phenomenon* for all more dependent forms of
electromagnetism and even for gravity itself. In his own way Reich was
struggling toward a grand unified theory of the weak and strong nuclear
forces (as in the Oranur experiment, which tested the effects of orgone on
radioactive uranium), and those of electromagnetism and gravity as well.

Of course, Reich wanted to show the continuity between his work in the early 1930s with his later work in bioenergetics and orgone biophysics. As noted, he had started his serious electrical experiments on the human body while in Oslo. The basic experiment involved placing electrodes on various parts of the body (tongue, nipples) and then measuring any change in electrical potential at the skin surface during and after sexual excitement. The results were positive for the claim that there was a direct causal relationship between sexual excitation and an increase in measurable electrical potential along the surfaces of the selected body areas. Anxiety proved to be measurable by the same method, but the directionality of the electrical flow was in the opposite direction, namely, away from the periphery toward the center. The fluctuations in electrical potential were from a few millivolts (mv), around 2, to 20 mv. A decrease in the skin-surface potential was measured in depression or anxiety, in which orgone (to use the later term) returned to the center of the body and left the periphery, where it would be present in the sexual function. Thus the anxious or depressed subject would lose mv from the skin surface in the course of the experiment, while the sexually excited would gain mv at the skin surface until the climax and then manifest a rapid drop-off of mv. Reich did not measure climax during intercourse, but rather climax in masturbation.

The connection between this research into the mv expressions of bioelectric energy and the earlier *Sexpol* work lay in the analysis of the intensity of the emotions as they in turn correlated to bioelectrical energy. Emotions *could* be quantified insofar as they had bioelectric manifestations:

Sex-economy occupied itself for a decade and a half with the vast field of psychic *emotions* before it made an important biophysical discovery: *The intensity of the sensations of pleasure, anxiety, and rage, that is, of the three basic emotions of any animal organism, was shown at the oscillograph, to be functionally identical with the quantity of the biological excitation in the vital apparatus.*[20]

Emotions, as manifestations of orgone, were thus energy systems in their own right and could have an intimate relationship to the body. Hence, the phenomenon of armoring must be manifest both in the emotions and in their corresponding muscular structures. We recall that Reich blamed Freud's jaw cancer on his muscular rigidity in the throat area—namely, his tendency to swallow his anger rather than to express it and thus relieve the orgonotic pressure. Anger and its suppression presented in the armoring of the second armor ring, that of the oral area. There was thus a continuum, with quantifiable and functional aspects, that connected psyche and soma. The immediate clinical observation of armoring (through the study of the body by mere observation or by some manipulation/palpation) could now be augmented with a bioelectrical measurement of anxiety and sexuality that revealed the flow of orgonotic pulsation from the center to the periphery and back again. Therapeutically, this represented a quantum leap forward.

The interlocutor O pushed ahead and enunciated his so-called "four-beat" formula. It is a description of the four stages that living matter goes through in a typical sexual cycle. At the same time, the four-beat movement "does not exist in nonliving matter."[21] For Reich this formula had the status of a natural law, like Newton's laws of motion or Darwin's principles of random variation and natural selection. O stated:

> The simultaneous identity and antithesis of living and nonliving matter is most easily demonstrated in the orgone-biophysical formula of living functioning. It is the basic formula of biological pulsation: MECHANICAL TENSION→ ENERGY CHARGE→ ENERGY DISCHARGE→ MECHANICAL RELAXATION. It applies to the pulsation of the heart as well as to the motion of the worm or the contraction of the vorticella.[22]

All living things, no matter how simple or how complex, went through this four-stage process of starting from a kind of sexual stasis (energy equilibrium), moving to a buildup of mechanical tension (which could be chemical or muscular), then to a parallel buildup of electrical charge, which in turn became discharged in coitus or its analogue, finally producing a relaxation of the mechanical apparatus with a return to a kind of sexual stasis. Using *this* formula, psychopathology would be redefined as any event or armoring that disrupted the free movement of the four-beat cycle. On the human level, whenever an analysand was blocked at the discharge moment, there would be a manifestation of castration anxiety, or fear of melting in the impending discharge, or a fear of bursting or of dying, or the reaction formation of sadism. At the other extreme, the Don Juan or nymphomaniac would go through the four-beat cycle without experiencing the depth structures that should be experienced in each beat. This would produce the well-known feeling of ennui in the sexual addict.

In a conceptual move very reminiscent of the Plato of the *Symposium* and *Phaedrus*, Reich argued that sexual attraction and desire are not those principles held to be primary by physics (which remained mechanistic) but are the underlying principles of the cosmos. Psychiatry had to be the place where the depth truth of the universe emerged, precisely because it worked in the sphere where bioelectric energy interwove with sexual desire:

> Does it not seem logical now that the discovery of the biological energy took place not in the realm of chemistry or physics, but in the realm of biopsychiatry? The guiding principle was not the functioning of the Diesel engine, but the *pulsation* of the heart, of a vacuole, or a protozoon. It was not the chemical compound, but sexual attraction, not the X-ray, but emotional excitation, not the flight of an airplane, but the flight of a bird or the movements of a fish, not the motion of an engine piston, but orgastic contraction, or the contraction of growth in the embryo.[23]

From this it followed, at least for Reich, that fellow researchers were oblivious to orgone energy because they were trapped in a metaphysics that was dualistic and mechanistic. The dualism expressed itself in the posited divide between the worlds of biology and physics, while the mechanism expressed itself in the use of analogies from machines rather than from nature in its more primal dimensions. The radicalness of Reich's naturalism drove him to probe into the nonmechanistic fundamental traits of the sexually striving universe. At the very least, one must appreciate the grand mythopoetic cosmic vision that was emerging from Reich's typewriter in the 1940s.

As his bioelectrical researches continued to unfold, Reich ran into some knotty problems over the differences between orgone energy and the well-known behavior of electromagnetic energy. One of his most pertinent discoveries was that this new living energy did not function through positive and negative polarities. Obviously, two positive magnetic poles will repel each other, while a positive and a negative magnetic pole placed together will attract each other. At the same time Reich was led to the conclusion that orgone energy moved in a slow wavelike fashion rather than in the rapid angular way that electricity functioned. Hence orgone was a wave pulsation that did not divide into polarities, although it would manifest synergistically and antagonistically. The antagonistic functionality of orgone was not, however, polar but dialectic, moving from stasis to expression and back again. From Reich's perspective, the polarity phenomena of electromagnetism were less primal than the dialectical waves of orgone. Or we could say that electromagnetic phenomena were species of the genus orgone and that their species-specific behavior was not fully pertinent to the genus.

One of the first concrescences of orgone was, as noted, the so-called bions that emerged in the transition from the inorganic to the organic. Bions could be produced by heating such things as beach sand, or through the process of organic decay. However they were generated, bions had very specific traits, besides being in the size range of bacteria, the smallest prokaryotic one-celled organisms.

> After having been made to swell [substances that produced bions], . . . the same substances show, particularly in the dark-field, a vesicular structure. The vesicles [bions] detach themselves. If viewed with apochromatic lenses, at a magnification of 3–5000x, their content appears blue or blue-green. The substances of origin, however, show their own color: coal appears black, iron blackish brown, etc. Every substance which has been made to swell and every living substance shows these two characteristics: *bionous, vesicular structure* and *blue-green* content.

> (E). At what stage do the pulsatory movements occur?
> (O). *When the membrane of the bion has become thin enough to yield to the internal impulse to expansion and contraction.*[24]

As one of the primary manifestations of orgone in action, bions exhibit traits that will be found in other forms of orgone. In place of positive and negative poles or charges, we see the "impulse to expansion and contraction," of which one manifestation is the flow of blood in the genitals before, during, and after coitus. The color of the bions happens to be the color of all forms of orgonotic pulsation. In his Forest Hills house, where he had set up a basement laboratory, as earlier in Oslo, Reich spent many hours alone in the dark to find out if he could see orgone directly—that is, without its form of concrescence in the bions (which required up to 5,000x magnification). After several hours he suddenly noticed that his entire body was surrounded by a blue–to–bluish gray vapor field of orgone (much like the aura as it has been analyzed in the Hindu traditions).[25] Later he became increasingly sensitive to manifestations of orgone in the atmosphere and even in deep space.

Thus far we have seen that orgone is, in Reich's account: (1) a nonpolar movement of expansion and contraction, (2) a wavelike pulsation rather than an angular and rapid propagation from a source, (3) the foundation of electricity and magnetism, (4) the inner pulsation of all living and nonliving things, (5) manifest in a blue-green wavelength, (6) found throughout the cosmos, and (7) potentially curative in its powers (as will be concretized in the orgone accumulator and orgone blanket). In the bionic sphere some bions will contain more orgone and some less. Those bions with the least amount of orgonotic charge (which is analogous to but not the same as electrical charge) can form into T-bacilli, which can cause bionous decay in their surrounding environment, leading ultimately to cancer.

Further phenomenological refinements followed from these initial forays into orgonotic pulsations. After much observation of orogne and its variations, Reich discovered that orgone was manifest in three different color fields. The first was that of blue-gray vapors (which can be seen in an orgone chamber after about twenty minutes), the second was that of blue-violet dots, while the third was that of straight yellowish rays. Vapors were the more obvious field phenomena that fluctuated through the entire environment, while dots were more intense manifestations within a localized visual field, and yellow lines were clearly, like the dots, more condensed versions of the vapors. Whatever the reader makes of this "phenomenological" evidence for three visual manifestations of orgone, it *is* something that can be seen under appropriate conditions. Obviously the vapors, dots, and lines could be internal optical phenomena, a kind of flotsam and jetsam of the optical nerve. But I am willing to say that the evidence points in the other direction—namely, that there is something both internal and external that has the features of pulsation and coloration.[26] For example, sunglasses actually dim the appearances of these optical phenomena while the use of magnifying glasses enlarges them.

Moving on to the second essay/dialogue in the series, Reich pushed the orgone theory into richer generic terrain by talking more and more about its cosmic status. Certainly orgone interacted with electricity and magnetism and might even be correlated in some way with gravity, which, of course, entails mass. Was there a way of converting orgone theory into a theory of mass and gravitation? Could Reich reground Newton and Einstein in a larger orgonotic gravity theory? Here one has to be much more cautious. Gravity is still difficult to analyze and may consist of waves of a very special nature. But if orgone is wavelike in its own special way, then there may be at least some family resemblances between one way of understanding gravity and Reich's understanding of orgone.

At the very least, if one follows Reich's presuppositions, one concludes that orgone is the life energy in all organic forms. But Reich, as a radical naturalist, utterly rejected the notion that orgone was a force that came to nature from a point outside of nature; that is, orgone was not supernatural or in any way connected with a patriarchal conception of deity:

> The specific biological energy does not exist "on the other side"; it is not metaphysical. It exists physically in the atmosphere and is demonstrable visually, thermically, and electroscopically. It functions biologically in the soil and in the living organism. There is a continual process of energy metabolism between the purely physical and the biological form of the orgone, significantly in the respiration of plants and animals.[27]

What I find especially interesting here is the immense problematic facing Reich, of both separating orgone from electromagnetic energy *and* working out the details of the ways in which orgone and electromagnetism must interact. My sense is that had he found himself working in a less hostile environment, one in which he could sit side by side with biologists and physicists on a daily basis, he and the team would have been able to work through this highly complex set of correlations. Yet again I will assert that in the future of even electromagnetic theory, some fundamental shifts may occur that will bring Reich's perspective, however underdeveloped, into at least dialogue status. So we see here that Reich is struggling with the thermal, visual, and electrical correlations of orgone, thus invoking classical thermodynamics, optical theory, and electromagnetic theory.

In the third essay of the series, Reich distinguished between two basic types of material substance vis-à-vis their respective relationships to the attraction or reflection of orgone: "(O) *Organic substances attract and absorb the orgone. Metallic substances reflect it.*"[28] This basic law of attraction and reflection became the theoretical foundation for the construction of orgone accumulators, in which organic and metallic materials would be layered inside a wooden shell or other nonmetallic material. For example, an accumulator, perhaps in the form of a human-size cabinet, would layer fiberglass with steel wool. This layering would guarantee that orgone would be gathered into a focus in the organic material, and then be reflected into the accumulator by the metallic material.[29] It should be noted that Reich used the term *organic* to refer to all nonmetallic materials.

Reich made a large-order extrapolation in this third essay/dialogue in which he firmly stated that orgone was the ocean within which electromagnetic waves were propagated. Optical phenomena, as electromagnetic phenomena, followed this principle by necessity:

> For the time being, it must be assumed that orgone is the medium in which the electromagnetic waves of light vibrate. This seems a justified hypothesis, not a "wild" one. The motion of radio waves is also to be ascribed to the orgone . . . That orgone is in motion is a definitely established fact. This motion is seen in the flickering in the sky and on objects. Certainly, orgone does not stay still like the water in a puddle. Furthermore, the motion seems to be of the nature of a *rhythmic* pulsation, again reminiscent of the wave. In the orgonoscope, we see moving light particles, and orgone heat is obviously produced by the mechanical retarding of this orgone motion. A good telescope clearly shows the wave-like motion in the orgone ocean at the magnification of as little as 60x.[30]

In the orgonoscope, the visual manifestations described above could be detected by the naked eye, while a telescope could open up the orgone ocean itself, both in galactic space and in deep space. The cosmology emerging here was one that affirmed the supremacy of life energy over the energies of death. The entire universe of space/time was envisioned as an emergent from the prephysical orgone ocean, the true waters of the deep from which creation emerged. Orgone represented the cosmic transition from firstness to thirdness. Reich further developed the evolutionary implications of this model in the 1950s.

In the fourth and final essay/dialogue in this series, Reich brought in the sexual model of his earlier years and applied it again to the orgone theory. He also staked out his claims about the dependency of gravity *on* orgone. It should be noted that throughout these four essays, Reich reported on his laboratory and naturalistic experiments as evidence for his cosmological speculations. In each case he argued that he was compelled to draw the conclusions that he did, about the differences between orgone and other forms of energy, by the ways in which forms of attraction and reflection appeared in his experiments. One striking fact to emerge from his extensive experiments was that orgone phenomena were measurably suppressed when atmospheric conditions were above 50 percent relative humidity.

Sexual attraction stands forth as the major motor force not only for biological systems but for the universe itself. Reich's position is similar to that of the physician Eryximachus in the *Symposium* who, when asked to define love, argued that the basic glue of the universe was *eros*, the energy that brought all things together, especially heaven and earth, the gods and the mortals.[31] While Plato struggled to distance himself from the sexual forms of *eros*, however, Reich privileged the sexual form as foundational *and* normative for all other manifestations of *eros* as orgone:

Biologists are familiar with a fundamental natural phenomenon which, right through to and including the 20th century, remained commonplace yet at the same time uncomprehended and mysterious. I am referring to the overwhelming force of attraction exerted on each other by both sexes throughout the animal and plant kingdoms. This force leads to the sexual act and culminates in orgastic, plasmatic convulsion in animals. It is a life-sustaining force. *This attraction is an orgone-physical function in the realm of the living.*[32]

Hence from the cosmic to the local there is a movement of attraction that culminates in some kind of orgonotic expansion, felt by us in the orgasm as the muscular and characterological armor gives way to the primal convulsions of libido. Organisms can obviously attract *or* repel each other, but the reason for such differences at the deepest level lies in the orgone field that underlies the more obvious mechanisms of attraction or repulsion, such as physical features (in sexual selection processes). In the human order, transference and countertransference fields are actually orgonotic fields—that is, they are merely one of the ways in which orgone interacts in the flexible space between the conscious and the unconscious. To fall in love (to be in bioenergetic attraction) is to enter into this transference-and-countertransference momentum. Yet, as noted, neither form of projection represents, either alone or in conjunction, a *sufficient* condition for genuine love. They may be *necessary* conditions, but other conditions must also be met, such as an awareness of the full autonomy of the Other (Kant's kingdom of ends) and the continual pursuit of self-transparency—the drive to make as many unconscious motives as possible manifest to the attending consciousness.

Back on the cosmic or at least planetary level, Reich argued that the magnetic field of Earth was a product of the underlying orgonotic field. The magnetic core of Earth was magnetized through orgone energy, and thus magnetism, like electrical radiation, was a product of the ground reality of orgone:

> The earth is surrounded by an *orgone energy field* which apparently extends far beyond the atmosphere and out into space. The effect of the earth's orgone field on the iron core of the earth must result in magnetization and the creation of two different magnetic poles, a north pole and a south pole of the earth. The earth's field of attraction is orgonotic and not magnetic in nature. *The magnetic north and south poles of the earth can thus be regarded as a polar functional effect of the orgonotic force field of the earth.*[33]

Given what Reich said elsewhere in these articles, the north and south polarities of the magnetic field of Earth could themselves *be* not orgonotic but a "functional effect" of the orgone field. The orgone itself is not polarized, although it does exhibit antagonisms and tensional variations.

Strict polarity takes place on the less primal level of electromagnetic phenomena.

What claims had Reich presented in these four brief essays? Clearly he was convinced that there was a conceptual and empirical divide between orgone and the other, better-known forces of nature. Yet he also carefully avoided slipping into panpsychism, the doctrine that all inorganic forms are really concrescences of mind or thought. He developed what might be called a *functional evolutionary monism*. The monism was functional in that it did not posit a primal substance as its principle of unity but instead argued that the world is one through a series of functional connections that did not have to be tied together through a system of internal relations. That is, there could be breaks and tears in nature, and nature was not a superorder or ultimate container. The evolutionary aspect of Reich's monism was clear in his sensibility to the complexities of organic ramification and probing in potentially hostile environments. An organism would ramify its own potentials and send probes out into the world to see which would be replicable in the long run—that is, live long enough to assure that the organism as a whole could reproduce itself. By the late 1920s it was known that the universe was expanding and that the evolutionary principles of biology might be applicable to the universe itself. Of course, this latter application became more sharply focused in the 1970s with the issue of baby universes, in which any number of potential universes could emerge out of the sea of possibility (orgone?), only some of which would survive under the twin pressures of natural variation and natural selection. If a potential universe had too much mass, for example, it would collapse back in on itself. If another potential universe had too little mass, it would expand to the point where dense objects might not form at all. Had he lived long enough to be aware of these newer physical cosmologies, one suspects that Reich would have placed orgone at a "location" prior to the big bang, again, as a type of firstness.

We have seen one of his most advanced discussions of orgone and its properties. But what of his more directly poetic vision, as it moved toward a religious cosmology in which universality and orgastic ecstasy were expressed in human orders? Did Reich have a religious vision in spite of his intense dislike for what he called "religious metaphysics," which he associated with the emotional plague? I have asserted throughout that he did have a kind of universalistic ecstatic naturalist religion and that it was the almost inevitable product of his views on sexuality. My argument goes like this: (1) Reich asserted that the sexual libido (the id) was the ground principle of human life; (2) he further asserted that the libido existed in a polarity between anxiety and pleasure; (3) from this notion he deduced that healthy sexual energy entailed the movement of the entire organism toward pleasure via orgastic release (coitus), (4) but that coitus could be successful only if the entire energy field of the psyche/soma was attuned to its social and material environments, environments themselves in need of reconstruction, (5) from which it followed that a connection with the larger environment enhanced the life of sexuality, and that (6) the larger the environment with which the connection is maintained, the larger the pleasure; from which it follows that (7) a sexual connection with the cosmos and its orgonotic fields is the deepest guarantee of the pleasure premium. My own twist on this argument is that hypothesis (7) is a fully religious hypothesis insofar as it brings in the entire realm of an ecstatically self-transforming nature (nature naturing). Reich's radical naturalism completely did away with the three Western monotheisms, with their patriarchal supernaturalism. In their stead he offered a new universal (nontribal) religion that was available to anyone (since there were no creeds) and that connected each psyche to the orgonotic pulsations that would help produce full sexual fulfillment.

The two source texts for the new ecstatic naturalist religion are *Ether, God and Devil* and *Cosmic Superimposition*. Together these texts present the fuller cosmic background that supports his new "religion." In the former book of 1949, Reich set up his contrast between orgonomic functionalism and what he now called "mechanistic-mystical patriarchal" thinking. Like many philosophers, he started to unfold and validate his new metaphysics by grounding it in a new epistemology. His epistemology was *existential* in that it stressed the role of the entire human lifeworld as the opener of knowing, rather than *analytic*, which would stress the role of more circumscribed knowledge claims. Existential epistemology wants to know what kind of human psyche or lifeworld is at play whenever there is a self/world correlation. Thus, each type of person will have a person-specific way of rendering the world intelligible. Analytic epistemology, in contrast, wants to know whether claim X has any warrantability as it can be established through accepted forms of validation. Obviously, the existential form is the more encompassing and has a more radical approach to our being-in-the-world and to the world in which our being-in is located.

Those who have read this far will not be surprised by the fascinating and evocative way in which Reich exhibited his existential epistemology. Put simply, the genitally potent person will have a different way of knowing, and hence a different metaphysics, from the neurotic and armored person. Again, I must stress that the term *metaphysics*, as I am using it here, has nothing to do with supernaturalist claims (or the "mechanistic-mystical") but really denotes the philosophical *activity* of probing into the grounding categories of the world. Hence there is no such thing as being "beyond metaphysics" (in the postmodern sense) or being antimetaphysical (as in certain analytic traditions). One either has a fruitful and generic metaphysics or a deadening and tribal one. Reich's is better than most, and his existential epistemology provides a good means of access to it:

> Orgonomic funtionalism represents the way of thinking of the individual who is unarmored and therefore in contact with nature inside and outside himself. *The living human animal acts like any other animal, i.e., functionally; armored man acts mechanistically and mystically. Orgonomic functionalism is the vital expression of the unarmored human animal, his tool for comprehending nature.* This method of thinking and working becomes a dynamically progressive force of social development only by observing, criticizing, and changing mechanistic-mystical civilization from the standpoint of the natural laws of life, and not from the narrow perspective of state, church, economy, culture, etc.[34]

One could also call Reich's approach here a *psychoanalytic* epistemology insofar as he wanted to show how a healthy unarmored person would, by definition, be open to the "natural laws of life" that the neurotic/armored person simply could not see. As per my discussion in the Preface, Reich realized that no "metaphysics" could emerge without a depth correlation with psychoanalysis; that is, the metaphysician (an agent who lives in each of us) cannot do his or her job properly unless the grounding work on the libido has been done. An armored person will see only as much of the world and its laws as the armoring allows. He or she must look out toward the world through darkened and opaque lenses that distort light waves in a variety of ways that are, unfortunately, unknown to that person. An unarmored person, by contrast, looks out into the world through lenses that are reasonably free from foreign bodies. We can put Reich's conclusion simply: the more genital potency a person has, the more of nature and its laws he or she will see. There is a tight fit between the healthy self and the orgonotic universe, a true micro-to-macrocosm structure.

As is always the case, however, whether one acknowledges it or not, there is a dialectic connecting one's metaphysics with one's epistemology; that is, there is a connection between what one thinks the world is made of and how one affirms what one thinks it is made of. For Reich this connection was a deep one. The post-1939 orgone theory emerged from his psychoanalytic discoveries of the orgasm and its bioelectric manifestations (which later proved to be secondary to the orgonomic foundation). Insofar as a person could experience the four-beat function in a healthy way, that same person would, by definition, be attuned to orgonotic energy. Hence it also followed that a neurotic and armored person simply could not develop a useful and rich metaphysics.

In his metaphysics, or more particularly his cosmology—that part of metaphysics that deals with the space/time universe and its possible grounds—Reich distinguished among three basic categories that are the chief contenders for the root principles of thought. The first two categories have long permeated Western thinking. Reich distinguished among: God, ether (in the sense of nineteenth-century scientific thought), and cosmic orgone. God had been characterized with the predicates soul, spirit, quality, and subjectivity, among others. Ether had been characterized with the predicates energy, body, matter, quantity, and objectivity, among others. But cosmic orgone energy transcended these posited nonrealities by exhibiting the traits of (1) primordial energy, (2) universal existence, (3) all-permeatingness, (4) originating ground of all energy, (5) originating ground of all matter, (6) biological energy in living beings, and (7) originating ground of the galactic systems. Orgone was the primal ground of all that there was, both material and living, and it even created galactic structures in giant vortices that punctuated the depths of space/time.

Reich certainly wanted to distance himself from any hint that he was reviving the ridiculed concept of ether as it had been dethroned in the Michelson-Morley experiments of the previous century. Ether could not be measured, while orgone could, albeit often indirectly. And God was a product of a controlling patriarchy that wanted to give cosmic status to the earthly father in the nuclear family. Thus ether was discredited scientifically while God was deconstructed via a matriarchal psychoanalysis. These twin negations then cleared the way for the more valid metaphysics of cosmic orgone energy. As stated before, orgone was not a deity, was certainly not a person, was not extranatural, and was not some kind of direct and willful agent in human history. Orgone was simply the pulsation at the heart of nature, and that fact alone called for a new religious consciousness, however named.

Reich's existential or psychoanalytic epistemology also called for a new relationship to the *object* of knowing. Instead of a "knowledge about," which would be detached and even voyeuristic, Reich called for a knowledge that would merge intimately with its object: "In order to investigate nature, we must literally *love* the object of our investigation. In the language of orgone biophysics, we must have direct and undisturbed *orgonotic contact* with the object of our investigation."[35] The way of knowing must correspond to what is known, and this can only be done by direct connection in which the subject/object split, the bane of most forms of epistemology, is overcome. So "knowledge about" (in the terms of Bertrand Russell) is replaced by what we can call "knowledge with." In more theological terms, Reich is reaffirming a classic doctrine, which asserts that only through grace (the "gift" of genital libido) can knowing of the ultimate (cosmic orgone energy) occur. In his transliteration of this doctrine, God speaks to us through sexual potency, which in turn makes an awareness of God's world—the world of cosmic orgone energy—possible. The "knowledge with" relationship is a form of the classical grace → inspired knowing correlation.

The relationship between sexuality and religion is certainly one of the most vexing, fascinating, and tension-filled of all cultural/biological relationships. Very few of the major religions have been comfortable with the power of sexuality (as if it were an alternative religion with its own form of ultimacy). The Tantric traditions, which are found in both Buddhism and Hindusim, have celebrated sexuality but often in a more sublimated form. (The "left-handed" Tantric school is more directly sexual, while the "right-handed" Tantric school shies away from the transgression of taboo boundaries.) For the three Western monotheisms, all deeply patriarchal, sexuality gets fully projected onto, for example, the serpent power of the underworld of chaos. Hence sexuality and religion are in a disjunctive class; that is, sexuality S = ~R (religion). For Reich:

The common principle of sexuality and religion is the sensation of nature in one's own organism. When natural sexual expressions were repressed in the human animal during the development of patriarchy, this produced a severe, unbridgeable contradiction between sexuality as a sin and religion as a liberation from sin. In primitive religion, religion and sexuality were ONE: orgonotic plasma excitation. In patriarchy, orgonity becomes "sin" on the one hand and "God" on the other. The functionalist understands the identity of emotions in sexuality and religion, the origin of the estrangement and the dichotomy it created, the fear of sexuality among religious people, and the pornographic degeneracy among the excommunicated. The mechanist and the mystic are a product of this contradiction, remain trapped in it, and perpetuate it. The funtionalist breaks through the barriers of this rigid contradiction by finding the common features in emotion, origin, and nature.[36]

Rather than being contradictory, sexuality and *true* religion had a common origin in the sense of orgonotic pulsation in the individual. The artificial separation that patriarchy placed between them came originally from the enforced marriage bond (as described by Malinowski) in which natural sexuality became commodified and torn from its animistic religious matrix. Reich retrieved a more positive conception of so-called primitive animism by understanding it as a genuine religion of nature and its pulsations as manifest in living things.

Animism (albeit radically transformed), allied to the new sciences, must come to replace monotheism with its one supernatural male deity who works out of an obedience/suppression model. To the scientific animist, "God" is located within the heart of orgonotic pulsations and is most fully encountered in the healthy four-beat function of sexuality. This "god" is neither male nor female in a *literal* sense but *could* be seen metaphorically as maternal, as the ground of being. Reich argued that this new "religion" had found the elusive *Ding an sich* (thing-in-itself) of Kant, namely, the depth reality behind appearances. Any student of Western philosophy will recognize some fascinating correlations with

Schopenhauer at this point, whose own thing-in-itself was the Will that behaved very much like Reich's sexuality.

For the rigid moralist and armored individual, animism is a frightening religious perspective because it entails that the self/world correlation is filled with chaos and uncertainty and involves transgression of hyper-moralistic boundaries and the loss of fear of the orgasm. The armored person requires a male deity to reinforce the castration anxiety stemming from the Oedipal drama and thus to repress the natural sexuality that needs to burst past the emotional and muscular armoring of the self. This deity has very clear rules delimiting the proper from the transgressive and has extremely powerful means for reinforcing this distinction, such as the threat of eternal punishment. The vagina/clitoris and the penis become the gateways to the darker kingdom where one is divorced from God's love and presence. The idea that one could encounter and enter into "God" in the orgasm is ruled out in principle, except during procreation between married couples. But even in this special case, sexual pleasure (the pleasure premium) is merely secondary to the potential creation of a new being.

Where, then, was the *devil* in this patriarchal rage against sexuality? As we have seen, the armored individual was ruled by the secondary drives that came from the repression of the primary instinct of life energy. One of the most intense emotional and behavioral manifestations of the power of the cultural/secondary drives was sadism, a drive that resulted, as noted, from a manic desire to burst through the armoring by any means possible. But the wall of the armor resisted this outward momentum, in turn generating the sadistic rage of the armored self. From this situation arose the realm of the demonic: *"I seriously believe that in the rigid, chronic armoring of the human animal we have found the answer to the question of his enormous destructive hatred and his mechanistic-mystical thinking.* We have discovered the realm of the DEVIL."[37] Obviously, the devil was within and was not an ontological structure in its own right. But patriarchal religion required a devil in some guise in order to work as God's other side. For Reich, as for Jung, the devil was actually an aspect of God and not a fully separate entity, such as a rebellious angel. The devil was God and God was the devil, but neither was necessary in a scientific animistic religion (what I have been calling an ecstatic naturalist religion).[38] A patriarchal god *required* a devil as its own Other, namely, as its mechanism for providing the "temptations" that were perverted forms of sexual/orgonotic energy.

What was at the heart of all genuine religion? Echoing Rank, Reich argued that separation from the maternal womb produced one of the greatest wounds in the human psyche. In a positive way, true religion understood and addressed this ontological wound and provided means for at least partially healing it:

All true religion corresponds to the cosmic, "oceanic" experience of man. All true religion contains the experience of a unity with an omnipresent power, and simultaneously of temporary, painful separation from this power. The eternal longing for return to one's origin ("return to the womb"; "return to the good earth from whence one came"; "return to the arms of God," etc.), for being embraced again by "the eternal," pervades all human longing. It is at the roots of man's great intellectual and artistic creations; it is the core of his longing during adolescence; it pervades all great goals of social organization. It appears as if man yearns to comprehend his separation from the cosmic ocean; such ideas as "sin" have their origin in an attempt to explain the separation. There must be a reason for *not* being united with "God"; there must be a way to unite again, to return, to come home. In this struggle between the cosmic origin and the individual existence of man, the idea of the "devil" somehow arose. It is the same whether one calls it "inferno" or "hell" or "hades."[39]

Reich argued that by the time the Greeks had perfected the art of writing in the classical period (although writing certainly was present in the archaic period), they had also entered into a polytheistic but fully patriarchal religion. As a consequence, their conception of Hades, the shadelike underworld that was but a dim analog to life aboveground, was inevitable. Without Zeus (or a male equivalent) as the reigning deity, no Hades would have been needed. A matriarchal polytheism would certainly have been fully animistic and this-worldly, affirming the values of an ecstatically self-forming nature.

All religion, whether genuine or perverse, lived in the dialectic of melancholy and ecstasy. The ejection from the womb produced a melancholy that was religious in depth and scope, while the promise of a return to paradise stimulated a longing that could be addressed either through sexual potency (which would connect the self back to the sacred), or through armoring and the devil (which would continue to separate the self from the sacred and cause unending anxiety, sexual stasis, brutality, and terror). But with the arrival of scientific animism (my linking of terms, not Reich's), genuine religion could at long last enter into the individual and social orders and proceed to transform the world into one that was fully cognizant of and attuned to the orgonotic pulsations at the heart of all things.

Reich concluded *Ether, God and Devil* with a summation of what he had learned about orgone by 1949. Since most of this material was more fully discussed in the four "Orgonotic Pulsation" essays, there is no need to fully examine his reiterations here. But two pieces stand out as demanding some brief attention and are also quite interesting for a fuller understanding of Reich's perspective. The first piece has to do with his extension of the orgone theory into astrophysics. We have noted his transformation of electromagnetic and gravity theories; what about the cosmos itself and its orgonotic pulsations?

If the "ether" represents a concept pertaining to the cosmic orgone energy, it is *not stationary* [contra Michelson-Morley], *but moves more rapidly than the globe of the earth.* The relation of the earth's sphere to the surrounding cosmic orgone ocean is not that of a rubber ball on stagnant water, *but of a rubber ball rolling on progressing water waves.*[40]

The universe of space/time was constituted by fast-swirling waves that permeated everything material and energetic. Hence the human organism in particular was "an organized part of the cosmic orgone ocean."[41] Reich's form of vitalism envisioned the entire cosmos as one vast ocean of orgone with varying densities, condensations, and speeds of rotation depending on region and type of concrescences involved. Theologically, his cosmological and astrophysical speculations pointed toward a world without an external creator god acting ex nihilo to generate its Other by an act of will. Nature continued to be its own source and eternally played out the rhythms and pulsations of orgone. And as noted, even with a big bang cosmology it was still possible to see orgone as a reality before, during, and after the big bang and in the state between universes.

The second piece in the concluding chapter of *Ether, God and Devil* has to do with the microcosmic representation of cosmic orgone in a scientifically controllable form. I have already discussed some of the features of the orgone accumulator and its manufacture. In concluding our discussion of *Ether, God and Devil*, I want to present Reich's own words on this most controversial subject:

The orgone accumulator is capable of concentrating atmospheric orgone energy by the arrangement of its layering. It consists of two or more (up to twenty) layers, each constructed of nonmetallic substance on the outside and sheet iron or steel wool on the inside. This arrangement influences the atmospheric orgone energy in such a manner that its movement toward the closed space is greater than toward the outside. An "orgonomic potential" is created from the lower level outside toward the higher level inside and is continuously maintained; the orgonomic potential can be demonstrated by the slower discharge of electroscopes on the *inside* and by the constant temperature difference *above* the upper metal place.

Concentrated orgone energy has many beneficial effects on living organisms, which I have tried to describe in my book, *The Cancer Biopathy*.[42]

Hence it was possible, given Reich's presuppositions, to compel orgone energy to concentrate in one spatial location, and it was further possible to measure this concentration in the behavior of the electroscope (a boxlike device that contained a vertical shaft, at the end of which were connected two very thin pieces of metal—these leaves expanded or contracted vis-à-vis each other depending on the level of orgonotic potential). Any living organism that sat (or was placed) inside an orgone cabinet would receive some of the benefits of the increase in orgone energy within the accumulator. Reich was, as noted, cautious in most cases about making too many grand claims about cancer cures and the like, but it is clear that he held very high hopes for the accumulator as one of the many tools that could be useful in the treatment of both mental and physical disorders.

In *Cosmic Superimposition*, Reich made even bolder claims about the nature of orgone and its role as the ground principle of the cosmos. During the period of the early 1950s, he became interested in such things as UFOs and weather modification (which involved using orgonotic shooters that would be pointed upward toward the clouds to produce rain). He traveled to Arizona in 1954 to investigate atmospheric conditions involved in desert formations, and carefully pursued the evidence for and against the idea that so-called flying saucers used a form of orgone energy for their propulsion systems. *Some* aspects of Reich's thinking during this final period suggest that some delusional ideas were entering into his framework, but there are a variety of explanations as to why this may have happened, the most reasonable being that his psychic inflation became entwined with an almost unbelievable series of external vilifications that decentered his professional and personal worlds. Again, there is absolutely no clinical evidence that Reich suffered from schizophrenia even during this period. (By definition, he would have had to develop the illness far earlier in his life.)

Reich advanced two concepts in this short book (actually, a collection of essays) that rounded out his metaphysics. The first was that of the "spiral wave" motion of all celestial and earthly phenomena, while the second was that of "superimposition," namely the conjoining of two distinct orgone systems into one. Superimposition would occur when a biological system became merged with its cosmic background—that is, one reality would be superimposed upon another. The basic stuff of the universe was "mass-free primal cosmic energy" that concresced into matter and electromagnetic energy. Reich wanted to integrate Kepler's model of planetary ellipses with his own conception of open spiraling among mass units: "From here the path of inquiry leads directly into a reconstruction of the planetary movements in terms of *open*, spiraling, mutually approaching and receding pathways, and no longer in terms of closed elliptical curves."[43] Further, the spiral/superimposition model would apply to such phenomena as sunspot cycles, the aurora borealis, hurricanes, tides, and all major weather events. For Reich this new model also applied to issues in celestial dynamics and cosmogony, although he didn't spell out the implications of orgone theory in full detail for theories of cosmogenesis.

For our purposes, since much of *Cosmic Superimposition* restated many of the conclusions of *Ether, God and Devil*, the most important essay is the final one, "The Rooting of Reason in Nature," in which Reich left some strong hints as to what a new orgonotic "religion" would look like. He created a brilliant cosmic and metaphorical religious perspective that linked human longing to the longing of orgone to become aware of itself (a model with strong family resemblances to Hegel's reflections on religion in the 1820s). Our hunger for knowledge was a cosmic hunger that infused itself, through superimposition, into our psyche:

> *The quest for knowledge expresses desperate attempts, at times, on the part of the orgone energy within the living organism to comprehend itself, to become conscious of itself. And in understanding its own ways and means of being, it learns to understand the cosmic orgone energy that surrounds the surging and searching emotions.*[44]

This was not to assert that primal cosmic orgone was conscious in the human sense (as that would entail a subject/object diremption) or that it had the form of a self, but that there seemed to be an inner propulsion within orgone to move into a secondary manifestation that was conscious of itself *as* orgone. This moment is what theologians would call "realized eschatology," in which the final realization of the meaning of the world appears in the individual in a clear epiphany. As the German theologian Friedrich Schleiermacher argued in 1799, "Nature creates its own admirers." Orgone, then, had a "drive" to create its own admirers through its superimposition onto finite forms of consciousness and self-consciousness.

The universe was rational, and since the healthy emotions within the self were natural and followed natural principles, the emotions were rational. There was no disjunction between reason and emotion; they were manifestations of each other in different gestalts or modes. The realm of the so-called irrational was nothing more than the realm of culturally produced secondary drives where emotions were indeed without reason or self-awareness. The mechanists and the irrational mystics had ridiculed the ancient perspective of animism, but "[i]n *Ether, God and Devil*, an at-

tempt was made to show that the primitive animistic view was closer to
natural functioning than the mystical and the mechanistic . . . The animistic view, and not the mystical, was a forerunner of functional thinking,
as expressed most clearly in Kepler's *vis animalis* that moves the heav-
ens."[45] Hence both the natural emotions and the religious perspective of
animism were fully rational and attuned to the laws of nature.

How did cosmic orgone energy make the transition from the nonliving
to the living? The leap into the realm of the living was through what could
almost be called a *self*-confinement of the orgone, if this concept is not
taken literally. This encapsulation was through the biological structure of
the membrane: *"The confinement of a bit of cosmic orgone energy by and
within membranes was the first clear differentiation of life from nonlife, or
organismic from nonliving orgone energy."*[46] At some further point in biological evolution, this energy developed the "capacity of perceiving its
own flow, excitation, expansion in 'pleasure,' contraction in 'anxiety.'"[47]
So we had a movement from the primal orgone ocean that condensed itself into stellar matter, forming primitive plasmatic flakes that evolved
into single-cell organisms. Within the upward curve of orgonotic pulsation (not through a divine agent), certain highly evolved streams of orgone
developed refined sensations of the two polar elements of pleasure and
anxiety. The movement of pleasure, as a basic feature of the universe per
se, was outward and expansive, while the sensation of anxiety, as anti-
growth and antievolutionary, was inward and nonadaptive. The only really
tragic product of the evolution of primitive orgone energy was that of the
secondary drives within the human animal that thwarted and even reversed the overflow of orgone. Hence Reich could now argue that patriarchy, which created the secondary drives, was an antievolutionary and
antiorgonotic function, one going against the very flow of the universe.

Reich brought his reflections in *Cosmic Superimposition* to a resound-
ing close by affirming that in the long run the results of orgonomic science
would conquer the emotional plague that was currently enveloping the
planet. Ironically, as in Judaism and Christianity, Reich affirmed a theology of history, a theology of hope that the kingdom of sexual justice and
pleasure would emerge from out of the horrors of previous history:

In this process of fighting the discovery of cosmic orgone energy, a
slow but most effective process of softening up the rigidities in the

armored character structures will inevitably take place. The hardest, toughest, and cruelest character structure will be forced to make contact with the basic fact of the existence of a life energy, and thus, for the first time in the history of man, the rigidity in the human structure will begin to crack, to soften, to yield, to cry, to worry, to free life, even if at first in a hostile, murderous manner. The help of medical orgonomists will do its share in the softening-up process.[48]

This encomium on the powers of medical orgonomy harked back to Reich's *Sexpol* work in medical and psychiatric clinics in Vienna and Berlin in the 1930s. The same almost messianic fervor for the liberating power within life energy was present in Reich from the beginning and remained with him right up until his death in prison. Did he see himself in the role of the religious prophet, even if such a self-identification would have otherwise suggested to him a pathological split in the psyche? My sense is that he was *pushed* into the role of prophet by internal forces (like psychic inflation) and the genuine experience of martyrdom visited upon him by, among others, the Food and Drug Administration. Structurally, the temptation is to follow out the logic of messianism until one somehow discovers that there may *be* a messiah and that that messiah may be closer to home than is comfortable.

Not everyone was able to follow Reich down the path toward a new natural religion of orgonotic pulsation. Even some of his otherwise sympathetic critics detected a break between the scientific Reich and the allegedly undisciplined nature mystic. The psychiatrist Eustace Chesser, in a chapter of his book on Reich entitled *Where Reich Failed*, states:

Reich not only attempted to reach a synthesis of the opposites of vitalism and mechanism, he laid the basis of a Nature-Mysticism. In view of his avowed hostility to mysticism, it seems surprising that he should develop in this direction. The intensified persecution of the last years undoubtedly affected his mental balance. In his book *The Murder of Christ* he identified himself with Christ. While in prison he attended some church services and wrote in a letter to his son: "I was deeply moved; I felt a new, universal faith in Life and Love, comprising monotheistic beliefs, races, etc., is

becoming a dire necessity to counterweight the 'Enemy of Man'."
In her biography of Reich his wife admitted that she had not been
able to understand this development as it seemed so far removed
from his thinking as she had known it.[49]

Chesser has it only half right. Reich was concerned with overcoming mechanism, not with integrating it with vitalism. Reich may have also misstated his own perspective when he referred to "monotheistic beliefs" as necessary in the current cultural crisis. His pantheism precluded any traditional notion of a monotheistic deity as world-creator or world-governor. Whatever the divine was for Reich, it was far more a manifestation of orgonotic pulsation than anything resembling a deity. Further, it should be clear that Reich's so-called religious thinking was implicit in his work from before the 1950s.[50]

The two remaining texts that we will look at here opened up the complex issue of Reich's self-identification and with how that self-image related to the issues of religious reality. In his very short book *Listen, Little Man!* (1946), Reich analyzed the little man within each person, just as he had done with the little Hitler within each German citizen in 1933. He indulged in some strongly messianic and inflated language concerning his own stature in the history of science, and the work can properly be seen as a compensatory document balancing his injured sense of self. In the second book, *The Murder of Christ*, he detailed a martyrology of Christ as it related to the seemingly eternal emotional plague. It does not require a hermeneutic distortion to see the text as a justification of Reich's own quite real martyrdom in his confrontation with the contemporary emotional plague of the U.S. government.

Listen, Little Man! was Reich's jeremiad against the postwar culture of the United States and its intense emotional armoring after the great conflagration that had just consumed its energies. The thematic texture of the monograph centered on the battle between the little man (fully armored and filled with castration anxiety) and the truly great man, who tried to open up scientific and sexual boundaries on the edges of experience. Even the great man had a piece of the little man within, and this could come out whenever he was exposed to the emotional plague for too long a period. But unlike the little man who had no idea that he was little, the great man fully understood his littleness and saw it as a temptation and a threat. Reich also talked about little and great women in a nonpatriarchal way, and he understood that the same personal and social logic applied to each gender, if not always in the same respect. In what follows I will include both genders even when Reich privileged the male, precisely because his deeper intent was to be inclusive.

The little man or woman is armored, fearful of novelty, a social conformist, addicted to authoritarian forms of leadership, and just barely tolerant of the fully healthy man or woman. Genius is tolerated, but only up to a point. It has to be a kind of "genius" that is not too threatening to the mediocrity within:

I know, I know, you want your "geniuses" and you're ready to honor them. But you want *nice* geniuses, well-behaved, moderate geniuses with no nonsense about them, and not the untamed variety who break through all barriers and limitations. You want a limited, cropped and clipped genius you can parade through the streets of your cities without embarrassment.

That's the way you are, little man. You can spoon it in to the last drop, you can help yourself and gobble it up, but *you can't create.*[51]

The role of the *scientific* genius, in particular, was fraught with distress coming from the innumerable little women and men who could not tolerate or understand the utter necessity of transgressing the boundaries of their emotional and muscular armoring so that truth could emerge. There was but a small step going from intolerance and unconsciousness to actual punishment. For Reich this step had almost always been taken in human history, and he thought that the history of science was but one thread of many in the history of martyrdom.

Here we see his more personal anger, directed toward the unfolding problems connected with his research and the reaction of local and national authorities:

"Did you hear that? He's casting aspersions on my martial spirit, on the honor and glory of my country!"

Be still, little man! There are two kinds of sound: the howling of the storm on a mountaintop, and your farting! You're a fart and you think you smell like violets. I heal your psychic affliction and

you ask if I'm in *Who's Who*. I understand your cancer, and your
little Health Commissioner forbids me to experiment on mice. I
teach your physicians to understand your case, and your Medical
Association denounces me to the police. You suffer from mental
disorder and they apply electric shock, just as in the Middle Ages
they would have applied the snake or the chain or the whip.[52]

The irony, of course, is that the little man or woman was inflicted with the
same punishments that were unleashed against the orgonomic scientist.
The scientist experienced rejection, alienation, loss of revenue, decreased research prospects, and continual social "shocks." The impotent
and sadistic little woman or man could be exposed to a more literal electrical shock in the name of reason and the conquest of the irrational. But
in each case the drive of the patriarchal and authoritarian society was to
eliminate irritants that disrupted its "smooth" functioning. Reich saw
himself as the unacknowledged savior of the little man or woman, an individual who was tragically driven by an unconscious and sadistic social
order mired in the secondary drives.

Throughout I have been asserting that Reich suffered from occasional
forms of psychic inflation. Needless to say, this claim will not sit well with
many of Reich's admirers. But how else can one interpret the tone of the
following passage:

Regardless of what you've done and will do to me, of whether you
glorify me as a genius or lock me up as a madman, of whether you
worship me as your deliverer or hang or torture me as a spy, your
affliction will force you to recognize sooner or later that *I have discovered the laws of living energy* and have given you an instrument
with which to govern your lives with the conscious purpose which
thus far you have applied only to the operation of machines. I have
been a faithful engineer to your organism. Your grandchildren will
follow in my footsteps and become wise engineers of human nature. I have opened up to you the vast realm of the living energy
within you, your cosmic essence. That is my great reward.

And to the dictators and tyrants, the crafty and malignant, the
vultures and hyenas, I cry out in the words of an ancient sage:

> I have planted the banner of holy words
> in this world
> Long after the palm tree has withered
> and the rock crumbled,
> long after the glittering monarchs
> have vanished like the dust of dried leaves,
> a thousand arks will carry my word
> through every flood:
> It will prevail.[53]

Here the messianic language is unmistakable. The arks will safely carry his holy words above every form of the emotional plague, and he will ultimately triumph. Neither the English nor the German text tells us who the "ancient sage" is, although, as suggested by Mary Boyd Higgins, it may be the thirteenth-century Persian poet Rumi. It would be hard to imagine too many significant scientists who would be likely to cast their life history in the posture of a world-conquering hero. Furthermore, this hero must best the little women and men who are out to destroy the great work. But I have also been arguing that Reich's psychic inflation was to a large extent a function of the failure of the outside scientific community to engage his work on the level that it demanded (at least in his eyes).[54]

Listen, Little Man! not only expressed a series of complaints against the antievolutionary forces of the mediocre but was a positive attempt to reexplain the origins of character structure and the rise of religion. As he noted in his preface, Reich had intended this work not for publication but for personal healing in the face of the "gossip and slander" that had begun, once again, to descend upon him from ill-informed sources outside his immediate research circle. About a year after the monograph was written, external events compelled Reich to publish it in translation: "The decision to publish this appeal as a historical document was made in 1947, when the emotional plague conspired to kill orgone research (n.b., not to prove it unsound but to kill it by defamation)."[55] Certainly some psychic inflation was predictable when the stakes were so high. From Reich's perspective, his entire life's work was under assault from the very people who, but for the emotional plague, should have been qualified to understand it. Since he could not convince them on scientific grounds, he sought to help them see their own entrapment in the plague world.

We have noted in several places Reich's distant relationship to his own Judaism. At the University of Vienna he had passed by the blandishments of Zionist political groups and Jewish cultural groups. He later blamed Freud's post-1920 antisexual theories (about the death drive and sublimation) on his ensnarement in patriarchal Judaism, and he himself never practiced the religion of his birth. In *Listen, Little Man!* Reich pushed his universalism and internationalism one step further and firmly rejected the idea that the Jews are or should be a special people:

> I am a biological and cultural mongrel and proud of it; in mind and body, I am a product of *all* classes and races and nations . . . I am moved by no feeling for the Jewish language, Jewish religion, or Jewish culture. I believe in the Jewish God no more than in the Christian or Indian God, but I know where you get your God. I don't believe that the Jews are God's "chosen people." I believe that someday the Jewish people will lose themselves among the masses of human animals on this planet and that this will be a good thing for them and their descendants. You don't like to hear that, little Jewish man. You harp on your Jewishness because you despise yourself and those close to you *as Jews*. The Jew himself is the worst Jew hater of all. That's an old truth. But I don't despise you and I don't hate you. I simply have nothing in common with you, at any rate no more than with a Chinese or a raccoon, namely, our common origin in cosmic matter. Why do you stop at Shem, little Jew, why not go back to protoplasm? To my mind, life begins with plasmatic contraction, not with rabbinic theology.[56]

Reich could see the god of Judaism only as a god who enforced the denial of libido and who was but a pale shadow of the orgone ocean that truly generated and sustained the universe and all that was in it. His perspective reminds one of the ancient writers of the Hindu *Unpanishads* (c.1500 B.C.E.) who pushed dramatically beyond *any* finite superimpositions on Brahmin. This absolute abyss was formless, truly nameless, devoid of features or traits of any kind, and could be only partially characterized by the simile of blissful pure light. For someone like Reich, the

Jewish and Christian gods must have seemed utterly small and tribal, deities emergent from armored projections rather than ontological agents worthy of devotion. He obviously was not fully conversant with the Christian mystical tradition or with the richer and deeper conceptions of God in Judaism, but he was more alert than most theologians to the demonic aspects of the patriarchal gods of both traditions. His own form of ecstatic naturalism (or scientific animism) drove him to see God (orgonotic pulsation or the orgone ocean) in the most generic terms possible.

Much of *Listen, Little Man!* took the form of angry and ironical refutations of some of the specific rumors that swirled around Reich and Orgonon. They represented the standard fare: Reich slept with his patients, Reich was a homosexual, Reich was a Communist or a cryptofascist, Reich abused children, or Reich was a medical quack peddling cures for all kinds of illness. He faced each rumor head-on, as was his perennial style, and ironically deflated them. In one sense this monograph comes across as a brave attempt to meet the plague directly, but in another sense it comes across as a prolonged cry against woundedness and against the mediocrity of almost all of humankind. This second dimension of the text gives us a picture of a deeply outraged and emotionally scarred man who had exhausted many of his financial, emotional, physical, and intellectual resources just to secure a place within the world of scientific culture. One senses that here was a man who wanted to be left alone to do his work, but who also, perhaps in spite of himself, stirred up the pot whenever he could so that he could then throw out his work as a challenge to the world of organized and well-funded science.

With all of this in mind, we have a natural and easy transition to an examination of the final text that will conclude our study of Reich's ideas. In a way, Reich's *sociological* theology of Christ was his act of finally situating himself in the history of science and in the history of religion. It was as if he and Christ represented two historical poles of an orgonotic religion that could now be fully expressed in a way that was simply unavailable to Jesus in the primitive culture of first-century Palestine. He and Christ were both ecstatic naturalists, and both were martyrs for the cause of the genitally and orgonomically healthy life. Reich was not interested in Moses; perhaps he had relegated that "historical" figure to Freud, but he had a deep sympathy for the alienated and wandering Jew who died on the cross under Roman (fascist) rule. This transference relationship to

Jesus makes clear sense when it is located in the overall trajectory of Reich's life.

Reich took a long, hard look at the Bible and was actually well informed about aspects of the history of theology and biblical interpretation. The Jesus who is about to emerge before us is certainly not the divine man of the Gospel of John, nor the apocalyptic and vengeful postresurrection judge of the Book of Revelation. He was more akin to the suffering servant found in the earlier Gospels of Mark and Matthew (written c.40–60 C.E.). In Reich's interpretation, the Hebrew Scriptures, upon which the gospels and epistles of the Greek New Testament were erected, presented the horrible history of human entrapment in the patriarchal plague that grasped the Hebrew writers. Yet these ancient texts gave few clues as to how humankind got *into* the trap. We were left with a sexually tinged patriarchal myth:

> There is so much the Bible tells about life in the trap, and *so little about how men got into the trap*. It is obvious that the exit out of the trap is exactly the same as the entrance into the trap, through which they were driven from paradise. Now why does nobody say anything about it except in a very few paragraphs which are as one to a million to the rest of the Bible, and in a veiled language which is meant to conceal the meaning of the words?
>
> The downfall of Adam and Eve is obviously, beyond any doubt due to something they did against the Laws of God in a *genital* way: "*And they were both naked, the man and his wife, and were not ashamed* (Genesis 2:25)."[57]

Reich was setting up a traditional dialectic, but with a dramatic twist. Traditionally, Jesus was sent or called by God to become the second Adam in order to redeem the sins of the first human couple. In Reich's more interesting and I think far more valid analysis, Adam and Eve were healthy and happy in the garden but were driven out by an evil god. Jesus served to reinforce the original position that Adam and Eve had to nature and sexuality in their purity *within* the garden of paradise. The serpent was fully redeemed by Reich (hinted at in 1921 in his dream of the blond anima figure) and equated with the phallus: "Every movement of the serpent is graceful, and many species are beautifully colored. In the serpent,

Satan first appeared as an angel of light. The serpent, thus, is a symbol of Life itself and the male phallus."[58]

But the real question for Reich was: why was there a forbidden tree of knowledge in paradise in the first place? What was God up to? Here, as before, Reich placed the blame squarely on God as the creator of the plague and the secondary drives. If Adam and Eve were orgonomically healthy before eating of the tree, they were sick and plague-ridden afterward. And the patriarchal god was behind it all, pulling the strings and setting up the serpent to be the instruments of "his" own devious power. Of course, all of this is a mythical structure, but it very well represented the transition into patriarchy and the restrictions against the id that followed. The role of Jesus, at this point, was to lead to the way back into paradise and the primary life-directed instincts and drives.

As before, we see two gods within the one patriarchal god, each alienated from the other. The "good" god, the true god of nature, was suppressed or even conquered by the "evil" god that was a projection of the armored individual, an individual who ironically derived much of her or his armoring from an introjection of the socially projected myth of a castrating deity. This was the trap in its most binding form. But Jesus Christ appeared to help the good aspect of God overcome its own bad aspect so that the god/nature equation (as in Spinoza) could return to human consciousness.[59] Without Jesus, God would not be able to find itself through the process of human coparticipation. And in the end evil was really a product of humankind because of the armoring that wouldn't let God's life force through. Of course, Reich was using the germ *god* as a shorthand designator for the nonpersonal orgonotic cosmic ocean.

Jesus, as understood properly by the genitally healthy individual, in Reich's account, brought us back into contact with the sacred energy currents that were always present in the Garden of Eden. At the same time he inverted the secondary drives so that evil was overcome:

The myth of Jesus Christ presents the qualities of "God," in other words, of the inborn, naturally given Life Energy, in a nearly perfect manner. What it does *not* know nor recognize is that Evil, *the Devil, is a perverted God, grown out of the suppression of the God-like*. This lack of knowledge is one of the cornerstones of the human tragedy ... *How can evil come from God's creation?* Here, in

each newborn infant, God was there, to sense, to see, to smell, to
love, to protect, to develop. And in each single newborn infant, to
this day, God was squelched, restricted, suppressed, punished,
looked upon with horror. This is only one of the many realms of the
chronic murder of Christ. *Sin (Evil) is being created by man himself.* This remained hidden.[60]

Humankind murdered the Christ within (it was a "chronic" condition),
just as it murdered the depth dimension of the true god of orgone and an
ecstatically self-transforming nature. Like Nietzsche, Reich insisted that
the history of theology was the history of attempts to both create and destroy the patriarchal deity that brutalized most of human history. For both
thinkers, God was indeed dead, but for Reich the true god would emerge
out of the death of the false god to redeem history. And of course, Reich
was this genuine god's prophet. Why else would he have used such strong
religious and theological language to talk about martyrdom and salvation
as he approached his mid-fifties?

In a more positive vein, we can ask: who then was Christ for the orgone
scientist? What made Jesus distinctive from everyone around him? Can
there be more than one Christ, and who gets a vote as to who fits the designation of a *new* Christ? Reich provided what I think were some clear
guidelines as to the nature of Jesus' "divinity" and uniqueness, but in such
a way as to keep the door wide open for new carriers of the divine infusion:

Christ gives freely. He can give freely since his power to absorb
life energy from the universe is boundless. Christ does not feel that
he is doing much by giving his strength to others. He does it gladly.
More, he needs this giving himself; he is full with strength to overflow. He does not lose anything when he gives to others richly. On
the contrary, he becomes stronger and richer by giving to others.
Not merely because of the pleasure of giving; he thrives on giving,
for his energy metabolizes faster; the more he gives off in strength
and love, the more new strength he gains from the universe, the
greater and closer is his own contact with nature around him, the
sharper his awareness of God, Nature, the air, the birds, the flow-
ers, the animals, to all of whom he is close, knowing them with his
orgonotic First Sense; secure in his reactions, harmonious in his

self-regulation, independent of obsolete "thou shalt's" and "thou shalt not's." He is unaware that other "shalt's" and "shalt not's" will break in later in a most tragic fashion and murder Christ in every single child.[61]

Jesus was an orgone accumulator who had the uncanny ability to directly transmit orgone energy to others. Although there is one biblical story about his anger at being suddenly drained of some of his energy by a touch from behind, the overall direction of his life was to give over the power of the orgonotic field within which he moved. The so-called miracle stories, such as his raising the dead, walking on water, stilling a storm, healing the demoniac, turning water into wine, and curing physical ills, were merely mythical ways of expressing wonder at the power of God's life energy within ordinary existence. There was no armoring in Jesus, and he had no experience of the power of armoring over almost all persons.

Christ loved children and women, sensing their greater closeness to natural orgonotic fields—and they in turn sensed the bodily orgonotic energy within him. He lived in his body but not in what Saint Paul a few decades later would call the "flesh." The "flesh" was the body in estrangement from itself, caught in the unending swirl of the secondary drives of lust, passion, sadism, narcissism, and so forth. The simple of the earth loved Jesus because they could see the life energy within him, even if they knew they might never fully attain it. And for Reich Jesus was also simple—that is, he did not contain some great messianic secret, to be told only to a few in his inner circle, nor was he a Dostoevsky-like hero who wrestled with his god and anguished over his impending fate. His only "secret" was that he was immersed within the bosom of nature and lived as a child of nature.

Reich rejected the idea that Jesus was a warrior-king in the tradition of the Macabees, or a zealot in the sense of his own first-century time. Rather, Jesus knew full well that there was no earthly way to overcome the occupying Roman forces, and he accepted the fact that his message worked along a very different time line. But the message was not about his person or "divinity" but about what he felt pulsating *within* himself:

Christ does not want to fight Caesar. He knows he cannot possibly conquer Caesar. But he also knows that Caesar will be long forgotten when what he himself feels in his body and what vibrates in his senses in harmony with the universe, will rule the world to the good of all men on earth. The Kingdom of God on earth, which is this feeling and vibrating of living Life in Christ as in all men on earth, is sure to come. It had been there, once upon a time.[62]

The Garden of Eden was reconstituted in the life and ministry of Jesus, who was its chief exemplar in the postfall epoch. Jesus was not a messianic warrior or prophet but a living concrescence of the full concentrated power of orgonotic pulsation. He lived his life naturally and simply and made no grand claims about himself as a leader or historical agent. His disciples, because of their emotional armoring, added their own readings to this life energy in their midst and thus inaugurated the ongoing tradition of misinformation about who the Christ really was. Many of them wanted a Son of Man from the house of David who would throw off the Roman yoke, while others wanted a man who would revivify the life of Judaism against its political corruption by the Pharisees and Sadducees. Amid all of these intense transferences and projections, Jesus remained quiet about his inner essence—he simply acted out of it.

The tortures imposed on Jesus did not reach down into his inner essence. Reich envisioned Jesus as a man who rose above his torments and rested content in the full power of his orgonotic connection, his "knowledge with" the orgone ocean. His whipping, the thorn of crowns, his social ridicule, all passed over his body and psyche as so many finite distractions of the world of the flesh. For Reich Christ endured these pains and humiliations even though he did not believe in the personal and conscious survival of bodily death. Christ's agony on the cross, in which he felt abandoned by his father (and he used *very* personal language in talking to his father), was not Reich's focus, as it would be for, say, a Lutheran theologian. There was almost a Gnostic reading of Christ as a being who did not really suffer in this world and who was an exemplar of a type rather than a struggling and anxiety-ridden individual. It was not the cross but the life of orgonotic pulsation that fascinated Reich.

In some highly poetic language (and the reader must remember that *The Murder of Christ* was written entirely in English), Reich linked Christ's life to that of all other things in the universe, producing what I would call a *cosmic* Christology. His point of transition from Jesus to the great orgone sea was through the concept of the "glowing silent force" within the suffering servant of humankind:

> The silent, calm glow of living Life cannot ever be destroyed by any means. It is a basic manifestation of the very energy that makes the universe run its course. This glow is in the dark night's sky. It is in the silent quiver in the sunlit sky that makes you forget bad jokes. It is the calm glow of the love organs of the glowworms. It hovers over the treetops at dawn and dusk, and it is in the eyes of a trusting child. You can see it in an airtight, evacuated glass tube charged from the air with life energy, and you can see it in the expression of gratitude in the face when you relieve sorrow in a man ill with the emotional plague. It is the same glow which you see at night on the surface of the ocean or at the tops of high masts [Saint Elmo's fire] . . . It is this glow which, in the feeling of mankind, unites Christ during his last agony with the great universe.[63]

Martin Luther might have said that Reich presented a theology of glory in which the emphasis was on how Jesus triumphed over the finite and merged with the infinite. Luther's own preferred theology of the cross stressed the sense of real death and the loss of divine connection as experienced by Jesus in the preresurrection moment of the cross. The theology of glory represented the Roman Catholic position, while the theology of the cross was an expression of the much deeper Protestant consciousness. Clearly, Reich wanted to align himself with a triumphant and healthy person for whom the cross was not so much his fulfillment as a symptom of the horrors of the emotional plague. Put differently, Reich would have been uncomfortable with any sense that Christ had a death drive or had accepted a way out of life as part of a divine plan he had made with a supernatural father.

Why exactly did the majority of people want Jesus' death? And why, when the final moment of crisis came, were all of his male disciples absent from Cavalry, while some of his closest women followers *were* present? And why was Jesus given the worst form of punishment possible, one not given to Roman citizens? Reich provided an answer to the first question that also shed light on the others:

Christ was killed in such a shabby way and he was defiled by a
sick and sickening crowd because he dared to love with his body
and did not sin in the flesh.

Christ was tortured because they had to destroy his truly godly,
i.e., orgonotic way of life, strange and dangerous to them.

They mocked him and laughed at him and threw ugly words at
him because they could not suffer to be reminded of godly life
within themselves.

Even the two thieves at their crosses nearby mocked Christ. In
this account, whether historically true or not, the Christian legend
has grasped an awful truth: "A thief is preferable to a godlike lover
of women." In the American South, they do not tar and feather Ne-
groes for theft, but for "rape of white women." . . .

The young, lively, beautiful, attractive Jesus Christ was killed
because he was loved by women the way a scribe never could have
been loved; he was killed because he was built and alive in a manner no Talmudic priest could ever suffer to continue to live. And
the Talmudists in later temples of creed as well as knowledge did
not suffer even the mention of this very core of the secret of the
murder of Christ.[64]

Sexual envy was one of the most potent engines of the emotional plague,
and the root for *this* form of envy was in the deeper envy toward those who
swam in the great orgonotic sea without manifest armoring. The armored
person hated what he or she most needed to become, and the murder of
Christ, as much an archetypal structure of the self as an actual historical
event, was reenacted with every child and in every society and shaped
human self-understanding. But this murder was hidden from consciousness and projected onto the Other. The long history of Christian anti-
Semitism can be partially explained by the belief that the Jews and not
the Romans had murdered Christ. If the Jews were doing what "we" do
but will not admit to, then "we" can develop a negative transference onto
them and load them with historical and even cosmic guilt. After all, "we"
would never have murdered Jesus.

Reich deliteralized the resurrection by translating it into a more Taoist
sense that all living things return after death to enter into the Tao or (Way)
of other living things. But Jesus' subjectivity or self-consciousness (the

concept of subjective immortality) had no continuity. Christ did not literally descend into hell and then rise and appear before several of his disciples. Rather, he merged once again with the orgone sea from whence he
had come. His "resurrection" can be felt in every birth, in every healthy
genital connection, in every pulsating work of art, in every moment of
truth telling, and in the powers of life within nature: "Life can not be
killed, ever. It hung from the cross bleeding in agony from many wounds,
but it is truly invincible. Having expired in one body, it will certainly
return in another body."[65] The return of Christ was not to be seen as a
physical return of an individual called Jesus in some space/time configuration, but as the perennial power of nature to spawn itself anew from its
own immolations.

In the course of *The Murder of Christ*, Reich reconstructed most of the
classical Christological doctrines in order to show a truer Christ who embodied orgonotic principles in his life and action. Jesus was no longer divine in a supernaturalist sense; nor could he violate the Newtonian causal
nexus by creating miracles. Like Schleiermacher, Reich affirmed that "all
was miracle" when seen from the standpoint of genuine and naturalistic
religious consciousness. His Jesus loved the life energy he sensed in children and women, and he was not afraid to fully use his body in a genitally
healthy way. The issue of the sexuality of Jesus had been continually denied by the orthodox as a threat to the very idea of a god/man, but Reich
knew that unless this primal dimension of his life was celebrated, Christ
would be irrelevant to the great task of conquering the antisexual emotional plague. While the suffering of Jesus was quite real, he rose above
it because of his intimate connection with the orgone ocean that healed
all of the breaks that he endured from the authoritarian social order.
Where the mature Schleiermacher (c.1821) spoke of Jesus' "perfect god-
consciousness" (a phrase used by Martin Luther King, Jr., in his famous
"Letter from a Birmingham Jail"), Reich spoke of the unbroken connection between Christ and the originating power of the world.

Like the twentieth-century New Testament scholar Rudolph Bultmann, Reich demythologized the written witness to the life of Jesus. Unlike Bultmann, he remythologized the Jesus story so that it could have
new life in the light of the great discoveries of orgonotic science. Reich
combined elements of the hero myth (going all the way back to his 1927
Genitality) with elements of his own martyrology. Yet he also probed into

aspects of Christ that very few religious scholars or persons of faith have seen or understood. Needless to say, we are not even sure which of the biblical sayings attributed to Jesus were ever actually uttered by him (perhaps as few as 10 percent), let alone which major and minor aspects of his life ever really happened. And this makes it likely that Christ's internal mental world is completely hidden from view. All Christologies are primarily literary creations that serve some deep philosophical, psychological, or theological need. Reich's literary creation had some striking features that opened up Jesus in such as way as to show *why* he had his extraordinary power over others (a fact that we do know to be certain). No one without some kind of unusual connection with the ground of the ecstatically self-transforming nature could have set fire to so many psyches so quickly and over such a large geographical area (thanks, of course, to the journeys of Paul). It is far less clear that Paul was an orgonotically healthy man. Any reader of his Epistle to the Romans should have serious pause about his abjections of sexuality and the life energy. His frenetic life was a far cry from that of the Christ who appeared to him on the road to Damascus.

By 1951 Reich had made some major theoretical advances beyond his European research into the bions and the cancer cell. For good or ill, he had "discovered" orgone and had probed into its correlations with electromagnetic energy and gravity, then extrapolated from orgonotics to astrophysics and cosmology. As I have argued from the beginning, Reich was consistent, logical, and rigorous in his thinking from the early 1920s until his last years. Direct lines of continuity extend from his work in psychopathology and neurosis to his conception of the spiral wave in galactic formation. Only a casual and fragmentary reading of Reich's astonishing output of published material could generate the view that he was guilty of wild speculation or that his texts demonstrated the traits of schizophrenia. This is not to say that Reich was right in all that he said—that claim does not follow from the preceding one—but rather that he cannot be tarred with the brush of madness or corrupted thinking. I do believe that he made some extrapolations from his data that were unwarranted or at least premature, but I have also become persuaded that he did the best he could in his isolation (whether self-caused or not) to work through some of the foundational issues in psychopathology, character, armoring, bioelectric systems, new energy forms, political structures, the history of

patriarchy, the history of religion, and cosmology. No other classical psychoanalyst, with the possible exception of Jung, even attempted to develop such an encompassing and rich categorial framework. When the
novice reader assumes that Reich took a great leap from text A to text B,
there are almost always texts (A1, A2, A3, and so on) that show that there
really was no leap, only the steady process of moving from one experimental conclusion to another. The more fully one plunges into Reich's
entire oeuvre, the more admiration one gains both for his dogged consistency and for his creative theoretical enframing of empirical data.

We will conclude this chapter with some brief biographical details
about Reich's struggles in the United States after his arrival from soon-to-
be-occupied Norway. His wife Elsa decided to remain in Norway rather
than to emigrate with Reich to New York. Since she was "Aryan," she
managed to survive the war years, but her relationship with Reich quickly
ended in divorce. There is little doubt that Reich carried a torch for her
until his death, but shortly after his arrival in America he met Ilse Ollendorff, the woman who was to become his third wife and the mother of his
third child, Peter. Reich moved into the house in Forest Hills, where he
created a laboratory in the basement and a meeting center for his research assistants on the first floor. Ilse Ollendorff Reich describes her
first encounter with Reich in October 1939, when she visited his house at
the encouragement of a mutual friend (Gertrud Gaasland, Reich's live-in
laboratory assistant):

> I met Reich briefly and was very much impressed by him, even a
> bit awed. He was a striking figure with his grey hair, ruddy com-
> plexion, and white coat. He showed me the laboratory, the house,
> and invited me to have a glass of wine . . . Reich [a few days later]
> talked to me of his children and of Elsa. He explained his separa-
> tion from her, saying that she had wanted to be independent and
> had feared that she might not be able to build up her own work
> again in the States, especially since she did not speak English
> very well. He told me that he was still very much attracted to her,
> but that the relationship had come to an end.[66]

Reich was quite honest with Ilse about his emotional situation and about
her potential secondary status vis-à-vis the haunting presence of Elsa.

But she developed a strong interest in the Austrian exile and married him on Christmas Day 1939. Shortly afterward she became one of his assistants in the laboratory in Forest Hills. In 1939 Reich was invited to join the faculty of the New School for Social Research in Manhattan. This new institute, largely created by the cream of the European exiles, could not offer a tenure-track position to everyone. Reich was a paid lecturer. He lectured on "Biological Aspects of Character Formation" to several dozen students, but his work was not as well received as he had hoped. Still, he managed to enter into the intellectual social scene of the city and to meet and converse with many of its leading psychoanalysts.

In the summer of 1940 Reich and Ilse took a New England vacation, winding up in Rangeley, Maine, which sits between two vast lakes, Mooselookmeguntic Lake and Rangeley Lake. The environment and weather so appealed to Reich that he and Ilse returned to the area. In 1942, by a happy confluence of circumstances, Reich was able to buy 150 acres of land just outside the town of Rangeley. He named his new estate Orgonon and immediately started construction on a series of buildings. He built a small home, a student laboratory, and an observatory for astronomical studies. (His personally designed telescope, a large refractor, was never built.) By the end of the 1940s Orgonon was more or less completed and became the locus of his research, lecturing, and mentoring. For a few years he continued to winter in Forest Hills and summer in Rangeley, but in 1950 he and Ilse moved to Maine full time. Their son, Peter, was born in April 1944 and was taken to Maine that summer. In the summer of 1946 Reich began to organize lecture series involving practicing physicians and advanced professionals.

Reich continued his habit of journal writing and intense letter writing. The recently published collection of this material provides invaluable insight into his inner war against the world and his growing disenchantment with the human kingdom. He shifted away from human psychopathology and even political psychology toward an encompassing philosophy of nature. In a journal entry of January 14, 1943, he wrote:

> Fifteen years ago my entire life and activities were anchored in political philosophy. In those days it was not wanted. Today, fifteen years later, I have lost all interest in political psychology; the most essential things have been said. Although political psychology is

now beginning to take root, I am in an entirely different place: I'm more interested in the radiation of the solar corona than in political psychology. I have become indifferent to man, *he is just too offensive*.[67]

Obviously Reich continued his passionate interest in finding a cure for the emotional plague, but he wanted to locate that cure on the cosmic level, since the political revolution had failed and would continue to fail without the power of the cosmic orgone ocean. Perhaps the ravages of the Second World War sharpened his sense of the strength of emotional armoring. The psychological war against the fascist plague had failed, and the world was now left with bloodshed and carnage. Reich's transition to a more cosmic setting made perfect sense given the ground that he had already covered with such thoroughness. He had regrounded classical psychoanalysis in its own rejected libido theory and had been ostracized from the kingdom. He had written a brilliant deconstruction of the entire Nazi psychological and mythic structure, only to have his book banned and burned. And he had found the correlation between the neurotic character structure and bioelectricity but had not yet found the cure for the plague. Consequently, orgonomic functionalism was driven by inner and outer necessity to probe into the larger physical and temporal background of the only energy in the known universe that could withstand the long-term effects of the plague.

Writing in his journal on Peter's first birthday (April 3, 1945), Reich revealed his own understanding of his parents' early deaths. He turned the tragedies into positive events that had goaded him toward the life of science: "I would very probably not have discovered the orgone if the death of my parents during the earliest years of my puberty had not catapulted me on a course toward independence. The sighting of the orgone required an especially high degree of intellectual independence."[68] His early forced separation from the grounds of nurture and authority drove him to seek substitute objects in the realm of cosmic nature. In his orgone theory he was able to refind his betraying mother and to tame his castrating father. During this period Reich developed an interest in the life and work of Isaac Newton, seeing in him a fellow seeker who needed a cosmic vision to heal personal Oedipal wounds. Newton's intense abjection of his mother is well known, as well as his fairly extreme manic-depressive dis-

order. Reich wrote that he was afraid to expose himself to Newton's mental life and that he sensed the same chaotic and hypomanic tendencies in
himself. Reich was correct that Newton linked gravity with God, just as
he himself wanted to link gravity (and everything else) with orgone. Newton got a much better post-Oedipal material maternal reality in his grav-
ity/God matrix than he had had in his autobiographical universe. Reich
got a less destructive Cecilie back through the encompassing power of
orgone. The Great Mother was purged of her evil betrayal as that evil
was relegated to the status of secondary sadistic drives. Both Newton and
Reich lived on the boundary where science and religion interacted, and
both probed into the Bible in order to find further evidence for their own
scientific theories (albeit using radical and nonliteral hermeneutic strategies). Newton looked for apocalyptic codes, such as that "found" in the
architectural plan of the Temple of Solomon, whereas Reich looked for
evidence of the rise and tyranny of patriarchy from the Genesis account
(c.1500–1200 B.C.E.) until its partial overcoming in the New Testament
(c.40–120 C.E.).

It was during this period (the 1940s and early 1950s) that Reich was
trying on one hero figure after another in his quest for self-identification.
His first transference had been to Freud in 1919, followed by Peer Gynt,
to be followed by Einstein, to be followed by the figures of Galileo, Kepler, Newton, and Christ. Not only was he testing his own measure against
the giants, he was also, I suspect, looking for some conjunction of genius
and martyrdom that reflected his own experience. Scholars remain
sharply divided as to whether Reich belongs among this august group, but
the issue of his martyrdom is much more complex and interesting, going
back at least, so the evidence seems to suggest, to his act of pulling off the
covers from his dead mother's body. How does one separate out external
causation in martyrdom from the internal projections and expectations
that may evoke it? That is, in what ways did Reich set up his own
tragedies, and in what respects were they visited upon him because of the
very nature of his research? While he was never forced to recant in
Galileo's sense, he did suffer financial and emotional losses because of
the independent line of his researches. But who martyred whom?

On January 6, 1946, Reich wrote about his own odyssey in a striking
passage that stressed his role as an exile and as a man burdened by far too
much mental exertion. He had now spent about six years in America, had

started his research colony in Orgonon, and was on the verge—unknown to himself—of becoming embroiled in a nasty and prolonged public castration drama:

> The road I have walked is long, extremely long. I began my journey through life as a young boy of only seventeen. From one province of Austria to the next, then graduation from the gymnasium, the war, medicine, natural science, love, suffering, illness, marriage, a child, then another child, a profession, a career, the discovery of the orgasm, the conflict with Freud, illness [at Davos], more strife, flight to Berlin, the founding of social psychology, war with the communists, conflict with the fascists. Flight from Berlin, conflict with the psychoanalysts, conflict on all sides, loss of the children, loss of my high position in the International Psychoanalytic Association, conflict with the mechanists, conflict with the genetic psychiatrists, flight from Norway, discovery and founding of abiogenesis [genesis from the nonliving], then cancer, the orgone, the spinning wave, cosmic orgonometry. Too much! Too much?[69]

This insightful yet painful narrative shows the emotional toll that his many displacements had taken on him. His honesty (in his own eyes) often forced him to stand between the Scylla of one extreme (such as red fascism) and the Charybdis of another (black fascism).

Starting in 1947, increased negative scrutiny was directed at Reich's work in orgone research and orgone therapy. What most vexed medical and government officials (both in Maine and in Washington) was the question of the curative powers of orgone accumulators. Reich and his assistants had built a number of these accumulators of varying sizes in their attempts to see if orgone in a more concentrated form could affect the metabolic and immune systems of living things. Some of the earlier accumulators were built as small "shooter" boxes that would send out a stream of orgone through a pipe and a funnel that could be placed on the desired part of the body. Most controversial were Reich's full-size orgone accumulators in which a patient could sit (on average from twenty to forty minutes a session) and experience the curative powers of orgone. The first really damaging blow to Reich's world of orgonotic research came in May

1947, when *The New Republic* published a highly critical article about Reich by Mildred Edie Brady, an ideologue and hack writer for Stalinist causes. She painted Reich with the brush of "contempt for the masses" and ridiculed his research as the product of a megalomaniac who only wanted sex from his disciples and money from the gullible masses. Unfortunately pieces of the article were reissued in both popular and technical journals, thus poisoning the waters around Reich.[70]

Had Reich been an academic or part of the intellectual elite, he would at least have had a chance for an open and intense debate; his followers might have taken up much of the defense for him (as, for example, Thomas Huxley did for Charles Darwin). But his strategy was to return to his work and to ignore as long as possible the plague that was slowly but unrelentingly gathering around Orgonon. Still, his three-week incarceration at Ellis Island in December 1941 and January 1942 reminded him that even in the land of democracy, especially under stress of war, civil and intellectual liberties could be curtailed. Further, Reich's work was coming into public view, and he was to be caught up in the growing hysteria against the new internal/external threat of intellectual and perhaps military invasion.[71] After all, just who was this Austrian who had once studied Hitler and who had been a card-carrying member of the Communist Party? Needless to say, anyone genuinely interested in Reich's views had only to read his writings or to interview him in an open and detailed way. But the Brady article had set the pot to boil, and there were to be no means for cooling it back down to room temperature. In this sense, Reich's final ten years took the form of a Greek tragedy insofar as the hero was visited with a fate only partially of his own making yet punishable nonetheless. If the gods of the authoritarian state wanted you to pay for your hubris, then you must pay the full measure and not half.

Shortly after the publication of the Brady article, the Food and Drug Administration (FDA) decided to take a long, hard look at its subject. Reich was astonished when three government agents showed up unannounced at Orgonon on July 29, 1952, to look over Orgonon and investigate the claims that had been made against Reich. An earlier visit by a local FDA agent three months after the article came out had produced very little that the FDA could use, but the agency was not about to let up its pressure on Reich. This time the search was on for the orgone box and Reich's alleged claims that it could cure cancer. He responded to the visit with intense anger but let the agents explore his research facilities. On February 10, 1954, persuaded by the FDA, the U.S. Attorney in Maine issued a lengthy complaint for injunction against Reich, his wife, and the Wilhelm Reich Foundation for fraud. Sharaf summarized the charges:

> Orgone energy was declared nonexistent; the accumulator was declared worthless. All Reich's American publications were regarded as promotional material for the accumulator. This was maintained even for works originally published in German prior to the discovery of orgone energy such as *Character Analysis, The Sexual Revolution,* and *The Mass Psychology of Fascism,* since Reich, either in a foreword or in added material, mentioned orgone energy in the English editions of these works.[72]

This sweeping and all-inclusive document gave Reich almost no room to continue to conduct his experiments or to use orgone accumulators in either an experimental or therapeutic way. The condemnation of his written work, especially by people who utterly lacked the mental ability to examine it in detail, presupposed that the government had a right to impose its views on basic research. Reich took the complaint very seriously and contemplated the best type of response to it.

After almost two weeks of deliberation, Reich decided to reject the court's demand that he appear as a defendant in a criminal trial. From his perspective, the district attorney was encroaching on territory that was out of bounds for even an authoritarian government. To add insult to injury, Reich's former *personal* attorney, Peter Mills, who had just been appointed to the position of U.S. Attorney in Maine, took on the case himself. That this was a stunning breach of professional ethics goes without saying; that Reich let the situation stand without legal protest is itself interesting; but that Mills never expressed any doubts about his dual role is astonishing. In a filmed interview many years after the trial, Mills expressed surprise that anyone would have asked him to recuse himself since he was finally in the position to enjoy his new powers.[73]

In his carefully worded four-page reply to the complaint, Reich appealed for the freedom of science from political interference and asserted that the court had no jurisdiction over fundamental research. He was going to refuse to appear in the Portland courtroom on the grounds that the

plaintiff (the FDA) had no right to be there in the first place. His appeal
to the autonomy of science was fully consistent with his general beliefs
about his own work and the history of science and its martyrs:

> I, therefore, submit, in the name of truth and justice, that I shall
> not appear in court as the "defendant" against a plaintiff who by
> his mere complaint already has shown his ignorance in matters of
> natural science. I do so at the risk of being, by mistake, fully en-
> joined in all my activities. Such an injunction would mean, practi-
> cally, exactly nothing at all. My discovery of the Life Energy is
> today widely known nearly all over the globe, in hundreds of insti-
> tutions, whether acclaimed or cursed. It can no longer be stopped
> by anyone, no matter what happens to me.[74]

His failure to appear forced the court to impose the injunction. Michael
Silvert, not a member of Reich's inner circle but a continual presence at
Orgonon, later violated the injunction by shipping orgone accumulators
across state lines. When Reich discovered his betrayal, he was furious.
The government response was to start a criminal contempt-of-court case
against Reich and make Silvert and the Foundation codefendants.

Judge John D. Clifford handed over the new case to Judge George
Sweeney, who set the trial date for April 30, 1956. This time Reich had to
appear because he had been arrested in Washington, D.C., for violating
the terms of the injunction. He served as his own attorney as well as the
attorney for Silvert and the Foundation. Colin Wilson, in his biography of
Reich, describes the situation of the first trial and its impact on the final
disposition:

> The hearings continued to drag on—October 10, October 18, No-
> vember 4—and Reich defended himself; he signed his motions as
> a "representative of the EPPO" (the Emotional Plague Prevention
> Office). He continued to talk about conspiracy and about the mis-
> representation of his ideas. With considerable patience, the judge
> kept explaining that the present case had nothing to do with either
> of these matters; it was simply a question of whether Reich had ac-
> tively disobeyed the injunction. He also pointed out that if Reich
> had wanted to present these arguments, he should have appeared

in court to answer the original Complaint. It was the nearest he came to telling Reich that he had mishandled the whole affair from the beginning.[75]

Even with Reich's intense eloquence, the jury found him guilty of violating the 1954 injunction. He was sentenced to two years in a federal prison, while Silver, the actual violator of the injunction, got one year. Most astonishing was the order to burn many of his publications and to send federal officers to Orgonon to destroy orgone accumulators and eradicate as many of Reich's publications as could be found. Later a more intensified assault was launched against Reich's books, and many more were incinerated in New York City.

Reich was placed in a private cell in the Lewisburg prison. He was given a psychiatric evaluation before his imprisonment, which asserted that Reich manifested paranoid schizophrenia, although he also "gave no concrete evidence of being mentally incompetent."[76] He developed a relationship with the prison chaplain and continued to write letters to family and friends. But his heart was weak, and he was not able to live out the full term of his sentence. Jim Martin sketches the final scene:

Wilhelm Reich was found dead in his cell at the 7 am head count in Lewisburg Federal Penitentiary on November 3, 1957, only seven days short of his parole eligibility. Fully clothed except for his shoes, his body was found lying on the prison cot. Dr. Lacovara came to the cell at 7:15 am and took the corpse to the morgue. At 9:20 am, Eva Reich was notified of her father's death . . . In Lacovara's opinion, Reich died of "coronary insufficiency with calcified aortic stenosis and generalized arteriosclerosis." The official cause of death was an [sic] heart attack.[77]

The body was taken back to Orgonon, where it was later laid to rest in a mausoleum overlooking the lakes and woods around Rangeley. A bronze bust of Reich was placed on top of the mausoleum. His body rests within a short walking distance from his observatory, which remains almost exactly the way it was on the day he died.

In the following decade Reich's ideas sank from view, and he was relegated to the margins of psychoanalytic and scientific thought—the legacy of the charge of schizophrenia still surrounded his image. But by the early 1970s interest began to revive in Reich's work on psychosexual dynamics and his theories of character armoring. His later speculations about cosmic evolution and the ubiquity of orgone garnered a few followers, but the body of serious research and reappropriation was focused on the less controversial material of the 1930s. The prospects for a deeper and more sustained dialogue with his vast body of research are brighter now than they have been at any time since his death.[78] New encounters with Reich may find a place for at least some of his more challenging ideas about the energy that may be behind cosmogenesis and the life of all organisms.

7

The Bursting Front of the New

My goal in this brief concluding chapter is to provide a categorial framework for locating Reich's ideas and to offer a prognosis about their future prospects in the domain where psychoanalysis intersects with semiotics, science, and metaphysics. Semiotics is an encompassing discipline that sees the world as being constituted by signs and their objects. A naturalist semiotics sees the referent of the sign to be real (to have secondness and thirdness) even if the object referred to is partially veiled from view. A postmodern semiotics (a contradiction in terms, in my view) sees the referent as a mere cultural or personal construct from the labile ground of language. Reich was firmly in the naturalist camp and explored the sign/object relation from a variety of evolving perspectives. He was a practicing semiotician even if he lacked the contemporary terminology for describing what he was doing.

His implicit philosophical anthropology culminated in the view that the human process is a concrescence of the orgonotic streamings found throughout the universe, and that the human turn toward self-consciousness opens up another layer or fold that dramatically complicates the semiotic processes of life. Self-consciousness, an ambiguous gift like the theft of fire by Prometheus, has dual implications, one pointing toward a profound sense of the lost maternal, the other opening up rage against that very longing. Reading the signs of one's own self is further complicated by the intrusion of the patriarchal order, which both creates and sustains the Oedipal conflict and castration anxiety.

Nature's self is thus a sign-reading animal that has to negotiate among ancient and highly differentiated sign systems not of its own contrivance. Each sign system is an actual infinite in its own right; that is, it is *actualized* in the world and unending. The orgonotic streams that Reich believed in are potential carriers of the actual infinite of signs, and orgone even leaves its own semiotic traces, particularly in the optical sphere. We are both in and of nature, and there is no possible way to extricate ourselves from our semiotic envelope. The actual infinite (unending signs in actualization) is manifest in innumerable ways, only some of which are available to human circumspection. But there is a robust continuum stretching from our own sensations of bioplasmic pulsations, to our symptom analyses, to the plague movements of the social order, to the spiral wave effect found throughout nature—especially in the galactic realm. We are the most sophisticated sign-interpreters in the currently known universe but also the most conflicted. In the animal kingdom sexual signs are interpreted and acted upon with nonanxious secondness. For us, by contrast, sexual signs are always ambiguous, fraught with danger, rarely brought to full interpretive completion, and a continual goad to the further production of stasis anxiety. All organisms (at least) are interpreters, but we are the *split interpreters*, with our sign systems in constant collision.

Moving beyond Reich, it has now become necessary to reframe the semiotic self within the context of a community of interpreters for whom all signs, unless they are private, are open to scrutiny and analysis. A mere natural or tribal community always fails to examine its most basic sign systems and strongly resists those who try to do so. Applying the ideas of Freud or Jung to the biblical texts, for example, is still an act that brings instant condemnation in many natural communities. A natural community jealously guards its signs and their interpretants (new signs that emerge from interpreters working on the original signs). Semiotic inertia is the only form of interpretive motion found in natural communities. But the powers of an evolutionary nature work against the rigidity of natural communities. Any sign *will* be changed whenever it is interpreted, no matter how infinitesimal the variation from the "norm." The analyst/ analysand relationship is one of the paradigms of how a community of interpreters can emerge from the dense background of the more pervasive natural community. New interpretants are encouraged, and dream material will compel the analysand into further interpretive acts regardless of what his or her so-called will decides. The evolutionary value of novel semiotic variation is obvious, provided that the new interpretants roughly coincide with the coevolving dynamic objects to which they are connected.

Reich did express contempt for the masses of people caught up in the plague, and he failed to find a social form of semiotic psychoanalysis that could function with smaller and larger groups. Like Jung he sensed the utter power of the great social Other, whether it be the plague or the collective unconscious in its infected state. But this massive Other can be brought closer to the realm of semiotic probing and circumspection. Interpretive codes and transitions can be clarified and the underside of sign systems can be illuminated through the techniques of semiotic psychoanalysis. The term I prefer to use for semiotic psychoanalysis is *psychosemiotics*, which denotes the processes through which the local and regional traits of the psyche are brought out of hiding and into the light of the waiting community of interpreters.

But the strategies associated with psychosemiotics require a revised conception of the constitution and functionality of the psyche. The Reichian model of contraction and expansion around the orgonotic energy of the nervous and muscular systems is quite powerful as far as it goes, but as we have noted, in moving toward bioelectricity Reich deprivileged the meaning approach that Jung had developed so successfully. Energy systems must be studied, but this focus puts the psyche on a fairly deterministic foundation. The meaning approach allows the mystery of the unconscious to remain, as it must, and invites the play of interpretants to cross from the unconscious to consciousness. Reich wanted a more controlled situation, whereas psychosemiotics lives fully within the emerging interpretants (potential thirds) of the psyche. There is a strong sense in which the otherness of the unconscious must not be violated by the drive toward too much clarity too soon. The quantitative conversion of psyche and soma to orgonotic pulsations runs grave risks if it turns its back on the plenitude of meaning that continually springs forth from the unconscious, which is both a scanning system of the lifeworld and a creating agent of new wholes.

The social dimension of psychosemiotics weaves meanings into and out of emergent communities of interpretation as they resist the natural communities within which they are embedded. If a natural community practices semiotic inertia, an interpretive community practices a centrifugal momentum in which interpretants fly outward to intersect with other potential interpretants in a larger unfolding of thirdness. This process is different from that of merging one's self in the orgone ocean because it requires deliberation, empathy, communication, intersubjectivity, and openness to the Not Yet (*noch nicht sein*). The community of interpreters protects and empowers the process of personal interpretation. This is not to say that the orgonotic approach is incompatible with psychosemiotics, but that it is only one mode, not to be privileged, whereby the psyche (personal and social) can gain evolutionary advantages and sexual well-being.

Should genital sexuality be the touchstone for psychosemiotics? Freud and Reich have left us with some very strong arguments and clinical research for assuming so. It is certainly clear that one should always look to where the resistances are, and to where latent negative transferences lurk—these resistances and transferences are almost always tied to the power of eros. The issue of sexuality is without doubt the most important within the human process, especially when manifest in its uniquitous neurotic character forms. Consequently, psychosemiotics will continue to privilege sexuality as the ground drive of the self-in-process. But it does not follow that the so-called sublimated forms of sexuality are merely secondary or linked to secondary drives. During certain phases of life, or during internal transformations of libido itself, other drives may assume functional or even structural priority. The drive toward creation may be even more encompassing than the sexual drive, which could be one of its instances, but this conclusion awaits further interpretive probing.

The self-in-process emerges out of the firstness of the physical womb and the womb of possibilities. It encounters the blunt edges of secondness as it negotiates its way toward enhanced meaning (thirdness). Sexual drives emerge in infancy, and the drive for meaning follows soon after. The self is less a plaything of its drives than a momentum that probes, challenges, and explores its environment. Each neurotic symptom is a goad to a new string of interpretants, even when it takes the form of repetition-compulsion. Each creative act restabilizes the organism/nature transaction and calls for further adjustments in an open future. The creative void into which interpretants are lured is the great Not Yet that makes meaning possible in the personal and social orders. This Not Yet is neither a *place* nor the realm of orgone but a clearing-away that makes room for interpretants. It is a processive infinite that houses the actual infinite of growing signs. The ultimate nonlocated location of the Not Yet has no qualities of its own other than that of serving relationally as a lure to semiotic and evolutionary self-organization on the boundaries of order and chaos.

Does radical naturalism really require that we assign a basic whatness to the world? Must we assume the strategies of classical, modern, and even postmodern metaphysics that always want to say: nature is X, whether that X be matter, spirit, energy, orgone, electromagnetism, ether, consciousness, eros, form, language, space/time particulars, or simple stuff? No. In a fully radical naturalism the concept of the foundational X completely disappears. Hence Reich's metaphysical privileging of orgone is relegated to a subaltern position, however important in its own right. All that can really be said about nature per se is that it is the constant availability of orders, not some superorder or primal foundation. Orgone may or may not be *in* nature, but it cannot be equivalent *to* nature.

What makes the orgone concept so interesting is that it straddles the divide between science and metaphysics. It emerged from Reich out of decades of preparatory research, and he felt that the cumulative evidence for its existence was overwhelming. But some of his claims about orgone went beyond the reach of his experimental protocols, and he extended the concept in highly metaphorical and poetic ways. This does not mean that the extensions were invalid; rather, he entered into a different order of discourse, one less continuous with the scientific than he assumed. In my final judgment I would say that the concept of cosmic orgone must continue to spur serious inquiry, that new scientific and research protocols must be developed for examining "it," and that the working paradigms of the life sciences must be open to transformation. The task of the metaphysician in this instance (and all language users have an operative metaphysics) is to analyze the generic claims of orgonotic science and to find translation mechanisms for rendering these claims into nonempirical yet still pragmatically useful ones.

In an ecstatic naturalist metaphysics—the unsaid within Reich's incomplete perspective—nature has no basic *what* but does have innumerable *hows*, innumerable ways of being. Had Reich been granted two more decades of life, he would, I suspect, have begun to open up this unsaid that runs through his framework like an underground spring. It is clear that Reich was a naturalist—that is, he denied the existence of a realm of the supernatural, and he affirmed that nature was self-created and continually self-creating. Nature was all that there was, but this primal fact had no moral implications either way. His naturalism was radical in that it dug beneath the various dualisms that marred the thinking of his era and strove toward the *Ursprung* that spawned the *hows* of the world and its orders.

Was his naturalism ecstatic? The term *ecstasy* as used here denotes the self-othering of certain natural/semiotic orders. An order of nature is ecstatic when it suddenly bursts forth with power and meaning in a way that grasps the center of the human psyche. That is, the order—say, a work of art or a sacred grove—becomes other to its own self-boundedness and emerges from out of itself to shake the roots of the attending psyche, especially in its unconscious dimension. As an epiphany of being (or manifestation of orgone, for Reich), the sacred order gives nature as a whole a deepened meaning. This is not to say, contra Reich, that nature per se is holy or sacred; rather, special sacred folds that represent a dramatic increment in meaning and power punctuate its innumerable orders. To encounter a sacred fold *within* nature—as by definition they cannot occur outside nature—is to activate the deepest transference and countertransference fields within the self. In concise expression, "no sacred fold, no religious transference or countertransference." Insofar as a sacred fold is seen *an sich*, the self must be changed. In formal terms: Sacred fold S entails transference and countertransference TCT. This relationship is fully symmetrical and goes in both directions. Thus S $\longleftrightarrow$ TCT. Neither can occur without the other.

Ecstatic naturalism is a form of radical naturalism that takes antidualism and the concept of the ubiquity of nature one step further. Nature, the constant availability of orders, is also the locus for those orders that are self-othering and that burst forth with newer folds of meaning and power. Reich envisioned these ecstatic orders as being orgonotically charged, and he may have been right (pending extensive future inquiry), but he did not grasp the more generic implications of his implicit and unsaid ecstatic naturalism. Clearly an ecstatic naturalist perspective has no place for a personal patriarchal god as the creator of nature ex nihilo. The sacred is in and of nature and is subject to entropy and the loss of meaning and power over time. But the spawning power of *nature naturing* is eternal and is not parasitic on the space/time universes that may come and go.

Insofar as Reich sought *the* ground of nature in his concept of the orgone ocean, he also sought *the* meaning that would unify the plague-ridden psyche. But if the former quest is abandoned, then the latter must fall by the wayside as well. My assertion is that nature has no ultimate ground of all grounds any more than it manifests some meaning of all meanings. Grounds come and go, always ordinally located—that is, pertinent to one or more orders but never to all. Meanings come and go, always tied to a specific psyche/sacred fold correlation, or to transactions of lesser semiotic density and scope. Ecstatic naturalism is the perspective that embraces the fragmentary quality of a mysterious and self-othering nature, only part of which is confined to the world of astrophysics and the space/time orders. My suspicion is that Reich's drive toward personal self-control also had implications for his metaphysics. Like Plato and Peirce before him, he projected the concept of self-control onto the universe at large. The vast orgonotic ocean (not ocean*s*) enveloped the fragile neurotic psyche and infused it with the power of self-control. The "flesh" was reintegrated with the "body," and psyche and soma were reconciled. But nature is many things besides this, and psychosemiotics must have the courage to face into a plural ground that is forever elusive in its own depths.

Philosophical anthropology has here become transfigured into psychosemiotics, the study of the entire self-in-process as but one of the innumerable sign systems in an infinite nature. The human process has species-specific traits that render it especially interesting to semiotic query. The inward turning toward consciousness and eventually self-consciousness are very late evolutionary products of a species that may be three million years old or more, but this dual turning represents one of the great punctuation points in evolution. Evolutionary psychology is probing into the questions as to how and why this infolding occurred, and its continuing researches are of great importance to psychosemiotics, but the more compelling set of questions has to do with the dialectic of self-infolding and self-othering. How does the evolutionary turn toward a consciousness aware that it *is* a self affect the momentum of self-othering in nature's ecstatic orders? That is, how does my having a centered ego and a self-aware psyche connect me to those epiphanies of meaning and power in nature that could be called "religious"? At the irruption of this question, the strategies of science, philosophy, theology, semiotics, and psychoanalysis (now psychosemiotics) converge.

Since semiotics is a governing framework for the discussion of whatever is manifest in whatever way it is manifest, it serves as the perspective that can translate and correlate other perspectives. All of science is semiotic, although it is other things as well. All of theology and philosophy are semiotic, although semiotics does not exhaust their "matter." And depth psychology is clearly semiotic through and through, yet it also contains realms that cannot be rendered semiotically. We must beware of falling into the trap of pansemioticism, which mistakes the functional power of semiotics for a full metaphysics of nature. Nature is indeed constituted by innumerable signs and their referents, but it is also an inexhaustible self-othering ground of fragmented grounds that cannot be made fully transparent to even the most robust semiotic analysis. My sense is that Reich was sometimes a pansemiotician in that he wanted to render the entire world into signs that could be publicly expressed to the relevant communities of interpretation. This quest is doomed to failure for the profound reason that nature is always "more" (William James) than can ever be signified about it. Nature always spills over the edges of our semiotic codes and contrivances.

In the twenty-first century my hope is that classical psychoanalysis can be reconfigured as a psychosemiotics that uses the powerful tools of a realist semiotics (in the tradition of Peirce) while also working out of a more successful and generic metaphysics of nature in its dual modes of *nature naturing* (nature continually creating itself out of itself alone) and *nature natured* (the orders of the world). Of the truly great pioneers of psychoanalysis, Reich and Jung stand out as having grasped the more encompassing and capacious metaphysical background of their probes into psyche and soma. Freud's analyses and conceptions, while path-breaking, seem somewhat restricted and self-limiting by comparison to the explosive works of Jung and Reich. While countless people around the world have embraced Jung, Reich has remained suspended in his own Not Yet. He remains a potency that has yet to emerge into its full scope and power. I strongly believe that his perspective, whatever its flaws, will be part of the emancipatory "bursting front of the new" that was evoked by the mystical Marxist philosopher Ernst Bloch.

Each component of the bursting front will work in dialectic with the others. A more open and radical science of life systems will enter into dialogue with psychosemiotics, which has a narrower but more dramatic focus of inquiry. In turn, theology will deconstruct its patriarchal delusions and wed itself to the philosophy of ecstatic naturalism. The sacred will be relocated to where it has in fact *always* belonged, the domain of nature in its sheer plenitude. And classical psychoanalysis will continue to serve as the wise older sister who pulled back the veil and helped us to see and confront the otherness and mystery within.

Notes

PREFACE

1. Reich learned to write in English in the late 1940s and early 1950s, although he started translating German into English in medical school. His written English is excellent. Both books were published together as Wilhelm Reich, *Ether, God and Devil and Cosmic Superimposition,* trans. Therese Pol (New York: Farrar, Straus and Giroux, 1951). They were reprinted in 2000 by New York: Welcome Rain.

2. Myron Sharaf, *Fury on Earth: A Biography of Wilhelm Reich* (New York: Da Capo Press, 1994). Sharaf wrote out of a fairly strong negative transference due to some personal sexual entanglements between Reich and Sharaf's girlfriend. At the same time he tended toward somewhat simplistic renderings of highly complex conceptual structures.

3. For good or ill, Reich often rewrote his earlier texts and added a lot of material from his later researches. As yet there is nothing equivalent to Freud's *Standard Edition* or Jung's *Collected Works.* His early *The Function of the Orgasm* is available in its original 1927 form in the translation *Genitality in the Theory and Therapy of Neurosis,* vol. 2 of *Early Writings,* trans. Philip Schmitz (New York: Farrar, Straus and Giroux, 1980). The 1940 German typescript can be obtained from the Wilhelm Reich Museum in Rangeley, Maine. The English text of this later edition is Wilhelm Reich, *The Function of the Orgasm,* vol. 1 of *The Discovery of the Orgone,* trans. Vincent R. Carfagno (New York: Farrar, Straus and Giroux, 1973). The German manuscript is also available in book form as *Die Entdeckung des Orgons,* vol. 1, *Die Funktion des Orgasmus* (Cologne: Verlag Kiepenheuer und Witsch, 1997). The original German book was published as *Die Funktion des Orgasmus* (Vienna: Internationaler Psychoanalytischer Verlag, 1927).

4. Wilhelm Reich, *Listen, Little Man!,* trans. Ralph Manheim (New York: Farrar, Straus and Giroux, 1974). Photocopies of the original German manuscript (*Reden an den kleinen Mann*) are available from the Wilhelm Reich Museum. See also *Reden an den kleinen Mann* (Frankfurt am Main: Fischer Taschenbuch Verlag, 2000).

5. I am very much aware that the move toward universalism and antitribalism contains

its own demons, especially in an age when various disenfranchised groups have struggled toward self-identity against colonial powers or reigning elites. My hope is that a dialectic can emerge in which postcolonial consciousness can engage with universalistic energies to break the hold of narcissistic tribalisms. On the negative side, one needs to be especially conscious of the dangers of subtle forms of, for example, anti-Semitism or of anti-Islamism that would chastise their particularistic elements. The solution I call for is for each tradition to find its own universalistic tendencies from within and to magnify them to the extreme, such as the mystical tradition within medieval Catholicism, or the Sufism within Islam, or the medieval and modern cabalism within Judaism, or the Transcendentalism within American Protestantism, or the universalistic message of the *Upanishads* (in my opinion, the greatest religious texts ever written) within Hinduism. This does not entail any loss of the rich liturgical content of each tradition, only the giving up of excessive ontological claims. My philosophical grounding for this universalizing move has its roots in Immanuel Kant's magisterial *Kritik der reinen Vernunft* (1781). See especially the new definitive translation, *The Critique of Pure Reason*, trans. Paul Guyer and Allen W. Wood (Cambridge, Eng.: Cambridge University Press, 1998). While as a naturalist I reject Kant's idealistic theory of knowledge, I honor his intense move away from the rage for the particular that was so brutally manifest in the religious wars that savaged Europe in the previous century. His own philosophical theology, as expressed in his 1793 *Die Religion innerhalb der Grenzen der bloßen Vernunft* (a book that was banned in its second edition) was the first truly emancipatory text to emerge out of the philosophical study of religion and consequently paved the way for the liberal theology of Friedrich Schleiermacher (1768–1834). See Immanuel Kant, *Religion Within the Boundaries of Mere Reason*, trans. George di Giovanni, in *Religion and Rational Theology* (Cambridge, Eng.: Cambridge University Press, 1996).

6. See especially Martin Heidegger, *Being and Time*, trans. Joan Stambaugh (Albany: SUNY Press, 1996). The first German edition is *Sein und Zeit*, in *Jahrbuch für Philosophie und phänomenologische Forschung* (1927).

7. See Ernst Cassirer, *The Philosophy of Symbolic Forms*, trans. Ralph Manheim (New Haven: Yale University Press, 1955). The first German edition is *Philosophie der symbolischen Formen* (Berlin: Bruno Cassirer, 1929).

8. I have developed the correlation of semiotics, psychoanalysis, and nature in two books, Robert S. Corrington, *Nature's Self: Our Journey from Origin to Spirit* (Lanham, Md.: Rowman and Littlefield, 1996), and *Nature's Religion* (Lanham, Md.: Rowman and Littlefield, 1997).

9. See Julia Kristeva, *Revolution in Poetic Language*, trans. Margaret Walker (New York: Columbia University Press, 1984). The original French edition is *La Révolution du langage poétique* (Paris: Editions du Seuil, 1974).

10. Wilhelm Reich, *The Murder of Christ: The Emotional Plague of Mankind* (New York: Farrar, Straus and Giroux, 1966). This book was written by Reich in English in 1951.

11. Reich visited Einstein at the Institute for Advanced Studies in Princeton, New Jersey, and subsequently wrote a series of letters to him that have recently been published in

Wilhelm Reich, *American Odyssey: Letters and Journals 1940–1947*, ed. Mary Boyd Higgins, trans. Derek and Inge Jordan and Philip Schmitz (New York: Farrar, Straus and Giroux, 1999). See especially the letter of February 20, 1941, on pages 63–80.

12. I engage in such an emancipatory reenactment in Robert S. Corrington, *An Introduction to C. S. Peirce: Philosopher, Semiotician, and Ecstatic Naturalist* (Lanham, Md.: Rowman and Littlefield, 1993).

13. For my own systematic correlation of psychoanalysis and metaphysics, see Robert S. Corrington, *A Semiotic Theory of Theology and Philosophy* (Cambridge, Eng.: Cambridge University Press, 2000).

1: FAMILY TRAGEDY, SEXUAL AWAKENING, AND WORLD WAR I

1. Wilhelm Reich, *Passion of Youth: An Autobiography: 1897–1922*, ed. Mary Boyd Higgins and Chester M. Raphael, M.D., trans. Philip Schmitz and Jerri Tompkins (New York: Farrar, Straus and Giroux, 1988), 39. The German edition, *Leidenschaft der Jugend* (Cologne: Verlag Kiepenheuer und Witsch, 1994) was published in 1994. The German version of this passage reads: "[E]lastische pralle Brust mit rosigweißer Haut ist das Schönste an der Frau. Daher liebe ich Gedichte, die in sinnlich-keuscher Begehr die Frauenbrust rufen, denn keine Sehnsucht kann bei mir so stark werden, als die nach der Frauenbrust, als Kopfkissen. Ich habe später viele keusche Nächte erlebt, in denen ich auf der Mädchenbrust ruhend, eng an sie und den Körper geschmiegt, vollkommenen Ersatz für den Koitus fand" (45). The first part of the autobiography, up to 1914, was written in 1922. In her preface to the text, Higgins stated that she brought out the previously unpublished material "in order to dispel the myths given currency by the various biographies that have appeared since [Reich's] death." One can't but suspect that Sharaf's *Fury on Earth* is one of the biographies that she had in mind. On his attitude toward his brother, Robert, Reich wrote in his journal on January 3, 1921, when Robert was about to leave Vienna: "What if I never see him again? I was still unable to resolve those infantile death wishes. My unconscious is full of horrible hatred toward him!" (146). The German reads: "Wie, wenn ich ihn nicht mehr sehe, oder er nicht mich! Ich war noch im Stande, mir diese infantile Todesphantasien sofort aufzulösen. Mein Unterbewußtsein ist mit entsetzlichem Hass gegen ihn geladen!" (166). Actually in the German text it says the opposite, that "I was still *able* to resolve those infantile death wishes," but this is obviously a typo.

2. Ibid., 25. The German reads: "Ich zählte ungefähr 11½ Jahre, als ich das erste Mal richtig koitiert u. zw. mit einer Köchin, die man von der Stadt her engagiert hatte. Erst sie brachte mich auf die zur Ejakulation nötigen Stoßbewegungen u. damals kam mir die Ejakulation so plötzlich u. unerwartet, daß ich erschreckt glaubte, es sei ein Unglück passiert. Von der Zeit an koitierte ich beinahe tgl. Jahre hindurch u. zw. stets am Nachmittage, wenn die Eltern schliefen" (27). The Schmitz-Tompkins translation leaves out an important element from the German. The end of the second sentence, instead of "at that time it had been an accident," should read "at that time the

ejaculation came so suddenly and unexpectedly that I was scared and thought it was an accident."

3. Reich, *Passion of Youth*, 42–43. The German reads: "Später habe ich über die Gewaltigkeit dieses Affektes oft nachgedacht u. konnte das (illeg) nicht lösen wie das möglish wurde, daß ich, der ich seit 3 Jahren Geschlechtsverkehr u. nicht gerade selten pflog, so außer mir geriet. War's das Milieu, die Kleidung, die rote Lazpe, die provozierende (illeg), der Dirnengeruch—? Ich weiß es nicht! Es war Sinneslust gewesen—*ich* hatte aufgehört zu sein—war ganz *Penis* geworden! Ich biß, retzte, stiß u. das Mädchen hatte ihre Not mit mir! Ich glaubte in (illeg) hineinkriechen zu müssen" (49).

4. See Paul Tillich, *Systematic Theology*, vol. 1 (Chicago: University of Chicago Press, 1951).

5. Myron Sharaf, *Fury on Earth: A Biography of Wilhelm Reich* (New York: Da Capo Press, 1994), 41; Ilse Ollendorff, *Wilhelm Reich: A Personal Biography* (New York: St. Martin's Press, 1969).

6. Wilhelm Reich, *Early Writings*, trans. Philip Schmitz (New York: Farrar, Straus and Giroux, 1975), 1:65–72. "*Über einen Fall von Durchbruch der Inzestschranke in der Pubertät,*" *Zeitschrift für Sexualwissenschaft*, vol. 7 (1920). The German book is *Frühe Schriften: 1920–1925* (Cologne: Vedog Kiepenheuer und Witsch, 1997).

7. Ibid, 1:66.

8. Ibid, 1:66–67. The German is: "[S]eit frühester Kindheit mit inniger Zärtlichkeit an der Mutter, die ihn oft vor tätlichen. Ausschreitungen des Vaters schützte. Die Ehe der Eltern war insofern keine glückliche, als die Mutter unter seines Vaters Eifersucht 'schrecklich zu leiden' hatte; er hatte schon als Fünf-bis Sechsjähriger häßliche Eifersuchtsszenen mit angesehen, es sei auch oft zu Tätlichkeiten seitens des Vaters gekommen, bei denen er sich immer als zur 'Mutter gehörig' gefühlt hatte. Leicht begreiflich, da er selbst so sehr unter der Knute stand und die Mutter innigst liebte. Sexuellfrühreif, schon mit 5 Jahren hatte es für ihn 'keine Geheimnisse' gegeben, und auch körperlich stark, vollführte er mit 11½ Jahren mit dem Stubenmädchen, allerdings von ihr dazu bewogen, den ersten Koitus. Vom 14. bis 18. Lebensjahr Onanie-Periode, abwechselnd mit Gelegenheitskoitus, im 15. Lebensjahr erste Äußerungen ganz geringer Minderwertigkeitsgefühle" (*Frühe Schriften*, 79–80).

9. Ibid, 68. The German is: "Als dann Mutter (oh, welchen Beiklang erhält jetzt dieses Wort!) aus dem Zimmer trat, aus dem ich keinen Lichtschein fallen sah, mit geröteten Wangen und irrem, unstetem Blick, da wußte ich: jetzt war es geschehen: ob das erste Mal, konnte ich natürlich nicht schließen. Ich wollte weinend, wie ich in der Ecke, von einem Schrank geschützt, dastand, auf die Mutter stürzen, doch auch das blieb aus, zu unser aller Unglück, denn ich trage die Überzeugung in mir, daß mein Anblick knapp nach der Tat sie zur Besinnung gebracht und, wenn auch etwas verspätet, uns die Mutter, und Vater die Gattin, gerettet hätte. Dies war die einzig mögliche Rettung!" (*Frühe Schriften*, 81).

10. Ibid, 1:69.

11. Reich, *Passion of Youth*, 29. The German reads: "Ich hörte Kuß, Flüstern die fürchterlichen Geräusche des Bettes u. darin lag meine Mutter u. 3 m dahinter stand ihr Kind u. hörte ihre Schande. Plötzlich Ruhe, offenbar hatte ich in meiner Aufregung Geräusch gemacht, dann beruhigende Worte seinerseits u. dann, dann wieder wieder oh. Nur Ruhe, Ruhe! Dieser nervenaufpeitschenden Tragödie gegenüber soll ich Übermenschliches leisten und "objektiv" urteilen! Welcher Hohn! Ein solcher Vorsatz! Aus jener katastrophalen Nacht erinnere ich nur soviel, daß ich zuerst ins Zimmer stürtzen wollte, doch von dem Gedanken zurückgehalten wurde, sie könnten mich töten! Hatte ich doch irgendwo gelesen, daß der Liebhaber jeden hinmache u. mit wilden Phantasien im Hirn schlich ich in mein Bett zurück, an Frohsinn geschädigt, im Innersten zerrissen für mein ganzes Leben!" (*Leidenschaft*, 31–32). A more accurate translation of the final part of the text would be: "With my brain filled with wild fantasies, I crept back into my bed, my cheerfulness undermined, my innermost being torn apart for the rest of my life!" The final English sentence from the quote "For the first time . . ." does not appear in the German manuscript.
12. Ibid.
13. Sharaf, *Fury on Earth*, 44.
14. Reich, *Passion of Youth*, 24. The German reads: "Die Prügel hatten mich nicht aufgeregt, war ich doch dran gewöhnt, umsomehr war ich wegen Mutters Verrat fassungslos. Sie hatte mich Vater ausgeliefert! Das konnte ich nicht verschmerzen u. verzieh es ihr auch niemals" (*Leidenschaft*, 25).
15. Sharaf, *Fury on Earth*, 44; Reich, *Passion of Youth*, 31–38.
16. Reich, *Passion of Youth*, 32n. This passage is missing in the German manuscript but appears in *Leidenschaft der Jugend*. The German is: "Wie logisch und vernünftig! Wie verkehrt mein Urteil 1919. Die Situation erscheint mir nun klar: Was Mutter tat, war vollkommen richtig. Mein Verrat, der sie das Leben kostete, war ein Akt der Rache: Sie hatte mich bei Vater verraten, als ich den Tabak für den Wagner genommen hatte, und nun verriet ich *sie*. Was für eine Tragödie! Ich wünschte, meine Mutter würde heute leben, um das Verbrechen, das ich in jenen Tagen, vor 35 Jahren beging, wieder gutzumachen. Ich habe ein Bild dieser noblen Frau aufgestellt, damit ich sie immer und immer wieder ansehen kann. Was für ein nobles Geschöpf, diese Frau—meine Mutter! Mag mein Lebenswerk meine Missetat wieder gutmachen. Angesichts der Brutalität meines Vaters hatte sie völlig recht" (*Leidenschaft*, 48).
17. Ibid., 38–39.
18. Ibid, 58. The section on the war years (53–67) was written in 1937. The German reads: "Ich meldete mich zum Heeresdienst, ein halbes Jahr früher als die gesetzliche Einrückung fällig war, und kam zunächst zu einer Abteilung, die Straßen baute und gleichzeitig in der Waffe übte. Das Einjährigenrecht hatte ich noch nicht. Mir fehlte das Abitur. Schüler der achten Gymnasialklasse konnten ein Notabitur ablegen. Man mußte den Stoff der letzten Klasse nachholen und eine etwas milder beurteilte Prüfung ablegen . . . Ich war gerade in der Offiziersschule. Wir waren 18-jährige Jungen, einige Tausend von der östlichen Armee. Wir hatten eine sechs-

wöchige Infanteristausbildung hinter uns und wurden nun in der Schwarm-, Zugs-
und Kompagnieführung geschult. Die Schulung war hart und streng . . . Zum Regi-
ment kam ich als Korporal zurück" (*Leidenschaft*, 64).

19. Ibid., 63. The German reads: "Die italienischen Gefangenen hatten Bordelle mit.
Eine ältere Frau und vier oder fünf Mädchen. Unsere Leute bekamen in der Reserve
'Bordellurlaub.' In Fiume und Triest blühte das Unternehmen in schauerlicher
Weise. Die Soldaten waren buchstäblich reihenweise angestellt, um zu *einem* Mäd-
chen zu kommen. Die italienischen Frauen wurden in unserem Lager einquartiert.
Am Tage hatten die Offiziersdiener und einige Mannschaftspersonen mit ihnen
geschlafen. In der folgenden Nacht nahmen die Offiziere sie in ihre Zimmer. Drei
Tage später marschierte eine ganze Kolonne ins Hinterland mit Tripper ab. Darunter
unser Hauptmann. So sieht die Moral aus" (*Leidenschaft*, 69).

20. See ibid., 91.

21. Ibid., 66. The passage is missing in the German manuscript but is available in the
book form. The German is: "Das Jus-Studium lag mir nicht. Ich ergriff es, weil man
darin rascher zum Broterwerb kommen konnte als anderswo. Es gab dreimonatige
Einpaukkurse zur ersten Staatprüfung, zum Romanum. Ich lernte fleißig, doch ohne
innere Beteiligung. Zwei Wochen vor der Prüfung, angefüllt mit Hunderten Para-
graphen römanischen und kirchlichen Rechts, traf ich zufällig auf der Rampe der
Universität einen alten Gymnasialkollegen. Er studierte Medizin. Da erwachte in mir
das alte naturwissenschaftliche Interesse. Die Jurisprudenz blieb liegen, und ich
übersiedelte auf die medizinische Fakultät. Es geschah halb unbewußt und unver-
mittelt. Ein guter intuitiver Akt, denn weinge Wochen später zerfiel Österreich und
mit ihm seine Rechtsprechung. Ich wäre kaput gegangen, da ich ohne jede materielle
Basis dastand" (*Leidenschaft*, 89).

22. Sharaf, *Fury on Earth*, 51.

23. For two important deconstructions of the "Einstein as the asexual wise man myth,"
see the magisterial Albrecht Folsing, *Albert Einstein*, trans. Ewald Osers (New York:
Penguin Books, 1997); the original German edition is *Albert Einstein: Eine Biogra-
phie* (Frankfurt am Main: Suhrkamp Verlag, 1993). See also the less magisterial but
delightfully informative Roger Highfield and Paul Carter, *The Private Lives of Albert
Einstein* (New York: St. Martin's Press, 1993).

2: MEDICAL SCHOOL, FREUD, AND THE EARLY PAPERS

1. For Freud's account of his 1885 time in Paris, see his letter to Jung of April 14, 1907,
(Letter 20F) in *The Freud/Jung Letters: The Correspondence between Sigmund Freud
and C.G. Jung*, ed. William McGuire, trans. Ralph Manheim and R.F.C. Hull, Bollingen
Series XCIV (Princeton: Princeton University Press, 1974), pp. 32–35.

2. Wilhelm Reich, *The Function of the Orgasm*, vol. 1 of *The Discovery of the Orgone*,
trans. Vincent R. Carfagno (New York: Farrar, Straus and Giroux, 1973), 35. The
German typescript from the library of the Orgone Institute in Rangeley, Maine, *Die
Entdeckung des Orgons*, reads: "Freud war anders, vor allem einfach im Auftreten.

Die anderen spielten im Gehaben irgendeine Rolle, den Professor, den großen Menschenkenner, den distinguierten Wissenschaftler. Freud sprach mit mir wie ein ganz gewöhnlicher Mensch und hatte brennend kluge Augen. Sie durchdrangen nicht die Augen des andern in seherischer Pose, sondern schauten bloß echt und wahrhaft in die Welt. Er erkundigte sich nach unserer Arbeit im Seminar und fand sie sehr vernünftig. Wir hätten recht, meinte er . . . Freud sprach rasch, sachlich und lebhaft. Seine Handbewegungen waren natürlich. Ironie klang durch alles hindurch" (36). Carfagno misses some of the poetry of Reich's German. I would translate *brennend kluge Augen*, not as "bright, intelligent eyes," but as "burning, wise eyes," and there is a different metaphysical sense if you translate *klang* in the last sentence as "sounded." Thus you would say, "Irony sounded through everything he said." Reich was *far* more of a poet than some of his translations convey. Reich's German typescript has a few typos that have been silently corrected here.

3. Myron Sharaf, *Fury on Earth: A Biography of Wilhelm Reich* (New York: Da Capo Press, 1994), 64.

4. To become a member of the Vienna Psychoanalytic Society, one had to read a paper and have its contents approved by the membership. Reich's paper was "Libidinal Conflicts and Delusions in Ibsen's *Peer Gynt*," in *Early Writings*, trans. Philip Schmitz (New York: Farrar, Straus and Giroux, 1975), 1:3–64. It was presented in October 1920.

5. The reader will want to examine the new translation of the *first* edition of this work, Sigmund Freud, *The Interpretation of Dreams*, trans. Joyce Crick (Oxford, Eng.: Oxford University Press, 1999). The introduction by Ritchie Robertson has a slight Jungian slant, pointing out, I think correctly, that Jung's dream theory is much stronger and more empirical than Freud's. As is well known, the first edition (*Die Traumdeutung*), which until now has not been available in English, was published in November 1899 but postdated to 1900 for the millennial impact. As is also well known, it was not a commercial success, selling around three hundred copies in its first years.

6. Wilhelm Reich, *Passion of Youth: An Autobiography: 1897–1922*, ed. Mary Boyd Higgins and Chester M. Raphael, M.D., trans. Philip Schmitz and Jerri Tompkins (New York: Farrar, Straus and Giroux, 1988), 78. The color combinations referred to in the first sentence are symbolic of various organizations, according to a translator's note. The German text is: "Kein Haß gegen Alles nichtjüdische, verständnisinniges Entgegenkommen den Anderen gegenüber, kein Streit, ob jüdisch od. hebräisch, ob blauweiß od. rotgrün, großzügig von außen nach innen u. gestärkt wieder nach außen, in weite Kreise. Weg mit der undurchdringlichen Mauer u. da das Wort, Kosmopolitismus Internationale in weitestem Sinne! Ich gestehe, zum ersten Male, seitdem ich ähnliches gehört und gesehen, stieg in mir etwas auf, eine Erklärung! Darum—haßte—ja haßte ich bisher nun diejenigen, welche den Juden zum Glück verhelfen wollten, nicht mit den Anderen, sondern über deren Leichen, nicht mit ihrem Einverständnis, sondern gegen deren Wille! Nicht ein: 'Wir alle sind'! sondern nur Wir! Endlich höre ich einen Mann, der zugleich Mensch ist u. Jude, nicht Chauvinist! Wir werden sehen welcher Art Früchte seine Intentionen zeitigen werden" (*Leidenschaft*, 79–80).

7. See the excellent book by Stephen Nadler, *Spinoza: A Life* (Cambridge, Eng.: Cambridge University Press, 1999). I do not invoke Spinoza casually here. I think that there are also some striking philosophical and *theological* parallels between the mature Reich and Spinoza, especially between Spinoza's view of *natura naturans* (nature creating nature) and Reich's view of cosmic energy. I will discuss this correlation and others in the final chapter.

8. Reich, *Passion of Youth*, 102. The German is: "Zweimal Onaniephantasien mit bewußtem Inzest auf die Mutter, von der ich nie den Kopf, immer nur Unterleib sah u. fühlte" (*Leidenschaft*, 113).

9. See John Kerr, *A Most Dangerous Method: The Story of Jung, Freud, and Sabina Spielrein* (New York: Alfred A. Knopf, 1993).

10. Reich, *Passion of Youth*, 125. The German is: "Kurz, Lore erklärte eines Tages, nun wäre sie fertig analysiert, nun wollte sie mich haben. Ich hatte keine große Lust. Mit Patientinnen soll man nicht schlafen, heißt es. Es ist auch zu kompliziert und gefährlich. Doch Lore war endlich 'sie selbst.' Sie könnte warten, meinte sie . . . Schließlich war se ja auch keine Patientin mehr. Und es ging niemand etwas an. Ich liebte sie, und sie wurde sehr glücklich. Am 27. Oktober 1920 schrieb sie in ihr Tagebuch als letzte Notiz: 'Ich bin glücklich. Restlos glücklich. Ich hätte nie gedacht, daß ich das je werden könnte—und doch. Vollste, tiefste Erfüllung. Vater haben und Mutter sein, beides zugleich in denselben Menschen. Ehe! Monogamie! Endlich! Nie gab es Koitus mit solcher Wollust, solcher Befriedigung, solchem Einssein und sich Durchdringen wie jetzt. Nie solche Parallelität in Anziehung des Geistes und Körpers wie jetzt. Und es ist schön. Und ich bin gerichtet, klar, fest und sicher—so lieb ich mich. Und naturwahr zufrieden! Nur eines: Ein Kind!!!!" (*Leidenschaft*, 142–43).

11. Ibid., 126. The German is: "Sie wußte, daß ich Lia liebte, anders als sie. Wir verstanden, daß man zwei Menschen gleichzeitig lieben kann, wenn man jung ist. Sie war nicht böse, ebensowenig wie ich Lia böse war. Es war gut zwischen uns. Doch mir hatten keinen Raum, um ungestört zu sein. Bei mir ging es nicht mehr. Die Wirtin war gefährlich geworden. Also besorgte Lore ein Zimmer bei einer Freundin. Wir liebten uns dort. Es war ungeheizt. Bittere Kälte herrschte. Lore erkrankte an schwerem Fieber mit gefährlichem Gelenksrheumatismus und starb in der Blüte ihres jungen Lebens acht Tage später an Sepsis" (*Leidenschaft*, 143). The English translation left out the sentence "We made love there," which appears right after the sentence "Lore got a room at a friend's."

12. Ibid., 145. The German is: "Diesmal ist's anders—denn ich bin die Ursache—da hilft kein Teufel!! Entsetzlich!! Wer sagt mir, was ich hätte tun sollen??? Ich bin die Ursache, aber kann ich dafür? Wer sagt mir, was ich bin??" (*Leidenschaft*, 164–165). In the translation the word *Teufel* is rendered as "soul," while in German it means "devil." A nonidiomatic English translation would be: "not a devil to help me." The German gives a stronger sense of the depth of despair than the English.

13. Sharaf, *Fury on Earth*, 60.

14. Reich, *Passion of Youth*, 152–53. The German is: "Es wird mir immer klarer, daß ich Anny Pink mit der Absicht analysiere, sie später für mich zu gewinnen, wie's mit

Lore war. Sie flieht die Männer, ich soll ihr zur Freilegung der Triebe verhelfen u. gleichzeitig erstes Objekt werden—Wie stell' ich mich dazu? Was habe ich zu tun? Analyse abbrechen? Nein, später keinen Verkehr! Aber sie, wenn sie's so tut, wie Lore u. an mich fixiert bleibt?—Übertragung anständig lösen!—Ja, ist Übertragung denn nicht Liebe, od. besser jede Liebe eine Übertragung? Ein junger Mensch soll keine Patientinnen in 20. Lebensjahr aufnehmen" (*Liedenschaft*, 173). Instead of the translation "Resolve the transference thoroughly," the German suggests: "Resolve the transference properly (*anständig*)."

15. Ibid., 147–48. The German is: "Ein Mädchen, lang, gelöstes Haar, loses Ärmelhemd, sprach mit kleinem, süßen Munde, ich küßte ihre Hand—lehnte Schulter an Schulter—Wange an Wange—und weit dahinter—hinter dem Graugold der Stadt öffnet sich der Himmel—zwei Hände—großknochig—Winken—man ruft—warum sollte das nicht möglich sein? Nein! Lustig auf u. schreiend, singend—Leopoldsberg—Kirche am Gemäuer—unter uns die Donau in der Tiefe—Kleider ab—u. nackt—wie nur Mütter uns geboren—tanzten—tanzten—hart am Abgrunde. Scherzo (Allegro)—tanzten—tanzten nackt—als Gottes Kinder in den langen Schatten unserer Leiber, die der stille Mond uns warf—Friede zog uns wieder u. ich barg den heißen Kopf in ihren weichen Schenkeln—deckte langes blondes Haar auf's Haupt—hart am Abgrund—während schlangengleich die Arme um- u. um sich wickelten u. mein Kopf, die weiche, weiße Brust fand. Ach ich armer Psychoanalytiker! Ich weiß ja doch, was all' dies heißt!!" (*Leidenschaft*, 168).

16. Reich's first and third wives were Jewish, while his second was not (interview with Mary Boyd Higgins, July 17, 2000, at Orgonon). His oil paintings, done after 1951, often show a blond anima figure emerging out of the great ground of a pulsating nature, having the same kind of breasts that Reich described as his ideal in his autobiography.

17. The hermeneutic concept that entailed probing into the inner life of the creator (writer) was devised by the liberal theologian Friedrich Schleiermacher. He contrasted this inner psychological method, as he called it, with an external textual method. See Friedrich Schleiermacher, *Hermeneutics and Criticism*, ed. Andrew Bowie (Cambridge, Eng.: Cambridge University Press, 1998). The various manuscript fragments and addresses were written between 1805 and 1833.

18. This volume will be the subject of the next chapter and is actually a translation of the *first* 1927 edition of *The Function of the Orgasm*.

19. Wilhelm Reich, *Early Writings*, trans. Philip Schmitz (New York: Farrar, Straus and Giroux, 1975), 1:73–85. "Der Koitus und die Geschlechter" originally appeared in *Zeitschrift für Sexualwissenschaft*, vol. 8 (1922). In *Frühe Schriften* it appears on pages 87–98.

20. Ibid., 1:77. The German is: "Von der leichtesten Potenzstörung, der Ejaculatio praecox, finden sich alle möglichen Übergänge bis zu den schwersten Formen, wie totaler Erektionsunfähigkeit. Die durch psychoanalytische Behandlung an solchen Kranken gemachten Erfahrungen zeigen . . . regelmäßig ein allen an Impotenz Erkrankten gemeinsames Merkmal: die Spaltung aller libidinösen Strebung in eine *zärtliche und*

sinnliche Komponente. Sie findet sich besonders kraß in jenen Fällen, die fakultativ impotent sind, wo z.b. die Fähgikeit zum Koitus immer bei der eigenen Frau, niemals bei Dirnen versagt" (*Frühe Schriften*, 90–91).

21. See Edward Shorter, *A History of Psychiatry* (New York: John Wiley & Sons, 1997), 53–59. The symptoms of syphilis start with sores on the penis or swollen lymph glands in the groin area. Once in the bloodstream, the spirochetes start their deadly work. "As the illness advanced, it might take one of two forms. If it affected primarily the spinal cord, it was known as tabes dorsalis (also locomotor ataxia), or wasting of the posterior part of the spinal cord. Tabes would cause lancinating pains to the abdomen as well as a high-stepping gait that patients described as 'walking on cotton.' . . . If the disease affected mainly the brain, psychiatric symptoms would be foremost, followed by dementia and paralysis . . . Both forms of neurosyphilis were invariably fatal." (55).

22. Reich *Early Writings*, 1:79. The German is: "Ejaculatio praecox und fakultative Impotenz treten am häufigsten zusammen auf, erstere sehr oft auch allein und bei allen Frauen; sie ist dann Ausdruck einer bestimmten unbewußten Angst, meist Kastrationsangst. Solche Patienten bringen Hemmungsvorstellungen wie: die Frau hat Zähne in der Vagina, am Grunde des weiblichen 'Schlauches' sei etwas, das nach dem Gliede schnappe u.a. Dort hingegen, wo ejaculatio praecox das Symptom fakultativer Impotenz ist, besteht daneben eine ausgesprochene Scheu vor dem Koitus mit einer Frau der eigenen Gesellschaftsschicht oder der angetrauten Gattin. Als Ursache dieser Scheu und der sonderbar ungestörten Potenz bei Prostituierten ergibt sich bei näherer Untersuchung regelmäßig eine Spaltung des einmal in der Kindheit begehrten ersten Lieblingsobjektes (meist der Mutter, Amme oder älteren Schwester) in zwei konträre Gestalten: die Dirne und die unerreichbare, idealisierte 'heilige' Frau, der man sich nur ehrfürchtig nähern darf" (*Frühe Schriften*, 92–93).

23. Ibid., 1:82. The German is: "Nicht also eine zweite Ejakulation ist die Forderung der Natur, sondern Koinzidenz von zärtlicher und sinnlicher Strebung" (*Frühe Schriften*, 95).

24. Reich, *Early Writings*, 1:86–124. "Triebbegriffe von Forel bis Jung" originally appeared in *Zeitschrift für Sexualwissenschaft*, vol. 9 (1922). In *Frühe Schriften* it appears on pages 99–143.

25. While Reich was aware of Jung's work, there seems to be no evidence that Jung, who had left the Vienna circle by 1914, was aware of Reich. This is confirmed by the fine book by John P. Conger, *Jung and Reich: The Body as Shadow* (Berkeley, Calif.: North Atlantic Books, 1988). It is helpful reading for anyone, like myself, who is happiest sharing the worlds of archetypal psychology and character analysis with some form of orgone analysis.

26. Reich, *Early Writings*, 1:92.

27. Ibid, 1:94. The German is: "Der Neurotiker ist sexueller Hyperästhet oder Perverser mit negativem Vorzeichen, d. h. Einer, der sein übergroßes order mit dem Realitätsprinzip . . . nicht zu vereinbarendes sexuelles Verlangen verdrängen mußte, ohne daß es ihm jedoch gelang, so daß die verdrängte Libido in Symptomhandlungen Abfuhr findet" (*Frühe Schriften*, 107).

28. Ibid., 1:101, 102. The German is: "In der Zeit durchschnittlich vom 5.–12. Lebens-
    jahre werden psychische Dämme, Reaktionsbildungen aufgebaut gegen jene Partial-
    triebe, die kulturell unannehmbar sind: Ekel gegen die Analerotik, Scham gegen den
    Exhibitionismus, wie überhaupt jede zur Moral gehörige psychische Bildung hier
    ihren Anfang nimmt. Diese Reaktionsbildungen werden unterstützt und beschleunigt
    durch die Erziehung in Schule und Haus wie auch ganz allgemein durch den Zwang,
    der dem Kinde bei seiner ersten Einführung in die soziale Gemeinschaft (Kinder-
    garten, Schule usw.) auferlegt wird . . . Des weiteren wird in diesem Stadium die
    Inzestschranke aufgerichtet, wahrscheinlich unter dem Rucke der Sexualein-
    schüchterung durch den Vater" (*Frühe Schriften*, 114, 115).

29. Otto Weininger, *Geschlecht und Charakter* (Vienna: W. B. Braumüller, 1903); English
    translation, *Sex and Character* (New York: AMS Press, 1975). For a fascinating ac-
    count of the impact of Weininger on Reich's fellow Austrian, the philosopher Ludwig
    Wittgenstein, see Ray Monk, *Ludwig Wittgenstein: The Duty of Genius* (New York:
    Free Press, 1990), especially 19–25.

30. Reich, *Early Writings*, 1:100. The German is: "Aus dem Ödipuskomplex resultiert
    dann durch die Hintansetzung durch den Vater, oft auch durch direkte Androhung
    des Penisabschneidens, die Kastrationsangst beim Knaben, aus dem Anblick des
    Gliedes beim Knaben der Penisneid beim Mädchen. Die Vorstellungen, der Penis
    wäre ihr abgeschnitten worden oder er sei noch klein und würde schon wachsen,
    spielen da eine große Rolle. Beide werden unter der Bezeichnung Kastrationskom-
    plex zusammengefaßt. Doch muß davor gewarnt werden, den Begriff der Kastration
    zu eng zu fassen, darunter nur das Abschneiden des Penis verstehen zu wollen,
    vielmehr gehört jedes Minderwertigkeitsgefühl, auf welchem Gebiet immer, zum Kas-
    trationskomplex" (*Frühe Schriften*, 112–13).

31. Ibid., 1:117. The German is: "Frauen lieben in der Mehrzahl in dem Maße wie und
    nur deshalb, weil man sie liebt" (*Frühe Schriften*, 130). The English translation
    should be even stronger: Women love "*only* because they are loved."

32. Ibid., 1:95n. The German is: "auch perverse Züge können durch mißglückte Ver-
    drängung entstehen, z.B. die homosexuelle Liebe zu femininen Jünglingen durch
    Wiederkehr der verdrängten Vorstellung, die Mutter habe einen Penis" (*Frühe
    Schriften*, 108n).

33. Ibid., 1:112–13. The German is: "*Ichtriebe* sind charakterisiert: 1. Durch An-
    erziehungsmöglichkeit in der *Ontogese*. 2. *Änderung der Objekte* mit Zeit und Ort. 3.
    Beeinflußbarkeit durch das *Realitätsprinzip*, d. h. Ausgehen auf später eintretenden,
    modifizierten, verminderten Lustgewinn. Die *Sexualtriebe*: 1. Durch die deutliche
    phylogenetische Entwicklung (in der *Ontogese lediglich Eindämmung*) 2. Immer
    dieselben Objekte, sonst Autoerotismus. 3. *Unverständigkeit* und *Unbeeinflußbarkeit*
    unterliegen dem *Lustprinzip*, d. h. Ausgehen auf Gewinnung von rascher, großer Lust
    (*Frühe Schriften*, 125).

34. C. G. Jung, *Psychology of the Unconscious: A Study of the Transformations and Sym-
    bolisms of the Libido*, trans. Beatrice M. Hinkle, Bollingen Series XX (Princeton:
    Princeton University Press, 1991). The original German text is *Wandlungen und*

Symbole der Libido (1912). Jung brought out a revised version in 1925, which is the version translated in the *Collected Works* under the title *Symbols of Transformation* (1952).

35. Reich, *Early Writings*, 1:125–32. "Über Spezifität der Onanieformen" originally appeared in *Internationale Zeitschrift für Psychoanalyse*, vol. 8 (1922). In *Frühe Schriften* it appears on pages 137–43.

36. Ibid., 1:125. The German is: "An Schwierigkeiten, die sich bei der Behandlung von Impotenten ergeben, kann man es lernen, der Onanieform erhöhte Aufmerksamkeit zuzuwenden" (*Frühe Schriften*, 137).

37. Ibid., 1:127. The German is: "das Schuldbewußtsein . . . hatte die Hand tabu gemacht" (*Frühe Schriften*, 139).

38. Ibid., 1:129. The German is: "Diese Onanieform deckte also seine masochistische Hingabe an die Kastration durch den Vater, den der Patient sehr liebte und haßte" (140).

39. Ibid., 1:131. The German is: "(1) Onanie auf dem Bauche liegend durch aktive Bewegungen des Beckens auf dem Leintuch oder einer improvisierten Vulva (Hemd, Polster usw.) ohne Zuhilfenahme der Hand. Hier scheint die männliche Einstellung sicher zu sein, die Phantasie auf das andere Geschlecht (wenn auch unbewußt inzestuös) gerichtet. Die Alloerotik ist hier die treibende Kraft. (2) Schon bei der Onanie im Bett, auf der Seite liegend, mit der Hand oder im Bade ist der autoerotische Einschlag stärker. Diese Onanieform ist unserer Erfahrung nach die weitaus häufigst geübte. (3) Prognostisch nicht sehr günstig zu beurteilen ist die Onanie auf dem Rücken liegend mit Lokalisation der Aktivität in die Hände während der Rumpf passiv bleibt. Die Erfahrung lehrt, daß diese Art der Onanie hauptsächlich von feminin eingestellten Männern geübt wird . . . Onanie vor dem Spiegel (narzißtisch), bei Lektüre von Vergewaltigungsszenen (dies sehr häufig), im Klosett, in öffentlichen Anlagen, wenn auch gut gedeckt hinter Sträuchern, mutuell mit Kameraden usw. usw., weisen auf pathologische Vorgänge im Umbewußten" (*Frühe Schriften*, 142).

40. Ibid., 1:132. The German is: "Onanie durch Zerren an der Klitoris (Peniswunsch)" (*Frühe Schriften*, 143).

41. Ibid., 1:133–42. "Zwei narzißtische Typen" appears in *Frühe Schriften* on pages 144–52.

42. Ibid., 1:134–35. The German is: "Im Grunde gibt es keine noch so scharf umschriebene Neurose ohne Spuren von Störungen der Gesamtpersönlichkeit. Das Minderwertigkeitsgefühl, die Begleiterscheinung sämtlicher Neurosen, die, narzißtische Narbe' (Marcinowsky), ist der konstante Ausdruck dieser Störung" (*Frühe Schriften*, 145).

43. Ibid., 1:136. The German is: "Der neurotische Charakter faßt die Analyse, das Hergeben von Einfällen, das Aufgeben von realen Befriedigungsmöglichkeiten im Sinne seines Kastrationskomplexes als Kastration auf und stellt früher oder später eine *negative* Übertragung her: der Analytiker ist ihm, in weit höherem Maße als dem Neurotiker, naturgemäß ein Feind" (*Frühe Schriften*, 146).

44. Ibid., 1:137–38. The German is: "Diesem ersten Typ mit *manifestem Minderwer-*

tigkeitsgefühl und *latentem Narzißmus* steht der zweite gegenüber mit *manifestem—* wie die Analyse ergibt, *kompensierendem—Narzißmus* und *latentem Minderwertigkeitsgefühl.* Er hat weniger Vertreter als der erste, ist schwieriger zu durchschauen und gibt bei Behandlung der Symptome die schlechteste Prognose. Es ist der auffallend und aufdringlich selbstsichere Mensch, der sich überall vordrängt, immer die erste Rolle spielen möchte, alles zu wissen glaubt, dabei keine Spur einer kritischen Instanz seinem Wesen gegenüber hat. Die Übertragung in der Kur ist minimal; was ihn an die Analyse fesselt, ist die Sucht, mit Erlebnissen, Gedanken, Wortspielen zu prahlen und im Analytiker einen willigen Zuhörer zu haben. Alle Übertragung fußt durchweg auf Identifizierung, er will alles selbst lösen weiß alles besser als der Analytiker. Ist im ersten Typ die exhibitionistische Tendenz verdrängt, kehrt sie nur als neurotische Scham und Verlegenheit wieder, so ist sie hier durchaus manifest, der große, mächtige Penis wird—symbolisch—immer wieder gezeigt" (*Frühe Schriften*, 148–49).

45. Ibid., 1:143–57. "Zur Triebenenergetik" originally appeared in *Zeitschrift für Sexual Wissenschaft*, vol. 10 (1923). In *Frühe Schriften* it appears on pages 153–67.

46. Ibid., 1:148. The German is: "Allerdings sind da die Übergänge von Lust und Unlust derart verwischt, die Phasen ineinandergreifend, daß man von 'lustvoller Spannung' sprechen zu können glaubt" (*Frühe Schriften*, 158).

47. Ibid., 1:151, which also contains diagrams. The German is: "Es ist für die Sexuallust charakteristisch, daß der partielle Abbau gleichzeitig ein Reiz zu Aufbau oder Spannungsvermehrung ist. Dies gilt aber nur für die Vorlust. In der Endlust werden die Spannungsdifferenzen immer größer. Abbau und Aufbau legen . . . größere pro- und regrediente Phasen zurück, bis die regrediente den erstrebten Nullpunkt erreicht hat und sich die progrediente von selbst erledigt, da beider Ausgangspunkt der 0-Punkt ist" (*Frühe Schriften*, 161).

48. I have taught this text in many contexts and find that younger students are less impressed with it (perhaps for obvious life-experience reasons), while graduate students seem more inclined to give it a hearing. Seminary students have clear theological antecedents to Freud's model and immediately invoke Augustine's *Confessions*.

49. Sigmund Freud, *Civilization and Its Discontents*, trans. James Strachey, *Standard Edition* (New York: W.W. Norton, 1989), 111. The original German edition is *Das Unbehagen in der Kultur* (Vienna: Internationaler Psychoanalytischer Verlag, 1930).

50. Reich, *Early Writings*, 1:158–79. "Über Genitalität" originally appeared in *Internationale Zeitschrift für Psychoanalyse*, vol. 10 (1924). It appears in *Frühe Schriften* on pages 168–88.

51. Ibid., 1:199–221. "Die therapeutische Bedeutung der Genitallibido" originally appeared in *Internationale Zeitschrift für Psychoanalyse*, vol. 11 (1925). It appears in *Frühe Schriften* on pages 208–30.

52. Ibid., 1:169–70. The German is: "Wir sehen uns sonst in der Analyse vor die Aufgabe gestellt, plastische, unverdrängte Triebkräfte gegen die verdrängten, starren, fixierten auszuspielen (Freud). Wir können ferner beobachten, wie die aus der Verdrängung befreite genitale Libido sich in den Dienst der Heilungstendenz stellt (Fall

1 bis 3), andere fixierte Triebkräfte im Übertragungskampfe oder rezenten Konflikten plastischer, anpaßungsfähiger werden und sich entweder der genitalen Hauptstrebung unterordnen oder auf irgendinem Wege zur Sublimierung gelangen" (*Frühe Schriften*, 179).

53. Ibid., 1:176. The German is: "Erektion, aktives Eindringten in eine Höhle, Mutterleibssehnsucht und rhythmische Ejakulation" (*Frühe Schriften*, 186).

54. Ibid., 1:203. The German is: "So gut wie keine Neurose ohne Störungen der Genitalfunktion" (*Frühe Schriften*, 212).

55. Ibid., 1:208. The German is: "Es ist anzunehmen, daß alle jene Don-Juan-Typen, deren Stolz darin besteht, recht viele Frauen zu besitzen oder ihre Potenz dadurch zu erweisen, daß sie möglichst viele Akte ('Nummern') in einer Nacht zustande bringen, nebst anderen Motiven (z.b. Suchen der Mutter, Rank) eine mächtige Impotenzangst kompensieren. Die Potenz solcher Männer ist sehr gering" (*Frühe Schriften*, 217).

56. Ibid., 1:214. The German is: "Starr auf dem genannten Standpunkt stehend, dürften wir keine Analyse durchführen, weil unsere Voraussetzung doch ist, den Patienten vom Lustprinzip weg zum Realitätsprinzip zu 'erziehen'" (*Frühe Schriften*, 223).

57. Ibid., 1:215–16. The German is: "Sämtliche Triebansprüche prägenitaler Natur sind als solche, d.h. soweit sie Anspruch auf Ausschließlichkeit erheben, realitätswidrig und können bei entsprechender Ichstruktur teilweise auf dem Sublimierungswege erledigt werden" (*Frühe Schriften*, 224).

58. Ibid., 1:216–17. The German is: "[D]ie Libido des ganzen Körpers strömt am Genitale ab. Der Orgasmus kann nicht als vollwertig betrachtet werden, wenn er nur am Genitale verspürt wird. Zuckungen der Gesamtmuskulatur und leichte Bewußtseinstrübung sind seine normalen Attribute und ein Beweis dafür, daß der gesamte Organismus an ihm teilhat" (*Frühe Schriften*, 225).

59. Ibid., 1:180–98. "Der Tic als Onanieequivalent" originally appeared in *Zeitschrift für Sexualwissenschaft*, vol. 11 (1925). It appears in *Frühe Schriften* on pages 189–207.

60. Ibid., 1:180. The German is: "[P]lötzliche, krampfhafte Exspirationen mit Erschütterung des ganzen Körpers, insbesondere des Kopfes und Halses und Hochziehen der Schultern: manchmal besteht nur ein leises Räuspern oder ein zuckendes Vor- und Aufwärtsschnellen des Kopfes" (*Frühe Schriften*, 189).

61. Ibid., 1:196. The German is: "[D]ie unerledigten Erregungen suchen einen symptomatischen Ausweg. Ist der eine versperrt, so wird der andere beschritten. Davon kann man sich bei jeder symptomatischen Psychotherapie überzeugen. Wird das Hauptsymptom suggestiv beseitigt, so tritt sofort oder später, je nach Stärke des Rapports, ein anderes an seine Stelle." (*Frühe Schriften*, 204).

62. Ibid., 1:222–36. "Eine hysterische Psychose in statu nascendi" originally appeared in *Internationale Zeitschrift für Psychoanalyse*, vol. 11 (1925). It appears in *Frühe Schriften* on pages 231–45.

63. Ibid., 1:222. The German is: "[E]ine neunzehnjährige Hysterika . . . infolge des Ausbruches einer kontinuierlichen psychotischen Spaltung . . . Die Patientin leidet seit mehr als fünf Jahren an Schlaflosigkeit und seit einem Jahr an einem konversionshysterischen Bauchschmerz" (*Frühe Schriften*, 231).

64. Ibid., 1:225. The German is: "Allmählich fällt ihr jedoch das am Vortage Gesprochene ein, und nun bricht mit allen Merkmalen kathartischer Explosion die verdrängte, in den Ausnahmszuständen wiedererlebte traumatische Situation durch: Zwischen ihrem fünften und siebenten Lebensjahr hatte sie bei einem jungen Lehrer Hebräisch gelernt. Eines Tages hatte er sie mit Alkohol betäubt; sie war mit einem stechenden *Schmerz* im Genitale erwacht und hatte sich nackt in seinem Bett liegend gefunden. Er kniete neben ihrem Bett, rechts von ihr, sein Kopf lag auf ihrem Bauch oberhalb der *rechten Leistenbeuge* (dem Orte des späteren Schmerzes) und hielt einen Finger in ihrer Scheide (daher der Schmerz beim Erwachen). Als er sie erwachen sah, warf er sich über sie; was dann geschah, weiß sie nicht mehr. Später glaubte sie, sich undeutlich erinnern zu können, daß er sein Glied gegen ihren Mund gepreßt hatte" (*Frühe Schriften*, 233–34).

65. Ibid., 1:231. The German is: "Die Patientin geht nicht aus, spricht wenig, sitzt in ihrem Zimmer und hält an ihrer Idee, nicht die Eva S. zu sein, fest" (*Frühe Schriften*, 240).

66. Ibid., 1:236. The German is: "Es ist ja bekannt, daß 'latente' Schizophrenien durch die Analyse zu manifesten werden können, was nur auf die vorhandenen Defekte im Ich beziehungsweise im Ichideal zurückzuführen ist. *In solchen Fällen ist es nun notwendig zu bremsen*, wenn die Assoziationen, die Erinnerungen, insbesondere die inzestuösen Konflikte *allzu rasch* bewußt werden, wie in unserem Falle. Es wird aufgefallen sein, wie viel und wie verpöntes Material in der kurzen Zeit von dreieinhalb Monaten zum Durchbruch kam. Das Überfluten des Bewußtseins mit verdrängtem Material muß ungünstig wirken, weil es nicht genügend verarbeitet werden kann, weil das Ich nicht genug Zeit hat, sich mit ihm *stückweise* abzufinden" (*Frühe Schriften*, 245).

67. Ibid., 1:235–36. The German is: "Ich habe mich nun überzeugen können, daß man mit der klassischen Regel Freuds bei allen milden Neurosen sehr gut auskommt, habe aber an Analysen von triebhaften Charakteren und schweren Charakterneurosen die Erfahrung gemacht, daß hier nur mit *unausgesetzter Analyse der Übertragung* Brauchbares auszurichten ist" (*Frühe Schriften*, 244).

68. Ibid., 1:237–332. The German edition is *Der triebhafte Charakter—Eine psychoanalytische Studie zur Pathologie des Ich* (Vienna: Internationaler Psychoanalytischer Verlag, 1925), 246–340.

69. Ibid., 1:245. The German is: "Man stößt in der Analyse des triebhaften Charakters auf Amnesien, die in nichts der typischen hysterischen Amnesie nachstehen. Andere Verdrängungsmechanismen, wie zerrissene Zusammenhänge genetisch zueinander gehörender Erlebnisstücke, verschobenes Schuldgefühl, reaktive Abwehr destruktiver Tendenzen sind beim triebhaften Charakter zumindest ebenso intensiv wie bei der Zwangsneurose . . . Von einer Schwäche der einzelnen Verdrängungen kann also nicht gesprochen werden, wir werden aber gerade die Frage, was denn die mangelhafte Abwehr bedingt, in das Zentrum der Abhandlung stellen und zu untersuchen haben, was am Verdrängungsmechanismus defekt ist, so daß Aktionen möglich werden, die bei der enfachen Symptomneurose niemals den Zugang zur Motilität erlangen" (*Frühe Schriften*, 253–54).

70. Ibid., 1:251. The German is: "Wir dürfen dann von einem hysterischen und zwangsneurotischen (eventuell schizoiden) Charakter sprechen, dem die Symptome aufsitzen, wie die Gipfel einem Bergmassiv. Der neurotische Charakter ist durch das Stadium, in welchem die Entwicklungshemmung vorfiel, ebenso in seinen Besonderheiten determiniert wie das neurotische Symptom. Der Zwangsneurotiker, welcher wegen seines Impulses, den Freund mit einem Messer von hinten zu erstechen, die Analyse aufsucht (zwangsneurotisches Symptom), weist dann auch den zwangsneurotischen Charakter auf: er ist pedantisch rein, ordnungsliebend, übergewissenhaft. Sowohl die Charaktereigenheiten als auch das Symptom tragen die Merkmale der sadistisch-analen Stufe an sich. Der Ausdruck 'triebhafter Charakter' kann dann nur eine spezielle Form des neurotischen Charakters meinen, nämlich eine *Störung der Gesamtpersönlichkeit*, welche gekennzeichnet ist durch mehr oder weniger *ungehemmtes Agieren*" (*Frühe Schriften*, 259).

71. See Note 9 in the Preface.

72. Ibid., 1:277. The German is: "Aber schon an der ersten Phase dieses bedeutsamen Prozesses setzen Versagungen ein: die Mutterbrust wird entzogen. Gewährung und Versagung stehen einander aber an jeder Entwicklungsstufe gegenüber, ja, die Fortentwicklung von Stufe zu Stufe ist allein durch die Versagung gewährleistet" (*Frühe Schriften*, 285).

73. Ibid., 1:279. The German is: "Die Inkonsequenz der Erziehung, mangelhafte Triebversagung auf der einen, auf ein Detailstück konzentrierte oder plötzliche, zu spät einsetzende Versagung auf der anderen Seite ist das gemeinsame Merkmal in der Entwicklung der triebhaften Charaktere." (*Frühe Schriften*, 287). The German version talks about the development of impulsive characters in the plural form and not in the singular form, as the English version suggests.

74. Ibid., 1:281–82. The German is: "Gerade solche Kranke weisen den typischen Befund polymorph-perverser Kinderspiele auf. Infolge der Sorglosigkeit der Umgebung haben solche Kranke weit mehr vom Sexualleben der Erwachsenen gesehen und verstanden, als es bei einfachen Neurosen im allgemeinen der Fall ist. Die Latenzzeit ist entweder überhaupt nicht oder nur sehr mangelhaft aktiviert worden. Bedenkt man die wichtige Rolle, welche die Latenzzeit in der Ichentwicklung des Menschen in Hinsicht auf Sublimierungen und Reaktionsbildungen zu leisten hat, so kann man den Schaden ermessen, der hier gestiftet wird. Da der triebhafte Charakter diese Latenz nicht erfährt, wird die Pubertät von extremen Durchbrüchen der Sexualität eingeleitet. Ein Ausgleich findet nicht einmal durch die Onanie oder durch sehr früh aufgenommenen Sexualverkehr statt, weil die ganz libidinöse Organisation durch Enttäuschung und Schuldgefühl zerrissen ist" (*Frühe Schriften*, 289–90).

75. Ibid., 1:314. The German is: "1. Manifeste Ambivalenz. 2. Keine reaktive Wandlung oder überwiegender Haß. 3. Isoliertes Über-Ich. 4. Mangelhafte Verdrängungen. 5. Sadistische Impulse ohne Schuldgefühl. 6. Charakter gewissenlos, Sexualität manifest, das entsprechende Schuldgefühl eventuell in neurotischen Symptomen verankert oder total verdrängt. 7. Das Ich steht beiderseits ambivalent zwischen Lust-Ich und Über-Ich, de facto Gefolgschaft nach beiden Seiten" (*Frühe Schriften*, 321–22).

76. Ibid., 1:327–28. The German is: "1. *Phase der fehlenden Krankheitseinsicht*: die pathologischen Reaktionen sind gleichsinnig mit dem wirksamen Über-Ich, oder die Isolierung des Über-Ich vom Ich ermöglicht die volle Unterwerfung des letzteren unter die triebhaften Strebungen. 2. *Phase der wachsenden positiven Übertragung*: der Patient macht den Arzt zum Objekt der Libido. Schon dadurch wird das alte Ideal auf die Objektstufe herabgedrückt; soweit narzißtische Libido daran gebunden war, wird sie in Objektlibido verwandelt. Das neue Objekt, der Arzt, kann insofern Grundlage einer neuen Über-Ich-Bildung werden, als er den Standpunkt des Realitätsprinzips vertritt und auch die bisher uneingesehenen Haltungen für realitätswidrig erklärt. 3. *Phase der wirksamen Krankheitseinsicht*: ein Stück des neuen, im übrigen durchaus inzestuös bewerteten Objektes, des Arztes, wird introjiziert, zum neuen Ichideal gemacht; das alte wird mitsamt seiner Quelle verurteilt. Jetzt erst kann die regelrechte Analyse einsetzen" (*Frühe Schriften*, 335–36).

3: THE FUNCTION OF THE ORGASM, AND LATE REFLECTIONS ON FATHER FREUD

1. Ilse Ollendorff Reich, *Wilhelm Reich: A Personal Biography* (New York: St. Martin's Press, 1969), 14.
2. Ibid., 15.
3. Myron Sharaf, *Fury on Earth: A Biography of Wilhelm Reich* (New York: Da Capo Press, 1994), 120. Unfortunately, Sharaf was not a strong theorist and often missed the deeper structural issues involved in Reich's works. But this trait is something his work shares with most of the secondary literature on Reich, which is simply lacking in theoretical firepower.
4. Unfortunately, an official critical edition is very expensive, and few scholars are qualified to undertake the editorship of such a multiyear project. Recent examples in this country have been the completed edition of the works of William James and the ongoing edition of the works of C. S. Peirce (which is a true masterpiece of scholarship).
5. Wilhelm Reich, *Genitality in the Theory and Therapy of Neurosis*, vol. 2 of *Early Writings*, trans. Philip Schmitz (New York: Farrar, Straus and Giroux, 1980). The original German edition is *Die Funktion des Orgasmus* (Vienna: Internationaler Psychoanalytischer Verlag, 1927).
6. Ibid, 11.
7. Ibid., 13. This connection between life and sex is basic to the Tantric perspective, which is part of both Hinduism (especially in Kashmir Shavism) and Buddhism (especially in Tibet).
8. Ibid., 27.
9. Ibid., 38–39.
10. Ibid., 60.
11. Ibid., 66–67.
12. Ibid., 71–72, 73.
13. Ibid., 75.

14. Ibid., 76.
15. Ibid., 77.
16. Ibid., 82.
17. Ibid., 78.
18. Ibid., 88.
19. Ibid., 92.
20. Ibid., 93–94.
21. Ibid., 96–97.
22. Ibid., 101.
23. Ibid., 108.
24. Ibid., 176.
25. Ibid., 177.
26. Ibid., 177.
27. Ibid., 178–79.
28. Ibid., 179–80.
29. Ibid., 191.
30. Ibid., 201.
31. Ibid., 216.
32. Wilhelm Reich, *Reich Speaks of Freud*, ed. Mary Higgins and Chester M. Raphael, M.D. (New York: Farrar, Straus and Giroux, 1967), 62, 61.
33. Ibid., 21.
34. Ibid., 63–64.
35. Ibid., 102, 103.

4: THE SEXUAL IS THE SOCIAL, AND *THE MASS PSYCHOLOGY OF FASCISM*

1. Wilhelm Reich, *People in Trouble*, part 2 of *The Emotional Plague of Mankind*, trans. Philip Schmitz (New York: Farrar, Straus and Giroux, 1976), 27. The German edition is *Menschen im Staat* (Rangeley, Me.: Wilhelm Reich Infant Trust Fund, 1973).
2. Wilhelm Reich, *The Invasion of Compulsory Sex-Morality*, trans. Werner and Doreen Grossmann (New York: Farrar, Straus and Giroux, 1971). The German edition is *Die Einbruch der Sexualmoral* (Cologne: Kiepenheuer und Witsch, 1972).
3. See Wilhelm Reich, *Beyond Psychology: Letters and Journals 1934–1939*, ed. Mary Boyd Higgins, trans. Derek and Inge Jordan and Philip Schmitz (New York: Farrar, Straus and Giroux, 1994), 33, where Reich states in a letter to Elsa Lindenberg on February 28, 1925: "Today I received a very kind letter from Malinowski. He is very enthusiastic about the *Invasion*. He is singing its praises everywhere and is using my theories in his lectures." In Reich's office at Orgonon there is a wonderful carved stick, hanging in a prominent place, given to him by Malinowski.
4. Reich, *Invasion of Compulsory Sex-Morality*, 153.
5. Ibid., 83.
6. Ibid., 45.

7. Ibid., 149.

8. Sigmund Freud, *Totem and Taboo*, trans. James Strachey, *Standard Edition* (New York: W.W. Norton, 1989). The first German edition was *Totem und Tabu* (Vienna: Hugo Heller, 1913).

9. Reich, *Invasion of Compulsory Sex-Morality*, 149.

10. Freud, *Totem and Taboo*, 194.

11. Reich, *Invasion of Compulsory Sex-Morality*, 165.

12. In my twenty-five years as an active member of the Society for the Advancement of American Philosophy, which meets every March to discuss classical and contemporary issues in pragmatism and liberalism, I have tried with very limited success to generate discussion about the unconscious and its role in social transformation. My colleagues always hear my subject as "the idea of religious heteronomy" rather than my intended concept of "unconscious irrational surges." Reich was correct that depth psychology and American pragmatic liberalism have very different trajectories, but it is still my hope that they can learn much from each other.

13. Wilhelm Reich, *The Mass Psychology of Fascism*, trans. Vincent R. Carfagno, (New York: Farrar, Straus and Giroux, 1970), xv. The German typescript, available from the Reich Museum, is *Die Massenpsychologie des Faschismus*. The German book, based directly on the museum manuscript, was published by Kiepenheuer und Witsch of Cologne and appeared in 1971. All of the following German quotes are taken from the subsequent 1997 edition of *Die Massenpsychologie des Faschismus*. The German for this quotation is: "Der Faschismus wäre, so heißt es, Rückkehr zum Heidentum und ein Todfeind der Religion. Weit davon entfernt, ist der Faschismus der extreme Ausdruck des religiösen Mystizismus. Als solcher tritt er in besonderer sozialer Gestalt auf. Der Faschismus stützt diejenige Religiosität, die aus der sexuellen Perversion stammt, und er verwandelt den masochistischen Charakter der Leidensreligion des alten Patriarchats in eine sadistische Religion. Demzufolge versetzt er die Religion aus dem Jenseitsbereiche der Leidensphilosophie in das Diesseits des sadistischen Mordens" (*Massenpsychologie*, 14–15). The book agrees word for word with Reich's typescript.

14. See Martin A. Lee, *The Beast Reawakens: Fascism's Resurgence from Hitler's Spymasters to Today's Neo-Nazi Groups and Right Wing Extremists* (New York: Routledge, 2000). This is an excellent book to read after exploring Reich's book on fascism. It goes into some detail about how the Roman Catholic Church helped leading Nazis escape to Spain, Portugal, and South America after the war, and it also tells the sorry tale of how the newly forming CIA sought out Nazi criminals to help them with anti-Soviet espionage. In addition, the book details how these very same Nazis helped to create neo-Nazi groups in America, some of which, like the Council of Conservative Citizens, a racist and anti-Semitic group often referred to as the "white collar Klan," have strong ties to some members of the Republican Party, such as Trent Lott, one of their keynote speakers in 1992 (see especially xix–xx).

15. Reich, *Mass Psychology of Fascism*, 27. The German is: "Die analytische Soziologie versuchte die Gesellschaft wie ein Individuum zu analysieren, setzte einen absoluten Gegensatz von Kulturprozeß und Sexualbefriedigung, faßte die destruktiven Triebe

als ursprüngliche biologische Gegebenheiten auf, die das menschliche Geschick unausrottbar beherrschen, leugnete die mutterrechtliche Urzeit and landete in einer lähmenden Skepsis, weil sie vor den Konsequenzen der eigenen Entdeckungen zurückschrak" (*Massenpsychologie*, 47). The English translation adds the prefix *psycho* to the German *analytische Soziologie*.

16. Ibid., 29–30. The German is: "Die Psychoanalyse von Menschen jeder Altersstufe, aus allen Ländern und jeder sozialen Schichte ergibt: *Die Verknüpfung der sozialökonomischen und der sexuellen Struktur der Gesellschaft und die strukturelle Reproduktion der Gesellschaft erfolgen in den ersten vier bis fünf Lebensjahren und in der autoritären Familie.* Die Kirche setzt diese Funktion später nur fort. So gewinnt der autoritäre Staat sein ungeheures Interesse an der autoritären Familie: *Sie ist seine Struktur- und Ideologiefabrik geworden*" (*Massenpsychologie*, 48–49). The English translation flattens the sense of *ungeheures Interesse* by using the term "enormous" when the deeper sense of *ungeheuer* connotes fear and the noun form *Ungeheuer* means "monster."

17. Ibid., 30.

18. Ibid., 37. The German is: "Aber neben dieser Rebellion gegen den Vater blieb die Hochachtung und Anerkennung seiner Autorität bestehen. Diese zwiespältige Einstellung zur Autorität: *Rebellion gegen Autorität mit gleichzeitiger Anerkennung und Unterwerfung*, ist ein Grundzug jeder kleinbürgerlichen Struktur am Übergang von der Pubertät zur völligen Erwachsenheit und besonders ausgeprägt bei materiell eingeschränkter Lebensführung. Von der Mutter spricht Hitler mit großer Sentimentalität. Er versichert, er hätte nur einmal in seinem Leben geweint, als nämlich seine Mutter starb. Aus der Rassen- und Syphilistheorie (vgl. Nächstes Kapitel) geht seine Sexualablehnung und die neurotische Idealisierung der Mutterschaft eindeutig hervor." (*Massenpsychologie*, 54–55). Here the English translation has "idolization" as its rendering of *Idealisierung* rather than the more accurate "idealization."

19. Ibid., 53–54. The German is: "Diese Stellung des Vaters erfordert nämlich strengste Sexualeinschränkung der Frauen und Kinder. Entwickeln die Frauen unter kleinbürgerlichen Einflüssen eine resignierende Haltung, die unterbaut ist von verdrängter sexueller Rebellion, so die Söhne neben einer untertänigen Stellung zur Autorität gleichzeitig eine starke Identifizierung mit dem Vater, die später zur gefühlsbetonten Identifizierung mit jeder Obrigkeit wird" (*Massenpsychologie*, 68). The term *Sexualeinschränkung* is translated as "sexual suppression," whereas the German conveys the very different sense of "sexual restriction."

20. Ibid., 91. The German is: "Bei den alten Griechen, deren geschriebene Geschichte ja erst mit dem vollentfalteten Patriarchat beginnt, finden wir in der sexuellen Organisation: Männerherrschaft, Hetärentum für die oberen, Prostitution für die mittleren und unteren Schichten, und daneben versklavte, ein elendes Leben führende nur als Gebärmaschinen figurierende Ehefrauen. Die Männerherrschaft, des platonischen Zeitalters ist durchaus homosexuell" (*Massenpsychologie*, 98). One could translate *durchaus homosexuell* as "quite homosexual" rather than "entirely homosexual," which comes closer to my argument in the text about the scope of homosexual practice in classical Athens.

21. Ibid., 100.
22. Ibid., 103. The German is: "Es ist also anzunehmen, daß dieses Symbol, das zwei ineinandergeschlungene Gestalten darstellt, auf tiefe Schichten des Organismus einen großen Reiz ausübt, der um so stärker ausfallen muß, je unbefriedigter, sexuell sehnsüchtiger der Betreffende ist. Wird das Symbol noch dazu als Sinnbild von Ehrenhaftigkeit und Treue präsentiert, so trägt es auch den abwehrenden Strebungen des moralistischen Ichs Rechnung und kann um so leichter akzeptiert werden" (*Massenpsychologie*, 106–7).
23. Ibid., 94. The German is: "Wenn hinter der Idee der Rassenmischung letzten Endes die Idee der Mischung von Angehörigen der herrschenden mit Angehörigen der beherrschten Schichten wirkt, so haben wir hier offenbar den Schlüssel zur Frage, welche Rolle die Sexualunterdrückung in der Klassengesellschaft spielt . . . Da die Sexualunterdrückung ursprünglich von den wirtschaftlichen Interessen des Erbrechts und der Heirat ausgeht, beginnt sie innerhalb der herrschenden Schichte selbst. Die Keuschheitsmoral gilt am schärfsten zunächst für die weiblichen Angehörigen der herrschenden Schichte. Dadurch soll die Erhaltung des gleichen Besitzes gesichert werden, der durch die Ausbeutung der unteren Schichten erworben wurde" (*Massenpsychologie*, 100).
24. Ibid., 137–38. The German is: "Die Gepaartheit von sadistischer Brutalität und mystischem Empfinden ist durchschnittlich überall dort anzutreffen, wo die normale orgastische Erlebnisfähigkeit gestört ist. Bei den kirchlichen Inquisitoren des Mittelalters, beim grausamen und mystischen Phillip II. von Spanien nicht minder als bei irgendeinem Massenmörder unserer Zeit. Wo nicht eine hysterische Erkrankung die unausgeglichene Erregung in ängstlicher Ohnmacht oder eine Zwangsneurose die gleiche Erregung in sinnlosen und grotesken Zwangssymptomen erstickt, bietet die patriarchlisch-autoritäre Zwangsordnung genügend Gelegenheit zu sadistisch-mystischer Abfuhr. Die soziale Rationalisierung solcher Verhaltensweisen verwischt das Pathologische" (*Massenpsychologie*, 134–35).
25. Ibid., 172. The German is: "Die zielbewußte Fernhaltung der Ergebnisse der Wissenschaft von den Massen der Bevölkerung und Affenprozesse wie in der USA fördern Demut, Kritiklosigkeit, freiwillige Entsagung und Hoffnung auf Glück im Jenseits, Autoritätsglauben, Anerkennung der Heiligkeit der Askese und Unantastbarkeit der autoritären Familie" (*Massenpsychologie*, 162–63).
26. An excellent book on the trial is the Pulitzer Prize–winning *Summer of the Gods: The Scopes Trial and America's Continuing Debate Over Science and Religion* by Edward J. Larson (New York: Basic Books, 1997).
27. Reich, *Mass Psychology of Fascism*, 187. The German is: "Es geht also nicht darum zu helfen, sondern *Unterdrücktheit bewußt zu machen, den Kampf zwischen Sexualität und Mystik ins Licht des Bewußtseins zu rücken, ihn unter dem Drucke einer Massenideologie zum Auflodern zu bringen und in soziale Aktion zu überführen*" (*Massenpsychologie*, 175).
28. Ibid., 191. The German is: "Ein weiterer objektiver Umstand, der mit dem früheren eng zusammenhängt, ist die rasche Zunahme der neurotischen und biopathischen

Erkrankungen als Ausdruck gestörter Sexualökonomie und die Steigerung des Widerspruchs zwischen realen sexuellen Anforderungen und alter moralischer Hemmung und kindlicher Erziehungssituation. Die Zunahme der Biopathien bedeutet Anwachsen der Bereitschaft, auch die sexuelle Verursachung so vieler Krankheiten zur Kenntnis zu nehmen" (*Massenpsychologie*, 178).

29. Ibid., 263–64. The German is: "Die Gedanken des Sowjetpatriotismus züchten und lassen groß werden Helden, Ritter und Millionen tapferer Krieger, die bereit sind, sich gleich einer alles verschlingenden Lawine über die Feinde des Landes zu stürzen und sie vom Angesicht der Erde hinwegzufegen. Mit der Muttermilch wird unserer Jugend die Liebe zum Lande eingegeben. Wir sind verpflichtet, neue Geschlechter von Sowjetpatrioten zu erziehen, denen die Interessen des Landes höher stehen denn alles und teurer sind als das Leben." (*Massenpsychologie*, 237).

30. Ibid., 262. The German is: "All unsere Liebe, unsere Treue, unsere Kraft, unser Heroismus, unser Leben—alles für Dich, nimm es hin, Du großer Stalin, alles ist Dein, Du Führer der großen Heimat . . . Wenn meine geliebte Frau mir ein Kind zur Welt bringt, so wird das erste Wort sein, das ich es lehre: *Stalin*" (*Massenpsychologie*, 236).

31. Ibid., 293. The German is: "Wir nennen die Beziehung eines Menschen zu seiner Arbeit, wenn sie ihm Freude macht, *libidinös*, die Beziehung zur Arbeit ist, da *Arbeit* und *Sexualität* (im engsten und weitesten Sinne) aufs engste miteinander verflochten sind, gleichzeitig eine Frage der Sexualökonomie der Menschenmassen; von der Art, wie die Menschenmassen ihre biologische Energie anwenden und befriedigen, hängt die Hygiene des Arbeitsprozesses ab. *Arbeit und Sexualität entstammen der gleichen biologischen Energie*" (*Massenpsychologie*, 263).

32. Ibid., 311. The German is: "Arbeitsdemokratie ist der naturwüchsige Prozeß der Liebe, der Arbeit und des Wissens, der die Wirtschaft, das gesellschaftliche und kulturelle Leben der Menschen regierte, regiert und regieren wird, solange es eine Gesellschaft gab, gibt und geben wird. Arbeitsdemokratie ist die Summe aller natürlich gewachsenen, sich natürlich entwickelnden und organisch die rationalen zwischenmenschlichen Beziehungen regierenden Lebensfunktionen" (*Massenpsychologie*, 276–77).

33. I derive this claim about Hegel from Alan M. Olson, *Hegel and the Spirit: Philosophy as Pneumatology* (Princeton: Princeton University Press, 1992).

34. Reich, *Mass Psychology of Fascism*, 322. The German is: "a) Die Menschheit ist biologisch krank. b) Die Politik ist irrationaler sozialer Ausdruck dieser Krankheit. c) Was immer im gesellschaftlichen Leben geschieht, ist aktiv oder passiv, gewollt oder ungewollt durch die Struktur der Menschenmasse bestimmt. d) Diese charakterliche Struktur ist durch sozialökonomische Prozesse entstanden und sie verankert, verewigt diesen Prozeß. Die biopathische Charakterstruktur der Menschen ist nichts anderes als erstarrter, autoritärer Geschichtsprozeß, biophysiologische reproduzierte Massenunterdrückung. e) Die menschliche Struktur ist vom Widerspruch zwischen Freiheitssehnsucht und Freiheitsangst beseelt. f) Die Freiheitsangst der Menschenmasse ist bio-physisch in Versteifung des Organismus und in charakterlicher Starre verankert. g) Jede Art gesellschaftlicher Führung ist nur der soziale Ausdruck der

einen oder der anderen Seite dieser Struktur der Menschenmassen. h) Es geht nicht um den Versailler Friedensvertrag oder die Ölquellen von Baku oder um 200–300 Jahre Kapitalismus, sondern um 4000–6000 Jahre autoritär–mechanistische Zivilisation, die das biologische Funktionieren der Menschen ruiniert hat. i) Geld- und Machtinteressen sind Ersatz unerfüllten Liebesglücks, getragen von der biologischen Erstarrung der Menschenmassen. j) Die Unterdrückung des natürlichen Geschlechtslebens der Kinder und Jugendlichen dient der Strukturierung williger Träger und Reproduzenten der mechanistisch-autoritären Zivilisation. k) Jahrtausende menschlicher Unterdrückung sind in den Fluß der Aufhebung geraten" (*Massenpsychologie*, 286). A better translation of *natürliches Geschlechtsleben der Kinder* than "natural sexuality of children" would be "natural sex life of children," shifting the emphasis to the entire lifeworld of the child.

5: *CHARACTER ANALYSIS*

1. Wilhelm Reich, *Character Analysis*, ed. Mary Higgins and Chester M. Raphael, M.D., trans. Vincent R. Carfagno, 3rd enlarged ed. (New York: Farrar, Straus and Giroux, 1972). The German edition is *Charakteranalyse* (Cologne: Kiepenheuer und Witsch, 1989), which is based on the manuscript owned by the Wilhelm Reich Infant Trust. All of the following quotes come from these editions. Fortunately, Reich located his new post–1933 material in a concluding third section so that the problem of historical layering is not an issue for us, although he did dot the earlier text with footnotes from 1945.

2. Ibid., 41. The German is: "Ganz allgemein kann gesagt werden, *daß man in der Analyse der Widerstände nicht früh genug eingreifen, in der Deutung des Unbewußten, von den Widerständen angesehen, nicht zurückhaltend genug sein kann.* Gewöhnlich wird umgekehrt verfahren: Man pflegt einerseits allzu großen Mut in der Sinndeutung zu zeigen und andererseits ängstlich zu werden, sobald sich ein Widerstand einstellt" (*Charakteranalyse*, 71).

3. Ibid., 56. The German is: "Wesentlich ist, daß man zunächst nur den *aktuellen* Sinn des Charakterwiderstandes durchschaut, wozu man das infantile Material nicht immer benötigt. Dieses brauchen wir zur *Auflösung* des Widerstandes. Begnügt man sich zunächst damit, den Widerstand dem Patienten vorzuführen und seinen aktuellen Sinn zu deuten, so stellt sich sehr bald auch das infantile Material dazu ein, mit dessen Hilfe wir dann den Widerstand auch beseitigen können" (*Charakteranalyse*, 87).

4. Ibid., 70–71. The German is: "Das Ich projiziert seine Abwehr gegen die Es-Strebung auf den Analytiker, der gefährlich, ein Feind geworden ist, weil er durch die unangenehme Grundregel Es-Strebungen provoziert sich bei seinen neurotische Gleichgewicht gestört hat. Das Ich bedient sich bei seiner Abwehr uralter Formen ablehnender Haltungen; es ruft zu seinem Schultz in der Not Haßregungen aus dem Es zu Hilfe, auch wenn es Liebesstrebung abzuwehren hat" (*Charakteranalyse*, 103–4).

5. Ibid., 80–81. The German is: "Im Laufe der Zeit . . . empfindet der Kranke das ständige Hervorheben seiner Affektlahmheit und ihrer Gründe als lästig; denn man hat allmählich genügende Anhaltspunkte gewonnen, um den Angstschultz, den die Affektsperre darstellt, zu untergraben. Der Kranke empört sich schließlich gegen die nunmehr von der Analyse drohende Gefahr, die Schutzinstitution der seelischen Panzerung zu verlieren und seinen Trieben, insbesondere seiner Aggressivität, ausgeliefert zu sein; aber indem er sich gegen die 'Schikane' empört, erwacht auch seine Aggressivität, und es dauert dann nicht lange, bis der erste Affektausbruch im Sinne einer negativen Übertragung, in Form eines Haßanfalles erfolgt. Ist es einmal soweit, ist das Spiel gewonnen. Sind die aggressiven Impulse zum Vorschein gekommen, so ist die Affektsperre durchbrochen, und der Patient wird analysierbar. Die Analyse verläuft dann in gewohnten Bahnen. Die Schwierigkeit besteht darin, die Aggressivität hervorzulocken" (*Charakteranalyse*, 114–15).

6. Ibid., 128. The German is: "Wenn es richtig ist, daß alle Neurosen auf der Basis eines neurotischen Charakters zustande kommen, und ferner, daß der neurotische Charakter gerade durch eine narzißtische Abpanzerung charakterisiert ist, so wirft sich die Frage auf, ob denn unsere Patienten überhaupt im Beginne einer *echten* positiven Übertragung fähig sind. Unter 'echt' meinen wir eine starke, nicht ambivalente erotische Objekstrebung, die die Grundlage einer intensiven, den Stürmer der Analyse trotzenden Beziehungzum Analytiker bilden könnte. Wenn wir unsere Fälle überblicken, müssen wir diese Frage verneinen und sagen, daß es eine echte positive Übertragung im Anfang gar nicht gibt, noch eben wegen der Sexualverdrängung, der Zersetzung der objektlibidinösen Strebung und der charakterlichen Absperrung, nicht geben kann" (*Charakteranalyse*, 168).

7. Ibid., 135–36. The German is: "Man möchte vom ökonomischen Gesichtpunkt die Aufgabe der Handhabung dahin formulieren, daß man eine *Konzentration aller Objektlibido in einer rein genitalen Übertragung* zu erzielen habe. Dazu ist nicht nur die Lösung der im charakterlichen Panzer gebundenen sadistischen und narzißtischen Energien nötig, sondern auch die Lösung der prägenitalen Fixierungen. Bei richtiger Handhabung der Übertragung konzentriert sich nach der Lösung der narzißtischen und sadistischen Strebung aus dem Gefüge des Charakters die dadurch befreite Libido auf die prägenitalen Positionen; es tritt dann eine Zeitlang eine positive Übertragung von prägenitalem, das heißt mehr infantilem Charakter auf, die den Durchbruch prägenitaler Phantasien und Inzestwünsche fördert und so der Lösung der prägenitalen Fixierungen dient. Alle Libido aber, die von ihren prägenitalen Fixierungsstellen analytische gelöst wird, strömt dann der genitalen Stufe zu, verstärkt wie bei der Hysterie oder erweckt aufs neue wie bei der Zwangsneurose, Depression usw, die genitale Ödipussituation" (*Charakteranalyse*, 176–77).

8. Ibid., 148. The German is: "Der Analytiker mag selbst leben, wie er es für richtig hält: Wenn er *unbewußt* starre moralische Prinzipien vertritt, die der Patient immer spürt, also etwa polygames Verhalten oder gewisse Liebesspiele selbst abgewehrt hat, *ohne es zu wissen*, wird er den wenigsten Patienten voll gewachsen und leicht geneigt,

dem Patienten irgendein Verhalten als 'infantil' vorzuhalten, das es an sich durchaus
nicht zu sein braucht" (*Charakteranalyse*, 191–92).

9. Ibid., 176. The German is: "als Prototyp der *zulänglichen* erweisen sich die *geni-
talorgastische Befriedigung* der Libido und die *Sublimierung*, als *unzulängliche* alle
Arten der *prägenitalen Befriedigung* und die *Reaktionsbildung*. Dieser qualitative
Unterschied drückt sich dann auch in einem quantitativen aus: Der neurotische
Charakter leidet unter einer sich ständig steigernden Libidostauung, eben weil seine
Befriedigungsmittel den Bedürfnissen des Triebapparats nicht adäquat sind; der an-
dere, der genitale Charakter, steht unter dem Einfluß eines ständigen Welchsels von
Libidospannung und adäquater Libidobefriedigung, verfügt also über einen *geord-
neten Libidohaushalt*" (*Charakteranalyse*, 225–26).

10. Ibid., 187. The German is: "An der Erscheinung fällt uns auf, daß die Reaktionsbildung krampfhaft und zwangsartig ist, die Sublimierung hingegen frei strömt. Es ist,
als ob hier das Es in Einklang mit Ich und Ich-Ideal direkt mit der Realität in
Verbindung stünde, dort hingegen bekommt man den Eindruck, als ob alle Leistun-
gen von einem strengen Über-Ich einem sich sträubenden Es aufdiktiert würden."
(*Charakteranalyse*, 238–39).

11. Ibid., 200. The German is: "Während die Entstehung einer Phobie ein Zeichen dafür
ist, daß das Ich zu schwach war, bestimmter libidinöser Regungen Herr zu werden,
bedeutet die Entstehung eines Charakterzuges oder einer typischen Haltung auf
Kosten einer Phobie eine Stärkung der Ich-Formation in Form chronischer Abpanzerung gegen Es und Außenwelt. Entspricht die Phobie einer Spaltung der Per-
sönlichkeit, so die Bildung eines Charakterzuges einer Vereinheitlichung der Person.
Sie ist die synthetische Reaktion des Ichs auf einen auf die Dauer unerträglichen
Widerspruch in der Person" (*Charakteranalyse*, 252).

12. Ibid., 207. The German is: "Der hysterische Charakter will also durch sein sexuelles
Verhalten zunächst festellen, ob und von wo die gefürchteten Gefahren kommen kön-
nen. Das zeigt sich besonders auch in der Übertragungsreaktion in der analytischen
Behandlung. Der hysterische Charakter kennt nie die Bedeuting seines sexuellen
Verhaltens, er lehnt dessen Kenntnisnahme heftigst ab, ist empört über 'derartige
zumutungeri', kurz, man merkt bald: was hier als Sexualstrebung imponiert, ist im
Grunde Sexualität im Dienst der Abwehr" (*Charakteranalyse*, 259).

13. Ibid., 212. The German is: "Historisch bestand zunächst eine zentrale Fixierung an
die sadistische-anale Stufe, also etwa im zweiten bis dritten Lebensjahr. Die
Erziehung zur Reinlichkeit war infolge ähnlich gerichteter Charaktereigenheit der
Mutter zu früh erfolgt, was mächtige Reaktionsbildungen, wie etwa extreme Be-
herrschtheit, schon im frühen Alter zur Folge hatte. Entsprechend der strengen Rein-
lichkeitserziehung entwickelte sich ein mächtiger analer Trotz, der zu seiner
Verstärkung die sadistischen Antriebe mobilisierte. Bei der typischen Zwangsneurose erfolgt dennoch ein Stück weiterer Entwicklung zur phallischen Phase, das heißt
die Genitalität wurde aktiviert, aber teils infolge der früh ausgebildeten Hemmung
der Person, teils infolge asketisch-kultureller Einstellung der Eltern bald wieder

aufgegeben. . . . . Es ist daher für die Zwangsneurose typisch, daß der Verdrängung der Genitalität ein Zurückweichen auf die bereits verlassene Stufe des Kotinteresses und der Aggression dieser Stufe folgt. Die analen und sadistischen Reaktionsbildungen pflegen sich nunmehr, in der sogenannten Latenzzeit, die bei Zwangscharaktern am besten entwickelt ist, zu verstärken und den Charakter definitiv zu formieren." (*Charakteranalyse*, 265–66).

14. Ibid., 217. The German is: "Der phallische-narzißtische Charakter unterscheidet sich schon in der äußeren Erscheinung vom Zwangscharakter und vom hysterischen Charakter. Ist der Zwangscharakter überwiegend gehemmt, verhalten, depressiv, der hysterische Charakter nervös, agil, ängstlich, sprunghaft, so der typische phallisch-narzißtische im Auftreten selbstsicher, manchmal arrogant, elastisch, kräftig, oft imponierend" (*Charakteranalyse*, 292–93).

15. Ibid., 236. The German is: "Der Masochist, weit entfernt davon, Unlust anzustreben, zeigt vielmehr eine *besondere Intoleranz gegen psychische Spannungen* und leidet unter einer quantitativ keiner sonstigen Neurose eignenden *Überproduktion an Unlust*" (*Charakteranalyse*, 292–93).

16. Ibid., 253. The German is: "Sein wahres Wesen, sein *Ich* ist durch die anale Fixierung in der Passivität festgelegt, durch die Hemmung der Exhibition überdies im Sinne der Sucht, sich zu verkleinern, verändert. Dieser Struktur des Ichs steht nun ein phallisches, aktives Ich-Ideal gegenüber, das nicht zur Realisierung gelangen kann, weil das Ich Konträr strukturiert ist. Die Folge davon ist wieder eine unerträgliche Spannung, die als weitere Quelle des Leidensgefühls hinzukommt und so den masochistischen Prozeß nährt" (*Charakteranalyse*, 311–12).

17. Ibid., 262. The German is: "1. Phase: 'Ich strebe nach Lust'; 2. Phase: 'Ich schmelze, das ist die befürchtete Strafe'; 3. Phase: 'Ich muß die Empfindung ersticken, um mein Glied zu retten'" (*Charakteranalyse*, 321).

18. Ibid., 275–76. The German is: "Angst ist also immer der einzig mögliche erste Ausdruck einer inneren Spannung, gleichgültig, ob diese durch eine Behinderung des Fortschrittes zur Motilität oder der Bedürfnisbefriedigung von außen oder durch eine Flucht der Energiebesetzungen ins Innere des Organismus zustande kommt. Im ersten Fall haben wir es mit Stauungsangst oder Aktualangst, im zweiten Fall mit Realangst zu tun, in welch letzterem Fall mit Notwendigkeit ebenfalls eine Stauung und dadurch Angst erzeugt wird. Es lassen sich also beide Formen der Angst (Stauungsangst und Realangst) auf *ein* Grundphänomen zurückführen, auf zentrale Stauung der Energiebesetzungen; nur ist die Stauungsangst ihr unmittelbarer Ausdruck, während die Realangst zunächst nur eine Erwartung von Gefahr bedeutet, die sekundär zur affektiven Angst wird, wenn sie durch Flucht der Besetzungen ins Innere eine Stauung am zentralen vegetativen Apparat herbeiführt" (*Charakteranalyse*, 379–80).

19. See the excellent book by Henri F. Ellenberger, *The Discovery of the Unconscious: The History and Evolution of Dynamic Psychiatry* (New York: Basic Books, 1970), 500–18.

20. See Sigmund Freud, *The Ego and the Id*, trans. Joan Riviere and James Strachey,

Standard Edition (W.W. Norton, 1989), 11–21. The German text first appeared as *Das Ich und das Es* (Vienna: Internationaler Psychoanalytischer Verlag, 1923).

21. Reich, *Character Analysis*, 292. The German is: "Die korrekt durchgeführten Charakteranalysen weisen bei aller unendlichen Mannigfaltigkeit in den Inhalten, Konflikten und Strukturen folgende typische Phasen in ihrem Verlauf auf: a. Charakteranalytische Auflockerung des Panzers; b. Durchbruch der charakterlichen Panzerung bzw. endgültige Zerstörung des neurotischen Gleichgewichts; c. Hervorbrechen tiefsten, schwer affekbesetzten Materials, Reaktivierung der infantilen Hysterie; d. Widerstandsfreie Durcharbeitung des durchgebrochenen Materials; Herausdestillierung der Libido aus den prägenitalen Bindungen; e. Reaktivierung der infantilen Genitalangst (Stauungsneurose) und der Genitalität; f. Hebung der orgastischen Angst und Herstellung der orgastischen Potenz; davon hängt die Herstellung der annähernd vollen Leistungsfähigkeit ab" (*Charakteranalyse*, 397–98).

22. Ibid., 297n. The German is: "Was die psychoanalytische Theorie das 'Es' nennt, ist in Wirklichkeit die physikalische Orgonfunktion im Biosystem. Der Begriff 'Es' drückt in metaphysischer Weise die Tatsache aus, daß in dem Biosystem etwas besteht, dessen Funktionen außerhalb des Individuums bestimmt sind. Dieses 'Etwas,' das 'Es,' ist eine physikalische Realität: die kosmische Orgonenergie. Das lebende 'orgonotische System' der 'Bio-Apparat,' stellt nichts anderes als einen spezifischen Zustand konzentrierter Orgonenergie dar" (*Charakteranalyse*, 403n).

23. Ibid., 371. The German is: "Denn die freigewordene Körperenergie versucht spontan *längs*wärts zu strömen. Sie stößt dabei an die noch ungelösten Querkontrakturen und vermittelt dem Kranken das unleugbare Empfinden eines 'Blocks,' ein Empfinden, daß nur sehr schwach oder völlig fehlte, solange es überhaupt keine freien plasmatischen Strömungen gab" (*Charakteranalyse*, 489).

24. Ibid., 399. The original is in English.

25. Ibid., 403. The original is in English.

26. Ibid, 422. The original is in English.

27. Handout from Conference on the Orgone Energy Accumulator at the William Reich Museum in Rangeley, Maine, July 17–21, 2000.

28. Reich, *Character Analysis*, 539. The German is: "*daß einzig und allein die Wiederherstellung des natürlichen Liebeslebens der Kinder, Jugendlichen und Erwachsenen die Charakterneurosen und mit den Charakterneurosen die emotionelle Pest in ihren verschiedenen Abwandlungen aus der Welt schaffen kann*" (*Charakteranalyse*, 372).

6: DISPLACEMENT, ORGONE, COSMIC RELIGION, AND CHRIST

1. Wilhelm Reich, *Beyond Psychology: Letters and Journals 1934–1939*, ed. Mary Boyd Higgins, trans. Derek and Inge Jordan and Philip Schmitz (New York: Farrar, Straus and Giroux, 1994), xx.

2. Ilse Ollendorff Reich, *Wilhelm Reich: A Personal Biography* (New York: St. Martin's Press, 1969), 44.

3. David Boadella, *Wilhelm Reich: The Evolution of His Work* (Chicago: Henry Regnery, 1973), 368.

4. Reich, *Beyond Psychology*, 7.

5. Ibid., 3.

6. Reich, *Wilhelm Reich: A Personal Biography*, 37.

7. Reich, *Beyond Psychology*, 197.

8. Myron Sharaf, *Fury on Earth: A Biography of Wilhelm Reich* (New York: Da Capo Press, 1994), 251.

9. Reich, *Beyond Psychology*, 215–216.

10. In particular, I mention the work of James Strick at Franklin and Marshall College; Bernard Grad at McGill University; Joseph Heckman at Rutgers University; James DeMeo at the Orgone Biophysical Research Laboratory in Ashland, Oregon; and Bernd Senf at the Fachhochsshule für Wirtschaft in Berlin, Germany.

11. Wilhelm Reich, *American Odyssey: Letters and Journals 1940–1947*, ed. Mary Boyd Higgins, trans. Derek and Inge Jordan and Philip Schmitz (New York: Farrar, Straus and Giroux, 1999), 67.

12. Ibid., 70.

13. Ibid., 35.

14. Ibid., 74.

15. Ibid., 218.

16. Ibid., 228. From an undated journal entry (probably in February 1944).

17. Ola Raknes, *Wilhelm Reich and Orgonomy* (Baltimore: Penguin Books, 1971), 148.

18. In essay seven of *A Pluralistic Universe* (Cambridge, Mass.: Harvard University Press, 1977), entitled "Continuity of Experience," James argues that our various encounters with the universe always hint of something "more" that turns out to be vitalistic and, in our context, orgonelike: "Every smallest state of consciousness, concretely taken, overflows its own definition. Only concepts are self-identical; only 'reason' deals with closed equations; nature is but the name for excess; every point in her opens out and runs into the more; and the only question, with reference to any point we may be considering, is how far into the rest of nature we have to go in order to get entirely beyond its overflow. In the pulse of inner life immediately present now in each of us is a little past, a little future, a little awareness of our own body, of each other's persons, of these sublimities we are trying to talk about, of the earth's geography and the direction of history, of truth and error, of good and bad, and of who knows how much more? Feeling, however dimly and subconsciously, all these things, your pulse of inner life is continuous with them, belongs to them and they to it" (129). It should be mentioned that James was a medical doctor who later became one of the most important philosophers of classical (1870–1930) Euro-American philosophy. He taught in the philosophy department of Harvard University. The relationship between his cosmology and that of Reich bears further creative examination.

19. Wilhelm Reich, "Orgonotic Pulsation (1)," *Orgonomic Functionalism: A Journal Devoted to the Work of Wilhelm Reich*, vol. 3 (Summer 1991), 23. This and the other three essays in the series were translated by Reich's first English-language translator,

Theodore P. Wolfe. Reich had a close working relationship with Wolfe, a native speaker of German, but it soured toward the end of Reich's life. The Wilhelm Reich Infant Trust Fund engaged several other translators to bring out new English versions of the originals. While out of print and hard to obtain, Wolfe's translations can still be found.

20. Ibid., 27.

21. Ibid., 31.

22. Ibid., 30–31.

23. Ibid., 36. It is interesting that some scientists are now attempting to make the diesel engine more efficient and less polluting by applying principles derived from genetics and evolution (via computer models). These frameworks entail working through the kind of adjustments that come from a natural selection process that "desires" efficiency. This represents a very important transgression of the old barriers between mechanistic and organic thinking. My own sense is that even quantum physics, with its uncertainty principle, remains mechanistic, even if it must fall back on "less desired" statistical language. Reich's functional approach clearly foreshadowed some of the major conceptual revolutions now in the making. This makes me more optimistic that the academic, clinical, and general therapeutic worlds are now more likely to give his work a fair hearing.

24. Ibid., 42–43.

25. W. Edward Mann, *Orgone, Reich and Eros: Wilhelm Reich's Theory of Life Energy* (New York: Simon and Schuster, 1973), 143–59, makes the connection between orgone and the human aura as described in the Hindu literature.

26. For what it is worth to the reader, I have experienced some of these colorations in the orgone room in Rangeley, Maine. In addition, I built an orgone blanket that has very strong effects, a bit like heat radiation, on my body. I am fully aware that experiences like these, no matter how intense, can have strong psychological causes. They could, for example, be manifestations of a positive transference to the subject of this book. It would be somewhat presumptuous, however, to assume that Reich could not be right about orgone and that his intense quest for *disconfirmations* was not a real part of his scientific methodology.

27. Wilhelm Reich, "Orgonotic Pulsation (2)," *Orgonomic Functionalism: A Journal Devoted to the Work of Wilhelm Reich*, vol. 4 (Summer 1992), 31.

28. Wilhelm Reich, "Orgonotic Pulsation (3)," *Orgonomic Functionalism: A Journal Devoted to the Work of Wilhelm Reich*, vol. 5 (Summer 1994), 37.

29. For an excellent and thorough analysis of the nature of the orgone accumulator, see *The Orgone Energy Accumulator: Its Scientific and Medical Use*, published by the Wilhelm Reich Foundation, 1951.

30. Reich, "Orgonotic Pulsation (3)," 43.

31. Plato, *Symposium*, trans. Michael Joyce, in *The Collected Dialogues of Plato* (Princeton: Princeton University Press, 1961). Eryximachus says: "And so, gentlemen, the power of *eros* in its entirety is various and mighty, nay, all-embracing, but the mightiest power of all is wielded by that *eros* whose just and temperate consummation,

whether in heaven or on earth, tends toward the good. It is he that bestows our every joy upon us, and it is through him that we are capable of the pleasures of society, aye, and friendship even, with the gods our masters" (541).

32. Wilhelm Reich, "Orgonotic Pulsation (4)," *Orgonomic Functionalism: A Journal Devoted to the Work of Wilhelm Reich*, vol. 6 (Summer 1996), 22.

33. Ibid., 31.

34. Wilhelm Reich, *Ether, God and Devil and Cosmic Superimposition*, trans. Therese Pol (New York: Welcome Rain Publishers, 2000), 11.

35. Reich, *Ether, God and Devil and Cosmic Superimposition*, 63.

36. Ibid., 107.

37. Ibid., 120.

38. See Robert S. Corrington, *Nature's Religion* (Lanham, Md.: Rowman and Littlefield, 1997), for the outlines of ecstatic naturalist religion.

39. Reich, *Ether, God and Devil and Cosmic Superimposition*, 121. For a fascinating study of Freud's correlation of the "oceanic feeling" with more genuine forms of mysticism, see William B. Parsons, *The Enigma of the Oceanic Feeling: Revisioning the Psychoanalytic Theory of Mysticism* (Oxford, Eng: Oxford University Press, 1999). In this book Parsons argues that Freud was actually more open to the religious dimension of mysticism than is often recognized, as can be seen in his correspondence with the French intellectual Romain Rolland, a disciple of Ramakrishna and Vivekananda.

40. Ibid., 141.

41. Ibid., 143.

42. Ibid., 155–56.

43. Ibid., 271.

44. Ibid., 278.

45. Ibid., 287.

46. Ibid., 291.

47. Ibid.

48. Ibid., 296–97.

49. Eustace Chesser, *Salvation Through Sex: The Life and Work of Wilhelm Reich* (New York: William Morrow, 1973), 90.

50. In their interesting if slightly flawed analysis of Reich and his psychological dynamics, Robert D. Stolorow and George E. Atwood argue that Reich had a split-off component to his psyche that stemmed from the suicide of his mother. This self-contained complex, so they argue, intruded itself in his written work again and again. In their psychobiographical analysis of *Cosmic Superimposition*, for example, they maintain, "The orgone in the atmosphere reacts to the presence of deadly orgone energy by surrounding and sequestering it into isolated pockets. The purity of the unaffected air is thereby safeguarded and preserved. The images of the feverish sequestering off of a deadly stale intruder vividly symbolize the splitting process on which Reich's life floundered; namely, the splitting off and repression of the image of his disappointing and sexually treacherous mother in order to preserve her as an idealized object, and

the splitting off and sequestering of his own disappointment, jealous rage, and moral indignation in order to preserve the image of an idealized, messianic self." See *Faces in a Cloud: Subjectivity in Personality Theory* (New York: Jason Aronson, 1979), 127. Basing their conclusions only on Ilse's previously discussed biography, with some hints from Peter's reflections, they make claims that go far beyond legitimate biographical data. I consider this argument to be an example of the reductive rather than ampliative, form of psychoanalytic reasoning. While his mother's suicide had a deep and long-lasting impact on his character, it certainly did not translate itself into the concept of negative orgone energy, for which he had, in his mind, direct empirical evidence; nor is his poetic cosmology a result of his ambivalence toward his mother's betrayal, but is rather a logical extension of all of his previous work, even though there are clear maternal components in his poetic vision. I owe my awareness of Stolorow and Atwood's book to Patricia J. Middleton, M.D.

51. Wilhelm Reich, *Listen, Little Man!*, trans. Ralph Manheim (New York: Farrar, Straus and Giroux, 1974), 45. The German text is *Rede on den kleinen Mann* (Frankfurt am Main: Fisher Taschenbuch Verlag, 2000) The German is: "Gewiß, gewiß, du willst daß es 'Genies' gibt, und du bist bereit, sie zu ehren. Doch du willst *brave* Genies, Genie mit Maß und Anstand und ohne Dummheiten . . . kurz, ein *passendes* und *wohlabmessendes* Genie . . . kein wildes, unzähmbares, alle deine Schranken und Beschränktheiten niederbrechendes Genie . . . Du willst ein Beschränktes, verkürztes, gestutztes und zurechtgemachtes Genie, um es, ohne zu erröten, im Triumphzug durch die Straßen deiner Städte zu führen. So bist du, kleiner Mann. Du kannst gut ausschöpfen und erschöpfen und auslöffeln und auffressen, aber *du kannst nich schöpfen*" (*Rede*, 50).

52. Ibid., 77. The German is: "'Hört, hört! Er besudelt meine Kriegsbegeisterung, die Ehre meines Vaterlands, die Glorie der Nation!' Schweig still, kleiner Mann! Es gibt zweierlei Töne, das Heulen des Sturms auf hoben Gipfeln . . . und deinen Furz! Du bist ein Furz, und du glaubst, wie Veilchen zu riechen. Ich heile deine Seelennot, und du fragst, ob ich in *Who is Who?* bin. Ich begreife deinen Krebs, und dein kleiner Medizinaldirektor verbietet mir das Experimentieren mit Mäusen. Ich lehre deine Ärzte, dich ärztlich zu begreifen, und dein Ärztevereinigung verleumdet mich bei der Staatpolizei. Du leidest an Verwirrtheit deines Geistes, und sie versetzen dir den elektrischen Schock, wie sie dir im Mittelalter die Schlange odor die Kette order die Peitsche versetzten" (*Rede*, 78–79).

53. Ibid., 127–28. The German is: "Was immer nun du mir angetan hast oder noch antun wirst, ob du mich als Genie verklärst oder als Wahnsinnigen einsperrst, ob du mich nun als deinen Retter anbetest oder als Spion hängst oder räderst, früher oder später wirst du aus Not begreifen, *daß ich die Gesetze des Lebendigen entdeckte* und dir das Handwerkszeug gab, dein Leben mit Willen und Ziel zu lenken, wie du bisher nur Maschinen lenken konntest. Ich war dir ein treuer Ingenieur deines Organismus. Deine Kindeskinder werden meinen Spuren folgen und gute Ingenieure der menschlichen Natur sein. Ich habe dir das unendlich weite Reich des Lebendigen in dir, deines kosmischen Wesens, eröffnet. Dies ist mein großer Lohn. Den Diktatoren und

Tyrannen aber, den Schlauen und den Giftigen, den Mistkäfern und Hyänen rufe ich
die Worte eines alten Weisen zu: Ich pflanzte das Paniere der heiligen Worte in diese
Welt. Wenn längst der Palmenbaum verdorrte, des Fels zerfällt, wenn längst die
strahlenden Monarchen wie faules Laub im Staub verwehn: Tragen durch jede Sünd-
flut tausend Archen mein Wort: Es wird bestehn!" (Rede, 124).

54. In his flippant and breezy The Life and Work of Wilhelm Reich (New York: Horizon
Press, 1971), trans. Ghislaine Boulanger, Michel Cattier claims: "Nearly all the texts
that Reich wrote in the United States were full of self-congratulatory remarks. He explained that his intellectual breadth eclipsed his enemies, who were mere mental de-
fectives . . . His thirst for recognition took an unpleasant turn when he implied that
he should be awarded at least two Nobel prizes, and complacently repeated the remarks to his disciples, who looked upon him as a messiah" (207).

55. Reich, Listen, Little Man!, ix–x. The German is: "Der Versuch seitens der 'seelischen
Pest' im Jahre 1947, die Orgonforschung zu vernichten (wohlgemerke: nicht als un-
richtig zu erweisen, sondern durch Ehrabschneidung zu vernichten), wurde zum An-
laß der Publikation der 'Rede' als eines historischen Dokuments" (Rede, 9).

56. Ibid., 32. The German is: "Ich bin ein biologischer und kultureller Mischling (mon-
grel), und ich bin stolz, das geistige und körperliche Ergebnis aller Klassen und
Rassen und Nationen zu sein . . . Mich bewegt kein Gefühl für jüdische Sprache,
jüdische Götterei, jüdische Kultur. Ich glaube an den jüdischen so wenig wie an den
christlichen oder indischen Gott, aber ich begreife, wo du deinen Gott hernimmst.
Ich glaube nicht, daß das jüdische Volk das 'einzige' oder das 'auserwählte' Volk
Gottes ist. Ich glaube, daß das jüdische Volk irgendwann einmal sich in den Massen
der Menschentiere dieses Planeten verlieren wird, zu seinem eigenen Gedeihen, und
dem seiner Enkelkinder. Das hörst du nun nicht gerne, kleiner jüdischer Mann, denn
du pochst so sehr auf dein Judentum, weil du dich selbst als Juden verachtest, und
jeden, der dir nahe ist. Der schlimmste Judenhasser ist der Jude selbst. Dies ist eine
alte Wahrheit. Doch ich verachte dich nicht, und ich hasse dich nicht. Ich habe mit
dir nur nichts gemein, oder nicht mehr gemein, als ein Chinese mit einem Wiesel in
Amerika: den gemeinsamen Ursprung aus dem Weltenall. Weshalb gehst du nur bis
Sem, und nicht bis auf das Protoplasma zurück, kleiner Jude? Für mich beginnt das
Lebendige in der Plasmazuckung, und nicht mit deinem Rabbinat" (Rede, 37–39).

57. Wilhelm Reich, The Murder of Christ (New York: Farrar, Straus and Giroux, 1966),
11.

58. Ibid., 12.

59. I am using the proper name Jesus to refer to the historical person (about whom very
little is actually known), while the title Christ is an honorific that was given to the historical person by the biblical writers. Paul Tillich's solution for dealing with this tension in designation works quite well: his phrase "Jesus who is the Christ" combines
the proper name and honorific in a more accurate way by showing that Jesus was the
one who was received as the Christ. Hence Jesus Christ is not a proper name and
makes little sense as a referent. But in this text I will use both terms interchangeably
in order to simplify matters.

60. Reich, *Murder of Christ*, 17.

61. Ibid., 19.

62. Ibid., 33.

63. Ibid., 146, 147.

64. Ibid., 153–54

65. Ibid., 160.

66. Reich, *Wilhelm Reich: A Personal Biography*, 51.

67. Wilhelm Reich, *American Odyssey: Letters and Journals 1940–1947*, ed. Boyd Higgins, trans. Derek and Inge Jordan and Philip Schmitz (New York: Farrar, Straus and Giroux, 1999), 173.

68. Ibid., 271.

69. Ibid., 322.

70. See Sharaf, *Fury on Earth*, 360–69.

71. On the overall social milieu surrounding Reich and his battles, see Jim Martin, *Wilhelm Reich and the Cold War* (Fort Bragg, Calif.: Flatland Books, 2000). Martin's book details the ways in which the Communists were in fact working against Reich and his research during the postwar period.

72. Sharaf, *Fury on Earth*, 418–19.

73. *Wilhelm Reich: Viva Little Man*, a documentary by Digne Meller-Marcovicz, produced and distributed by Natural Energy Works, Ashland, Ore., 1987, 2000. The video is ninety minutes in length.

74. Wilhelm Reich, *Selected Writings: An Introduction to Orgonomy* (New York: Welcome Rain, 2000), 539.

75. Colin Wilson, *The Quest for Wilhelm Reich: A Critical Biography* (New York: Anchor Press/Doubleday, 1981), 227.

76. As quoted in Martin, *Wilhelm Reich and the Cold War*. Martin sources the quote as coming from "Documents dating from early FBI assessments of Reich as a national security risk [, which] contained Otto Fenichel's privately spoken slander" (419).

77. Ibid., 415, 416.

78. As an example, see the video *Man's Right to Know: The Wilhelm Reich Story*, 2002, the Wilhelm Reich Infant Trust.

Acknowledgments

While this has been a profoundly interesting book to write, I have been fraught with emotional ambivalence about its subject matter. Fortunately a number of people have rendered assistance to me along the way and have helped to enhance my narrative on the evolution of Reich's life and thought. While there have been some sharp disagreements, my interlocutors have always been gracious and thoughtful in rendering comments. First, I should like to thank Mary Boyd Higgins, director of the Wilhelm Reich Infant Trust and editor of the English translations of Reich's books, for her careful reading of the manuscript. She has always been willing to make hard-to-find material available to me and to discuss relevant biographical data.

Among Reichians I should like to thank Amaro Reyes, M.D., for his clinical perspectives on Reich; our discussions have proved to be quite valuable. Patricia J. Middleton, M.D., helped me refine my psychobiographical reflections and has been a good friend. James Strick, professor of the history of science, helped me to see the implications of Reich's scientific research for both biology and physics and correct some of my early misconceptions. He also made suggestions as to specific wordings. Andrew Kahn read the manuscript carefully and made some tart, focused comments.

The work of my friend Carl Fulwiler, M.D., Ph.D., combines psychiatry and neuroscience in such a way that he still remains friendly to depth psychology. Our innumerable conversations over several decades have shaped the background of my thinking. My friend Kathryn Kimball, a professor of creative writing and literature as well as a gifted poet, has helped me to find more judicious and creative ways of rendering my thoughts. To my editor at Farrar, Straus and Giroux, Paul Elie, I am especially grateful for showing me many ways to make my text and my ideas clearer and richer. And finally, I must thank my wife, Sara Henry-Corrington, professor of art history, for her comments on the manuscript, for our many conversations on the relationship between psychopathology and the arts, and above all for pursuing her own work and thereby providing a goad to my efforts.

Index

DATE DUE

GAYLORD			PRINTED IN U.S.A.